the funeral planner

GOES TO
WASHINGTON

Saving the nation with just a BlackBerry
and awesome shoes

LYNN ISENBERG

THE FUNERAL PLANNER GOES TO WASHINGTON

Focus Media, Inc.

ISBN 0-9778923-5-2

First published as a Mira paperback 2009
First published as a Focus Media, Inc. paperback edition in 2010

Visit Focus Media at www.focusmediamarketing.com

Printed in the U.S.A.

Author Photo by Megan Schoenbachler

Table of Sponsors

The Dignity Memorial Network®
Legacy.com®
Eternal Image™
ForeThought®
GoDaddy.com®
1800Flowers.com®
EchoSign
Heardable.com
DNA2 Diamonds
Cadillac Travel Agency
Got Kosher, Inc.
Andiamo's Italia Restaurants
BTB Burrito
Eagles Nest Restaurant
First Capital Funding Tribute to Nancy Newman
The National Hospice Foundation

Note: Sponsorship Ads and Valuable Offers located at the
back of the book.

www.booksandbrandsinc.com

Be sure to check out these other titles in the series.

LYNN ISENBERG

Lynn Isenberg (www.lynnisenberg.com) is an Author,
Multi-Media Producer, and Brand Strategist in
entertainment media (film, TV, digital, publishing, live
events). Her books and work have been featured on
The Today Show, Fox News, The New York Times, and
in other media globally. She holds a BA in Literature &
Film from the University of Michigan and a Masters in
Spiritual Psychology. Isenberg is the founder-CEO of
Lights Out Enterprises™ and The Tribute Network, the
author of four novels and two non-fiction grief guide-
books, and creator of The Funeral Planner Digital
Series. Her Screenwriter-Producer credits include
MGM/UA's "Youngblood," Tri-Star/Columbia Pictures'
"I Love you to Death", "True Vinyl", and the Fine
Living Network's popular series "I: Design." For more
information visit www.thetributenetwork.com.

Prologue

The president of the United States turns to me and in a direct, matter-of-fact manner says, "I want you to head up the House Bereavement Specialists Committee. Now."

I stand on the White House lawn, staring at him, not sure if I've heard him correctly and if I did, wondering why he is talking to me, let alone asking me to do things like head up a House Bereavement Specialists Committee. Do I look like Moses standing behind a burning bush? I don't think so—even if Moses really was a girl and the history books got it all wrong to purposely and cagily, I might add, shift society from the core of its matriarchal beginnings to its current underpinnings to set the stage for a well-entrenched patriarchal society—but I'm getting off point. There's no burning bush, no empty can of oil burning for eight days straight, no large red bodies of water separating on cue here, only a blistery wind whipping brown hair over my eyes. I quickly brush it away for the fourth time.

"We've got a crisis on our hands," says the president. "A *grief* crisis."

True. Our great nation has been crippled by grief. Not only were natural disasters, corporate and government scandals getting everyone down, but the death of the beloved first lady two months ago had tipped the scales, launching the nation into a deep depression.

Haley Stone was no ordinary first lady or ordinary lady for that matter, but a woman with the subtle and humble grace of Audrey Hepburn, the elegance and poise of Jackie Kennedy Onassis and the innocence and courage of Princess Diana. She had been tireless in her work to solve the nation's problems and she used merit, never entitlement, to do it. Though no one ever said it, it was tacitly acknowledged that she carried the charisma for her husband's vote into office, offending no one while remaining true to her ideals.

Her death was sudden, like an unexpected natural disaster or an act of terrorism. In the nine months before her death, she had finalized a plan to solve the nation's homeless issue, leaving the impression that her work on earth had been completed in that final gesture. Exhaustion seeped in, pneumonia took over, and in three days she was gone. Her prominent legacy was the Poverty Reform Bill that now rested in the hands of Congress.

Everything Haley Stone did in life was done with meticulous forethought, and so it had been no different in death. In good health, she had quietly and confidentially approached Lights Out Enterprises to document her pre-need wishes. That's how I came to meet President Andrew Stone, while privately preplanning the first lady's fanfare goodbye. He was cordial and polite as was his style, one which did not include loquacious or effusive descriptions.

The funeral service that my partner Richard Wright and I

were unexpectedly called in to execute was dignified and graceful like the first lady wanted. The clergy conducted a traditional affair filled with psalms and hymns and prayers. There was only one thing missing; no one talked about her. I wondered how the absence of telling stories about the departed would affect the nature of healing in the grievers. Haley also loved life and specifically requested a celebration in the form of a good ole fashioned American outdoor picnic. I figured people would talk openly about her in a more relaxed setting, like a picnic, but the event never happened. The outspoken opinions of the smooth-talking Tyler Simmons, President Stone's political advisor, caused that particular aspect of the pre-need plan to be immediately dismissed. Simmons cited that a celebration of the first lady's demise would be considered crass; an extravagant event in poor taste that would most surely leave the president vulnerable to critics who would weaken his popularity and inevitably jeopardize his chance for a second term in office. The president was overcome with grief and unable to comment on the matter. Thus, Haley Stone never got her picnic and the country remained unhealed and in a state of despair.

And now this. The popular secretary of state Mr. Jonathon Darcy unexpectedly dies on the cusp of ending nineteen painstaking months of successful Middle East peace negotiations.

Jonathon Darcy was in good health at sixty-nine years of age. There was nothing wrong with him. Except that his wife of fifty-two years had died three months ago. Lights Out Enterprises had been hired by the terminally ill Mrs. Darcy to preplan it, having heard about us through Haley Stone's secretary.

I vividly remember Richard Wright turning to me at Mrs. Darcy's funeral. Richard and I stood next to each other on top of Mount Mansfield in Vermont with fifty other mourners. Jonathon and Dorothy Darcy had climbed Mount Mansfield together every anniversary of their fifty-two year marriage. Her pre-need wishes were to take one final journey to the top of the mountain and have her husband cast her ashes to the wind. As Jonathon Darcy carefully unscrewed the lid of the urn to spread his wife's ashes, Richard Wright took one look into Mr. Darcy's eyes. Within the nanosecond of a blink Richard leaned into the crook of my neck and whispered, "Three MTL."

Richard was known to make predictions on survivorship of one spouse once the other had passed away, but I had no idea how his record held up. I knew enough to decipher his code for "three months to live". Nevertheless, I shook it off as an overreaction, that he too was caught up in the nation's collective consciousness to mourn alongside Mr. Darcy.

But Richard had pegged it right. The country's most popular junior leader, who by all accounts, with his steadfast and just rationale, his disarming negotiating skills and his insightful understanding of all parties on all matters, was without question the silver lining that would carry the president into his next term. That role was even more pronounced upon the passing of Haley Stone.

Only Mr. Darcy had died of a broken heart.

The result of his unexpected demise along with the first lady's two weeks prior had remnants of a double-strength emotional tsunami. A nation overcoming one catastrophe after another, a nation counting on a wise foreign affairs specialist and a treasured first lady—who both die so soon; leaving a nation bereft with grief. And the president of the United States picks *me* to fix it? Why not the Dali Lama? Or Tony Robbins? He's inspirational. Why me?

The president breaks his intense glare into my eyes for a quick glance at the lawn, catching sight of my footwear. When he looks up at me, he seems even more positive than before that he's got the right person to fill these shoes.

I stare back at him wondering again *why me?* And who else could fill these shoes? Then I notice my shoes. Elegant, sophisticated and extremely unusual high-heeled pumps that Eve Gardner had mysteriously acquired for me moments before I was to arrive at the White House. I had no idea where she got them or what brand they were. Of course there was no questioning Eve, whose fashionista sensibilities earned her not only the role of my former protégé, but stylist, as well.

She simply slipped them on me and declared, "You're golden."

Right about now I preferred pewter and wished the muted sun would stop peeking behind gray October skies and remain in sight long enough to shed some consistent warmth into my bones.

"Excuse me, sir, but with all due respect, I think there are more spiritually inclined people suited for this kind of work."

"I want you." He suddenly looks like that famous animated drawing of the government's Uncle Sam in red, white and blue wagging his finger at me.

"Can I ask why, sir?"

"I need someone who's got a vision on grief."

"A *vision* on grief? What am I supposed to do? Pass out tissues with Mr. Darcy's name on them? I mean, just what are my objectives, sir?"

"Get rid of the grief," he balks. "Hampstead will set you up. Office, staff, balloons, whatever you need. Just get rid of it. I'm counting on you, Madison Banks."

Get rid of it…whatever that was supposed to mean. Of course, with an office in the White House and a staff of my choosing at my disposal, I figured I was about to find out. Although nothing could have prepared me for a position inside the confines of our political power center or how one diminutive entrepreneur-turned-funeral planner might impact the sphere of influence affecting the nation and its ripple effect worldwide.

Had I noticed the brand name of the shoes Eve had procured for me and imbued it with some sort of premonition, I might have had a clue. And yet it wasn't until I kicked the gold heels off my aching feet at midnight inside my hotel room at the Hay-Adams, where the president insisted my team and I stay, that I noticed the engraved inscription beneath the instep.

It read *Messiah*. Who in the world would name a pair of shoes Messiah? At least I wouldn't be alone. There must be hundreds of other people wearing them, I thought, before drifting off to a deep sleep. But I couldn't have been more wrong.

1

I awaken and lie still in bed as the first rays of consciousness take hold of me. As per my custom, I roll over for pen and paper but stop myself in midroll.

"Oops. The Serenity Prayer," I say aloud.

I resume a resting position. I promised my friend and business associate Sierra D'Asanti that I would say the prayer for at least one month before starting my day. She thought it might help me learn to relax and create a less hectic pace for myself. After three days I hadn't seen any benefits. But a promise was a promise.

"God grant me the courage," no, that's not right, "God grant me the strength," that's not it, oh, yes, I remember now. "God grant me the serenity to change," no… "God grant me the serenity to accept the things I cannot change," yes that's it, "to change the things I can," no, wait, "the courage to change the things I can and the wisdom to know the difference." Whew. I wonder why I have so much trouble remembering such a simple prayer. Before I can answer, I fall back into my compulsive habit of picking up a pen and notebook to write the day's action plan.

Yesterday's memories stir in the background making a slow advance to the front lines of my mind. Oh yes, the president of the United States of America appointed me to head up a House Bereavement Specialists Committee. My job: Obliterate Grief. I write: *Action Plan to Obliterate Grief.* Step 1: Identify Grief; Step 2: Not sure.

I pause, holding my pen…just how does one obliterate an emotion, especially an emotion as devastating as grief with its internal conflagrations and its untidy paroxysms of insidious indescribable pain. Are there such things as weapons of grief destruction? I have known the devastation of grief and its arduous protracted struggle. It took me over a year to begin to confront the loss of my uncle Sam and my best friend from college, Tara Pintock. How will we as a nation survive those other losses? What can we learn from them? And more importantly, how can we grow from them? Without growth, there is only stagnation and a slow backward decline of the heart and soul.

The newspapers hit my door with a loud thud. It's 5:30 a.m. I immediately step into the hallway of the Hay-Adams Hotel to retrieve the newspaper. The headline blares: "President taps Funeral Planner Madison Banks as Grief Czar." Oy.

I glance at the article but the headlines beside it catch my immediate attention. "Nation Grieves for Darcy." The article includes a lengthy biography on Mr. Darcy and mentions the time and location for the funeral taking place the following day. Another headline reads, "Tri-States Devastated by Midwest Tornado." Wisconsin, Illinois and Indiana suffer fifty billion dollars in damages from the ravaging tornado that hit the area last week. Hundreds have been killed, resulting in homelessness on the scale of Hurricane Katrina. They might as well rename the newspaper *The Grief Update and Forecast.*

In the last four years, America had been struck by Hurricanes

Katrina, Gustav and Ike, Hurricane Ivan, floods, wildfires, one natural disaster after another, the effects of global warming, not to mention the continued aftermath of 9/11 and the unrelenting fear-induced threats of nuclear attacks. It was as if God or some higher power had turned us into one collective entity named Job to test our faith. If that were at all true then the article on the flip side of the front page proved that our nation was failing miserably. The headline read, "Widespread Depression Responsible for Record Low GNP." I scan the story citing record high sales of antidepressants across the country. Great. We would all become grief zombies. Even I was not immune to the cornucopia of grief that seemed to spread emotional tidal waves of suffering across the country. And I wondered where I might find refuge from its psychological pain until I recalled it was my job to create the refuge.

Another thud hits the ground outside my door. This time I retrieve the *Financial Street Journal*. The front page headline reads like a déjà vu. "Funeral Planner becomes Nation's Grief Czar." Oy. Again.

I need a cup of coffee. I reach for the phone to order room service when it starts to ring. I stare at it. Who else has read the paper at this hour? With trepidation, I pick up the receiver and gently close my eyes.

"Hello?"

"Yes, I'd like to speak to the newly appointed grief czar."

"Very cute, Victor."

The sound of Victor Winston's voice still sends a thrill of curiosity and contentment down my spine, just as it did the first time I met him at Nate & Al's Deli in Beverly Hills, California, two years ago.

I remember Victor Winston eating lunch with venture capitalists Johnny Bright and Bobby Garelick. Johnny Bright teased me about being efficient while he himself failed to discern the difference between efficiency and effectiveness. Victor chimed in to clarify the matter by quoting the great business management leader Peter Drucker.

With one perspicacious glance, Victor seemed to get the whole of me. His style supported me in a seamless manner. And he was still doing it to this day. I wasn't aware of how Victor's voice affected me in that moment inside Nate & Al's Deli. It wasn't until later that I recognized the impact his choice of words and his tone of voice had on me.

The next time I saw Victor, six months had passed. I was making my official business plan presentation to Johnny Bright and Bobby Garelick. Johnny and Bobby happened to invite Victor to sit in on the meeting. I was pitching Shepherd Venture Capital for a first round investment of substantial funds for Lights Out Enterprises. I explained that Lights Out Enterprises was about "celebrating a life" as opposed to "mourning a death" in terms of funeral planning, and specialized in catering to the pre-need market. "Creating Meaningful Experiences to Remember" was the tagline. Lights Out Enterprises would offer experienced design consultation, high-end digital production services, high-end talent relations and customized merchandise as "funeral favors." I had done my homework and pointed out the facts and figures reflecting a growing industry of twenty-eight billion dollars which would rise as baby boomers aged. I walked them through the various components of the business I had envisioned. Revenue generation would come from consultations to individuals and funeral homes, customized digital life story tribute films and personalized branded merchandise.

Victor remained silent during my entire ninety-minute pitch. Johnny and Bobby were agape at the numbers. Yet, the two of them ultimately dismissed the concept out of their own preconceived fears around death and an incorrect hunch that it might only end up as a *dying* trend.

When Johnny and Bobby left the room and I stood alone in a puddle of rejection, Victor spoke to me for the second time. Again, he used metaphors, parallelism and similes. "Keep your eye on your vision," he had said, and "I hope Lights Out sees a lot of light...and knock 'em dead," underlining his words with a tone of voice that possessed a tacit, unwavering faith. In what, I wasn't sure.

It wasn't until the third time Victor spoke to me that I pinpointed my attraction to him. Six more months had passed. Once again, I stood in the lobby of Shepherd Venture Capital but this time I came better prepared. I carried with me a completed prototype; a life story video produced by Lights Out Enterprises. This was not a cookie-cutter slide show that some funeral homes had embarked upon. This was the tribute video for my beloved uncle Sam who gave me the first seed money for my business. It was a highly personalized video and it was sacred to me.

I asked the receptionist to inform Johnny Bright that I was in the lobby. However, unbeknownst to me at the time, Johnny had already stolen my business plan, quit Shepherd Venture Capital, and joined forces with my archnemesis, Derek Rogers, to launch a competing business called Tributes in a Box.

"Johnny Bright quit with no forwarding information and Bobby Garelick is out of the country on business," said the receptionist.

I stood in the lobby feeling naked and tired, and out of sheer desperation asked the receptionist if *anyone* was around. And then in the distance I heard Victor's voice. "I'm here," was all he said. It was in the way he said it, with his uncanny gift to create an emotional safety net along with an undeclared belief in who I was.

It turned out that Victor had taken my earlier presentation quite seriously and done a little digging on his own to verify the merit in my cause. And, well, to make a long story shorter, Victor became the sole venture capitalist to underwrite an official first-round investment for Lights Out Enterprises. Since

then, he's become my fiancé and never stopped believing in
the business, or in me.

"How on earth did you swing an appointment like this one?"
Victor asks over the phone line, bringing me back to the present.

"I didn't swing it. I was chosen. Reluctantly, I might add.
What do I know about healing a nation? I'm just an event
planner in funeral clothes."

"Well, you can't let the president down. Nor the country,
I might add. We're all counting on you now, Madison. No
pressure or anything. But I don't have to tell you that everyone is in a state of despair. The flight attendants, teachers, the
guy selling newspapers on the corner...there's a terrible malaise
in everyone's eyes. The quality of work is shameful, too. No
one cares about anything anymore. It's as if our country has
lost its sense of self and with it all of our pride."

"I know. Arthur Pintock ordered his employees to go home
yesterday because they couldn't focus on their jobs." Arthur
Pintock was the CEO of Pintock International, the world's
leading mortgage lender, and the father of my best friend from
college, Tara Pintock. It was the lack of personalization at
Tara's funeral that inspired Lights Out Enterprises. Arthur
Pintock became one of my first lead-generating clients. It
turned out to be a life-altering experience for him. His initial
tribute video woke him up to the fact that while he had developed the most powerful mortgage lending company in the
world, he had undermined his personal life into a state of
shambles. He set out to change his modus operandi and went
on sabbatical from Pintock International to discover himself,
and well, eventually he returned to his company with a fresh
perspective on living a life of balance. And he joined the
advisory board of The Tribute Network division of Lights Out
Enterprises, convinced that its Web site could attract a niche
market on the scale of YouTube as an advertiser-supported

sharing site for life celebration videos. Somehow, Arthur had managed to create a fulfilling life and was even courting his former wife, Grace Pintock. The death of Tara had been the final straw in pulling their marriage apart. But he was determined to make amends and renew his marriage with Grace. I wondered how many people, including myself, would have the strength and courage to rewrite their life story, a much harder task than embarking on a whole *new* story.

"Have you started writing an action plan?" asks Victor.

"Yes, as a matter of fact I have…notes here and there… while I oversee the final plans for Mr. Darcy's funeral service. Where are you right now?"

"Austin. I've got a meeting lined up with an advertiser who might be interested in The Tribute Network."

"That's great." I jump to my feet. "When is it? With the time difference I'm sure I can hop on a plane and meet you there in time to make the presentation and—"

"Stop. You're doing it again."

"What?"

"Micromanaging me, Maddy. I'm a big boy. I can handle it. Besides, it's a long shot because we don't have enough traffic on the site yet. But I've got other meetings in Austin so I figure it's worth a try. And besides, you already have a job. Cure a nation. Plan a funeral. How much do you think you can possibly take on?"

"But I…I need to…"

"…to stop overscheduling so you don't have to feel a false sense of importance. Isn't that what you're supposed to be working on at your meetings, how to value yourself outside of work?"

He was right. In fact, Victor was right most of the time, which sometimes really irked me. Was I that lost in my own circuitous path that I had to always get back on track via his insights? Was I not good enough to find my own way?

I take a deep breath and pull out my sheet on *Definitions of a Workaholic* I found on the Internet several months ago when I thought I might have an issue.

The thought that I might have work addiction issues became apparent when Victor took me river rafting for a long weekend. Any non work-related activity made me uneasy and agitated. I was all too eager to check my BlackBerry for e-mail messages every time we stopped along the river to have lunch or camp out. When Internet connectivity became impossible I went into withdrawal, searching for any scrap of paper I could find to make notes to myself about work. When that didn't happen, I resorted to scratching ideas in the sand with a stick. I talked to Victor incessantly about the next item we needed to address to continue the expansion of Lights Out Enterprises and The Tribute Network. The clincher was when we rode the rapids and I continued to talk about business above the din of smashing waves and the moment where we nearly capsized. That's when Victor strongly suggested I seek help. I agreed to do so.

I decided defining the problem was the best way to start and found all kinds of definitions for the ailment on the Internet. I shared my secret with Sierra who sent me a copy of the Serenity Prayer with instructions to memorize it and repeat it every morning. I also printed out a schedule of gatherings in the area of Los Angeles where I live as a reminder to go to one. But so far, I just hadn't had time. I was too busy working. What a cruel and strange cycle.

I unfolded the paper with the twelve definitions on it. There they were, staring right at me:

Number One: You find it hard to love and accept yourself. What if that was true? Was I working for love and acceptance? If so, then from whom? My parents? Victor? The president? No, not the country. That's too many people to get approval from.

Number Two: You use work to gain approval, to define yourself, to justify your very existence. Okay, there might be some truth in that. I had the best intentions to go to a conference and find out, but then

Mrs. Darcy passed away and there were simply too many details to take care of. Maybe it *was* time to go to a class. How bad could it be? I had no idea what to expect. Except that I knew there had to be more to life than working, even if I truly believed my work to be exciting and adventurous.

Number Three: You use work to get an adrenaline fix. Oh my God, that's me. It's like I'm a work junkie.

Number Four: You use work to escape your feelings. That sounds familiar. I work so hard I don't have time to feel. Is it all one big form of avoidance? Maybe work is my form of Prozac?

"Victor. I think I'm trying to run away."

"From what?"

"My fears."

Gentleness coats his voice. "What are you afraid of, Maddy?"

"That…I'm not good enough to be the grief czar."

"Sure you are, Madison Banks. Just go with your strengths."

"My strengths?"

"Yes, that's why you've been chosen…so to speak."

I glance at the golden Messiahs on the floor; the heels are twisted together. The shoes look as if they've been wrestling with each other all night and from sheer exhaustion now lay still in a tangled heap.

"What are my strengths?"

"You said it earlier." He pauses.

"Victor, I really don't have time for conundrums. Can you just give it to me as you see it?"

"No, because it's not about how *I* see it, Maddy. It's about how *you* see it."

I sigh into the phone. He had slipped me another pronoun-twist.

"Look," he continues, playing therapist with me. "If your strengths aren't obvious to you, don't sweat it. They'll reveal themselves no matter what you do."

"Mmm…thanks for the obtuse advice, Victor."

"You're welcome. I'll catch up with you later. Good luck, my grief czar."

As he hung up the phone, it hit me. In those last three words of his was the answer to phase one of my action plan to heal the nation.

The Hay-Adams Hotel

0800 hours. Richard Wright sits across from me at a breakfast table in the hotel's posh restaurant known as Lafayette. Beautiful murals depicting Washington in the 1800s line the walls. Clean white linens adorn our table with delicate cups of coffee and tea laid out for us.

"I'm so grateful you're here, Richard. I couldn't do this without you."

Richard smiles at me. "I gotta tell you, Maddy, I never thought my career as a funeral director and bartender in Clark Lake, Michigan, would bring me here, helping conduct a service for a head of state. If only your uncle Sam could see this, he'd be real proud of you."

"Yes. He'd be proud of you, too, Richard. I think he brought us together for a reason. We make a good team. So tell me. I only have five more minutes. Is everything in order for Darcy's funeral tomorrow?"

"The only thing I don't have under control is the press."

"Don't worry. The White House will handle that."

Richard hands me a piece of paper. "Here's a checklist," he says. "If you have any questions, call me. I'll be prepping things for us at Gawler's Funeral Home."

"Is all the electrical in place?" I ask.

Richard nods.

"Did you walk through the woods?"

He nods again. "I did."

"And everyone knows the timing?"

"All but one."

"Who?"

"They wouldn't say. A cousin of Mr. Darcy's, I think."

"Well, let's make sure we prep whoever it is on their time limit before they reach the microphone," I say. "Geez, it's like producing the Academy Awards."

Outside the window a limo pulls up to the front of the hotel. I check my watch. The White House escort is right on time. I throw on my coat. "Gotta go. I'll touch base with you later."

Richard gives me a warm hug and I'm off to my next appointment.

Once I'm seated inside the limo, I turn to the driver. "Excuse me, how long does it take to get to the White House from here?"

He turns to me with a warm smile, punctuated by sadness in his eyes, "'Bout ten minutes."

"Thank you," I reply. "Do you think you could be so kind as to put on National Public Radio?"

"No problem," he says, and twirls the dial.

"…Mr. Simmons, can you tell us more about the legacy Jonathon Darcy will leave behind?" asks the interviewer.

"John Darcy leaves behind rare qualities of insight and risk in Americans I don't think we're likely to see for a long time."

"What do you mean by insight and risk, Mr. Simmons?"

"Well, for instance, there's a bill in Congress that John was passionate about that has to do with prison reform."

"Prison reform? We'll be talking to behind-the-scenes Washington socialite Elizabeth Anderson, about her theories on reforming institutions such as prisons in the next hour. Was Mr. Darcy working with Ms. Anderson on this issue?"

"They may have spoken to one another, Bob, I'm not sure. I know Elizabeth Anderson has some strong opinions on the matter, and I'm surprised she's granting you an interview. She rarely speaks to the media. So, I'd say you're showing off, Bob."

"Well, I'm just doing my job," says Bob, chuckling.

"With respect to prison reform or the Middle East, the fact is that John wasn't afraid to go on record, take on tough issues and make risky decisions. His motto was to always try and if it doesn't work, recognize it and move on."

"What kind of risk was he intending to take with this prison reform bill, if I may ask?"

Before I can learn about examples of Mr. Darcy's unusual insights and risks, the limo driver pulls to a stop. "We're at the White House, ma'am," he says.

I look at the mammoth blinding structure in front of me. As I maneuver out of the car, my lean leg with a Messiah pump touches ground and I ask, since when did I become a "ma'am"?

The White House

At 0900 hours I am escorted through the corridors of the White House by Walter Hampstead who everyone fondly calls Hampstead. Hampstead is thin, almost gaunt with short cropped peppered hair and a thin moustache. He walks with a smooth gait and is perfectly coiffed, like Victor. He is the real CEO of the White House, not in the sense of being the elected CEO of the country, like President Stone, but the employed CEO of the actual White House itself. He has been there for nearly three decades and five presidents. Apparently, he's the man who hires and fires every employee on the grounds from the crew of gardeners to the round-up of secretaries as well as five full-time chefs. He's the person who coordinates and manages all the details it takes to actually run what happens behind the front-line business of our nation's capital.

We continue to walk in silence, which makes me uncomfortable, or maybe it's the series of off-beat looks he gives me now and again; sort of like the way the hotel manager in the movie *Pretty Woman* looked at Julia Roberts' character for the first time. Maybe my wardrobe is askew. Perhaps I should have checked with Eve Gardner before leaving the hotel. But that's ridiculous. I'm probably imagining things.

I turn to Hampstead. "So, um, how many rooms are actually in the White House?" I ask.

"One hundred thirty-two rooms...thirty-five are bathrooms."

"Wow. That's a lot of doors."

"There are four hundred twelve doors to be precise."

"Oh. How many windows are there?" I ask.

"There are one hundred forty-seven windows, Ms. Banks, twenty-eight fireplaces, eight staircases and three elevators." He sends a smug smile my way.

"Hmmph. Interesting facts and figures."

"Tell me what you need, Ms. Banks, and I'll have it for you within twenty-four hours," he states, as he leads me down the Cross Hall of the White House.

The heel of my Messiah pump creates an echo against the marble floor. Hampstead's shoes on the other hand are eerily silent. In fact, I've never seen such supple leather on men's dress shoes before. We pass by a row of columns, a grand staircase, and portraits of former recent presidents lining the walls. But the most striking object in the room is the circa 1938 Steinway grand piano with gilded eagle legs and decorations of American music and dance.

The BlackBerry clipped to my belt begins to buzz and ding as we pass a small group of dignitaries on a White House tour. Hampstead glares at me. I glance back and slip the phone out of its holster to silence it and quickly review messages. The screen is bloated with e-mails from family, friends and colleagues. By now, they've all seen the headlines. I make sure there's nothing urgent, like a pre-need client suddenly shifting to a time-of-need client, and then turn the phone off.

We round more corners and pass by a room filled with statues. Hampstead seems to resemble them. His face is smooth like porcelain. There are hardly any creases around his eyes, which makes me suspicious. How can you have a job like that and not worry about security, rogue employees, or training new staff all the time? I wonder what his turnaround rate is. He looks like he runs a tight ship. Maybe his turnover rate is nil? Hence, no wrinkles, only loyal servants who work and behave in orderly fashion twenty-four-seven. Is that possible? If it is, I want to know his secret.

"Your temporary office will be in the Roosevelt Room," says Hampstead. "Of course, you'll have to move during our morning staff meetings until I can relocate you, since there are only two meeting rooms in the West Wing."

He opens a door and reveals a windowless rectangular room. I guess this room lost the lottery ticket on window rationing. That must explain the giant skylight overhead. A large conference table overwhelms the room with a multimedia center on one wall. On the other wall are two large plaques of Theodore and Franklin Roosevelt. Above the fireplace is a painting of Teddy Roosevelt on a horse during his days as Commander of the Rough Riders in the Spanish-American War. On the mantle rests a Nobel Peace Prize that I become fixated on.

"That happens to be the first Nobel Prize ever granted to an American. Teddy Roosevelt received it in 1906 for his mediations that ended the Russian-Japanese War of 1905."

"Oh," I say, realizing Hampstead is a treasure trove not only of White House facts and figures but every piece of American history that goes with it. As I walk around the conference table I notice a giant stuffed fish on the floor along with several empty aquariums. "What's the historical reference to that?" I ask.

He grins at me. Aha, the hint of a sense of humor lies behind those piercing eyes.

"The Roosevelt Room was formerly known as the Fish Room," replies Hampstead. "Franklin Roosevelt decorated the room with several aquariums and fishing trophies. John F. Kennedy caught that giant sail fish on a fishing trip and added it to the room. President Stone wants to bring some of the original artifacts back to life here. Those will be out of your way by the end of the day."

"President Stone likes to fish?" I ask.

"It's where he does some of his best thinking," reveals Hampstead.

How perfectly appropriate, I think. I can feel Uncle Sam's presence as an enveloping ray of sunlight suddenly peers through the skylight. Perhaps Uncle Sam is with me now. I look up and wink, maybe to myself and just maybe to Uncle Sam, too.

"He has quite a collection of lures," adds Hampstead.

"Really? So did my uncle Sam. He used to manufacture them."

"Isn't that a coincidence," he says, dryly. "The two of you can compare notes on fish hooks."

"Do you know if he has the moonglow jig in his collection?"

Hampstead stares at me for a long beat. "I'm afraid I don't." He crosses over to a mahogany door. "This door leads to a hallway, which leads to the Oval Office." He pauses to stare at me. "President Stone wants you close by." I slowly nod my head. "You have quite a job ahead of you, Ms. Banks. The president is in a vulnerable place right now."

"I can only imagine what he's going through," I reply.

"I think that's why he chose you, Ms. Banks. Because he thinks you can." He allows the weight of his words to sink in.

"Well...imagination is one resource I never seem to be missing."

Hampstead's shoulders relax and he offers me a knowing smile. My answer seems to have pleased him. "For now, use the phone at the end of the conference table. Directions are underneath it. If you need anything at all, call me. Soon, I'll have an office ready for you, with room for two full-time staff members."

"Thanks."

Hampstead turns to leave, then hesitates. "Good luck, Ms. Banks. And welcome to the White House." He closes the door behind him.

Sitting alone in the Fish Room, I wonder how much luck I'm going to need. Before I can set up my laptop and return phone calls and e-mails, there is a knock on the door.

"Come in."

The president's press secretary enters the room. I stand up to greet him. He's about five foot seven inches with a thick stream of jet-black hair cropped neatly on his round head. He holds out his hand for a firm shake.

"James Damon. Pleasure to meet you, Ms. Banks," he says. "We have a situation. The media is all over this story. They want to meet you and ask a few questions."

"I have to talk to the press?"

"They want face time. It's standard."

The mahogany side door abruptly opens and President Stone walks in. He surveys us. "James. Madison. Have you been briefed?"

"I was just getting to that, Mr. President," replies James.

"I'd like to introduce Madison to the feeding frenzy, if you don't mind."

"Excellent idea, Mr. President." James smiles.

The president faces me. "Well, Ms. Banks. Have you got anything worthy to announce yet?"

"Sir, I was just getting started on a concept based on—"

"Let's hear it," says the president. He sits down, giving me his full attention.

"Um. With all due respect, sir. And Mr. Damon. I'm not comfortable discussing my concepts without signed NDAs." I could see from the president's and Mr. Damon's dumbfounded stares that my peculiar statement required further explanation.

"I've been burned too many times. People stealing my ideas. And I made a vow to myself." A long pause ensues, "…which actually, brings up the question of legislation that would protect intellectual property in its earliest stages of—"

"Mr. Damon," the president interrupts. "Could you please give Ms. Banks and me a moment? And bring me an NDA form to sign for Ms. Banks."

"Do we have any?" asks James.

"Create one," says the president.

James nods and leaves the room. The president looks me square in the face. "What have you got for me, Madison?"

"My Grief Day."

"My Grief Day. What's that? Some sort of code for D-Day?"

"No sir, it's a national holiday…that I invented…for the purposes of addressing grief head-on."

"What's the theory behind this?"

"I'm basing the concept on the theory of homeopathy."

"Homeopathy? The principle of *similar suffering* to cure one's ills."

"Yes, sir."

"Madison, are you familiar with the twenty-million-dollar duck story?"

"Was it covered in *The Financial Street Journal,* sir?"

"The *dilutions* from the heart and liver of one duck were manufactured to supply enough homeopathic products to amass a profit of twenty million dollars in the course of one year. That is to say, the effectiveness of homeopathy might not be anything more than a placebo."

"Sir. If I may point out. Homeopathy doesn't necessarily have to mean small amounts. You said one duck's parts were diluted. I'm talking about the opposite of dilution. I'm talking full strength. My Grief Day isn't about taking a private minute during the day to remember our pain. It's about laying our grief wide open, together, as a country…to recognize our pain, to share our pain and to celebrate the good that comes of it. Grief can be an opportunity to learn about ourselves. If we don't grow from our grief, then what purpose has it served us?"

The president sits there thinking, seemingly immobilized by his personal grief. I can see it in his eyes. Memories alive again with the pang of reality alongside them. The reality that that memory can't be touched, that the first lady is forever intangible now. I breathe quietly, wishing I could make her real, wishing I could make his pain go away.

"Mr. President," I venture. "I believe that aside from experience itself, 'story' is the best way a human being can learn and grow. My Grief Day is one way to get there."

He slowly nods under the spell of a pregnant pause. Then he raises his eyes toward me and quietly comments, "I like this idea, Madison. If you don't mind, I'd like to pick the date to be recognized as our national grief day."

The Press Room

The place is packed with reporters. A sea of video cameras is almost all I can see as arms stand cocked in midair, poised to stretch to the sky. James Damon stands at the microphone, announcing the president. President Stone takes the podium and speaks to the crowd.

"Ladies and gentlemen of the media, allow me to introduce a woman of extreme imagination and intelligence, who will be heading the House Bereavement Specialists Committee, acting in a role our great country needs right now as grief czar, if you will. Please welcome, Ms. Madison Banks." He turns to me and nods. His smile is composed oddly of masked grief and desperate hope.

I nervously walk toward the podium, praying I don't trip. But then I remember the brand name of my shoes and my confidence returns. "Hello…everyone," I say with as much aplomb as I can muster.

Multiple hands shoot up. James Damon points to different people, anointing his picks with the momentary power to question.

A woman stands up and addresses me. "Julie Waters from BBS News. Ms. Banks, how do you intend to handle the situation across the country, where people are so depressed they're unable to function at home or at work? And its result in record-high sales for prescriptions of antidepressant medication?"

I lean into the microphone and reply, "We have a plan that will speak to the situation—" Before I can get another word in, James Damon anoints another cocked elbow in the middle row of the crowded room.

A gentleman rises from his seat, "Roger Duke from *The New York Chronicle*. Ms. Banks, will your plan help the Gross National Product to rise from its current all-time low since 1935?"

"That is my intention—" Before I can finish, James Damon cleverly picks another reporter who is only too eager to chime in and cut the other reporter off.

"Gary Kaye from *The Austin News*. Ms. Banks, who will you be appointing to your committee?"

"I'm appointing people who are experts in their fields and who have been with me from the beginning of Lights Out Enterprises, Richard Wright, Sierra D'Asanti, Eve Gardner, Arthur Pintock and Victor Winston."

"Don Chapin, *Financial Street Journal*. Can you describe your plan to alleviate the nation's despair?"

"The plan does not set out to alleviate our country's pain or to ignore it..." James Damon starts to point to another hand, but I keep talking, "...but to embrace it. And to do that we're creating a national holiday called My Grief Day. A day to pay tribute to our losses, both personal and public."

"Do you have a date?" someone hollers.

"December twenty-first," I reply.

"Julie Waters again. Who chose the first lady's birthday?"

"I did," says the president from the side of the room, his voice beginning to crack. There's a small tear in the corner of his eye.

"Mr. President! Who will replace Jonathon Darcy in the Middle East peace negotiations?" shouts an anonymous rogue reporter.

The president takes a deep breath and responds, "With all due respect, Mr. Darcy's funeral service is tomorrow. I believe the answer to that question can wait until after we have properly paid our respects to the life and contributions Mr. Darcy has made to his family and friends, and to our country and the world. Peace negotiations will be suspended until John...rests in peace...that's all I have to say right now." His voice cracks again, revealing traces of anguish.

James Damon steps in. "That's all for now, folks." He guides the president and me out of the room.

The president takes another deep breath to recompose. "I think that went well."

"Yes, good job, Madison," James says.

"I think you're a natural," the president offers. "When will I meet your committee?"

"Tomorrow."

"Good. I'll look forward to it."

From the White House, I race over to Gawler's Funeral Home to go through a practice run with Richard. All is in place. Four hours later, I return to the hotel. Only once I'm back in my room, I can't rest. I work obsessively on finalizing last-minute details for the funeral and on a variety of sketches for My Grief Day. I'm still hyped up from the adrenaline of what occurred today. I wonder how it went for Victor and shoot him a quick e-mail to say hi, ask him about the meetings, and tell him I miss him. I hoped he might surprise me and show up, but our opposing schedules seem to create a constant wedge between us.

I turn my attention back to my work when there's a knock on the door. I open it to find Eve Gardner standing in front of me. She has a nasty scowl on her face.

"What'd I do now?" I ask.

"As a graduate of my company, Fashion Therapy 101, you do not get in front of national media coverage wearing the outfit you had on today, except for your shoes of course, which I'm sure no one saw, at least not the cameras." Eve barges in and I have a déjà vu all over again.

"What was wrong with my outfit?" I turn around to watch her pour herself a glass of water.

Eve takes a sip and then shoots me a dirty look. "First of all, you forgot all about the double C's—color and coordination... Purple earrings with gold pumps? Haven't you learned anything at all from me? And where do you get off wearing velvet with linen? Major faux pas! I nearly OD'd on OMGs!"

"What's an OMG?"

"IM for Ohmygods. Where have *you* been?"

"Obviously, in the closet, picking out the wrong outfit. What's the big deal about velvet and linen?" I'm truly puzzled. "You make it sound racist. And who cares?"

"The American Fashion Association, that's who cares."

"There's such a thing?"

"No. I made it up. But there might as well be for people like you who are so...so...fashion challenged. Actually, there is an organization called AAFA. The American Apparel and

Footwear Association, but they don't deal directly in matters of good taste. They're about trade shows and lobbying for legislation on behalf of the clothing industry—"

"Eve, excuse me," I say, interrupting her. "I have a lot more important things to do than worry about attire."

"Really?" asks Eve.

I have a feeling I'm about to be interrogated.

"Let me ask you something," she says, circling pompously around me in her haute couture outfit, beige feathered hat and all. "Have you thought about what colors you're going to use to represent My Grief Day?"

"What's wrong with black?"

"In the context of grief, it's morbid. That's what's wrong with it. Not to mention passé. Meanwhile, you intend to celebrate the nation's grief? Is that not correct?"

"Well, sort of," I reply.

"And you intend to make it a national event. Is that not correct?"

"Yes, in a manner of speaking."

"And do or do not national events require socialization?"

"They do."

"And when you step outside your house to quote socialize and celebrate end quote with your fellow human beings, what is the first thing you do?"

"You greet them."

"Before that. Before you step outside."

"You put your socks on?"

"No. Before that."

"Brush your teeth. Okay. Floss."

She rolls her eyes for the third time, waiting for me to figure it out.

"Eve, I don't have time for twenty-one questions."

"You put your clothes on, Madison...unless you're at a nudist colony."

"Eve, what is the point of this?"

She holds up a finger. "I'm not done." She looks at me and squints. "What makes you pick the clothes you wear on the day you wear them?"

I stand there thinking. Challenged. But if this is another God blessed conundrum I'm going to scream. Okay, what's my decision-making process as I picture myself standing in front of my closet in the morning? "Mood," I reply, feeling like I nailed it. "And the type of appointments you have that day."

Eve folds her arms together and stares at me as if she's won something or other. "I rest my case."

"What case?"

"That clothes are representations of our emotions, of our selves, of our culture, of our nation. We don't walk around in turbans and veils. And you want to create a national event without giving a smidgen of thought as to how people should prepare for it? When you go to a wedding what do you wear?"

Her style was relentless. "A dress or long skirt," I answer, thinking that Eve really missed her calling. Prosecuting attorney would have suited her just fine.

"When you go to a ball game what do you wear?"

"Blue jeans and a T-shirt."

"When you go on a hike up a mountain, what do you put on?"

"Hiking shoes and khaki pants."

Eve slows down her pace and nods her head at me. "You are mixing grief with celebration. Will people be sitting? Standing? Running? What's the uniform? What are people supposed to *wear* to My Grief Day?"

"I…I hadn't thought of that…yet."

"Right. Meanwhile, you are now the spokesperson for bereavement and thus you represent the grief brand. What's it going to be?"

I sigh. Fashion was clearly something out of my realm.

"Pink," I blurt, hoping that will shut her up. But her eyes pop open wide and she beams at me.

"Perfect. It's bright and soft at the same time. Hot or pastel?"

I shake my head. "I don't know. Pastel."

"That's good, Madison. I like that. That's very, very good! Fine, once you've designed the activities for the event, I'll come up with the fashion…in pink. In the meantime, let's just pray the media doesn't have a heyday in the papers and on the Net at your expense."

And with that, Eve breezes out of the room.

"Wait. Where are you going? You want to go over the details one more time for tomorrow?"

She turns around. "It's not one more time. It's thirty-six more times. I've been counting. Richard, Sierra and I have it all covered. You can actually stop worrying. All you have to do now is remember to wear the outfit I put together for you. Details are in your inbox. Enjoy your evening off."

"Where are you going all dressed up like that?"

"I'm off to a vigil for the first lady with this really cute senator's aide I met in the lobby. Bye." She smiles and heads for the elevator.

"Okay. Thanks. Have a good…vigil."

I order in room service for dinner while sending out e-mails confirming arrival times and security check-ins for the service and then rack my brains for a table of contents to the overall MGD plan. Then I get stumped. My energy dries up. Suddenly, the high of the day dissipates to a flat line as I stare at the empty screen on my computer. The clock reads 8:40 p.m. and I'm still working. Something is pathetically wrong with me.

I am always working as if tomorrow might never come, and the rest of my whole life has to be lived in each and every day that I wake. My theory behind this kind of behavior rests on the assumption that this pace and form of multitasking is necessary in case one does not happen to wake up the next day. What if there is no tomorrow? I *have* to accomplish everything I've ever wanted to do in this very moment. What a terribly stressful way to live life, I realize. Why do I feel this way? What is it that compels me to work so hard? And does it matter? Do I matter? With all the grief and disaster in the world, in this country, and around me, is my work really making a difference? Of what value is it? Of what value am I?

My self-esteem is about to break down the evening before Jonathon Darcy's funeral. I know I have to do something about it. I glance at my desk and the piece of paper with the definition of work addiction on it. It's that time. I search the Internet for a workaholics' gathering that might be taking place somewhere in the vicinity. Luckily, I find one at a place called the Westside in Georgetown. If I hurry I can make it on time and accomplish one *more* goal before the night rolls in and the tomorrow I think might never come won't have a chance to stop me. Although I had no idea how long a night could last, or how valuable and deep its shadows could touch one's soul.

2

The large yellow handwritten sign indicates the Workaholics Anonymous meeting is on the second floor. I leap up the staircase and find a second sign with an arrow pointing the way. I arrive ten minutes late. There's a fairly beat-up conference table and makeshift chairs. Only two other people are there; a pale man in his fifties who removes paperwork from a portable plastic file folder. The other person is a young well-dressed woman in her forties. We silently nod to each other. The sounds of footsteps reveal a third arrival. A young man in his late twenties appears.

The man in his fifties looks at the clock. It reads 9:17 p.m. "Well, shall we get started?"

The three of us nod.

"Hi. My name is Stephen and I'm a recovering workaholic."

The woman speaks. "My name is Rachel. I'm a workaholic."

The young man says, "I'm Brian. Workaholic."

By now, I've caught on and respond, "Madison. Workaholic."

Stephen smiles and says, "I remind everyone that this is an

anonymous meeting so that truth and clarity may be present and help guide us on our path to recovery. Who would like to read the definitions of a workaholic?"

Rachel agrees. Stephen hands her a laminated piece of paper. As Rachel begins to read, the sound of more footsteps pound upon the staircase. A man in his sixties appears and quietly sits down.

My mind wanders from the disruption, wondering how everyone is able to find the time to pull themselves away from their work to make it here at all, let alone on time. Rachel is on definition Number Five when I start to listen again.

"We work incessantly, at the expense of our health, relationships, recreation and spirituality. Even when we are not actually working, we obsess over our next task, hence denying ourselves the enjoyment of a balanced and varied life," she repeats.

That hits home as I can't remember the last time I saw my Michigan family. I think about my beloved dog, Siddhartha, who has become the adopted love-child of my mother because of my crazy work schedule and the constant traveling I do between Los Angeles, Michigan and now Washington, D.C. I miss Siddhartha in the most terrible way. I must make a trip to see her. Then I think about the last time I worked out at the gym. Over three months ago. Not good. I really do need to get an iPod so I can listen to the news while running on the treadmill and kill two birds with one stone. I'll have to try that. But then there's all that time it takes to make all those choices that require time to download. Hmm.

Rachel continues reading. *"Number Six. We rely on work to cope with the insecurities that are the natural order of life. Hence we overdo everything, creating even more work than necessary by expending unnecessary time and energy on worrying, overplanning and over-organizing resulting in an unwillingness to surrender control and an inability to delegate to others, which in turn causes us to lose our spontaneity, creativity and flexibility."*

I squirm in my seat as I recall the details of my compulsive morning action plans and how trusting others to help me do my job is so painful for me. Why? Do I have trust issues? I trust Sierra. She always comes through for me. And so do Victor and Richard and Arthur. Eve is consistently inconsistent but still there is a degree of consistency in that. Maybe I don't belong here after all. Or so I thought until Rachel gets to the next definition.

"Number Seven. We measure our sense of self-worth by what we do, not who we are. Because we are so busy doing, we have become out of touch with being. Our need for approval through work overrides every other aspect of ourselves, jeopardizing a well-balanced human being for a one-dimensional existence."

Oh my God, was I becoming one-dimensional? Was my self-worth determined by my actions in the workplace? If I didn't have work, who would I be? I shudder in my chair.

"Number Eight. We induce adrenaline highs inside our bodies by attracting stress and intensity into our workplace. When the crisis subsides, we suffer from withdrawals resulting in anxiety and depression that wreaks havoc on our peace of mind."

I didn't know work could actually be equivalent to a drug that creates adrenaline highs. Who knew? Instead of popping pills or gulping martinis, you could knock an extra five hours off at the office and be good to go with a false sense of approval and self-worth until it wore off and you had to repeat the cycle all over again. And yet, the competition inherent in democracy's work ethic is the foundation of capitalism. So how do you *work* around that?

"Number Nine. We lie to ourselves and to others about the amount of work we do. In fact, we secretly hoard work to insure that we will always be busy and never be bored. We fear free time and vacations because we find them painful instead of refreshing."

"Oh my God. That's me!" I blurt out.

Everyone stares at me with a knowing look and a reprimanding brow.

"There's no cross talking," Stephen insists.

I nod and quickly settle down wondering how does one be without being bored? But then my phone vibrates. I sneak a peak. It's the White House calling. It must be Hampstead. Maybe my new office is all set up and he's got the keys for me.

"Excuse me," I whisper, and hit answer. Everyone looks at me, appalled. Apparently this is a big no-no, bringing outside work inside a work addiction meeting. But it's the White House calling.

"Madison Banks speaking," I answer, realizing I've just blown my anonymity. I look at my watch. It's ten o'clock.

"This is President Stone."

"Yes, President Stone."

My newfound work addiction colleagues stare at me with an odd combination of amazement and annoyance.

"I think I need, uh…"

"Yes? Hello?"

Someone else gets on the phone with him. "Ms. Banks. This is Hampstead. We have a private matter to discuss. The president is…having a…difficult moment. Would there be a private grief support group that he could attend to discuss his feelings. Can you please look into finding the right person or situation for him?"

"With all due respect, Mr. President and Hampstead, I personally wouldn't recommend a grief support group at this time. I believe the wound is too fresh. It would be like putting a cast on a broken leg before having the surgery to heal it. I'm not saying grief support groups are not valid. They are! Very much so! But according to Richard Wright, timing is a very important consideration. He has very strong reasons for waiting."

I turn to the faces staring me down in continued dismay and amazement. I cover the mouthpiece and whisper to them. "I'm so sorry! I'll just be another minute."

Back to the conversation at hand. "If you go too soon, while your wound is still fresh, you're likely to have unrealistic expectations for recovery that could inhibit your healing process.

Richard recommends a six-month to one-year minimum wait time before entering into a grief support group."

"I'm not sure I'm seeing the analogy here, Ms. Banks," says the president in a faint voice.

"Well…think of it as if you were going to invade a country for having weapons of mass destruction before you've identified that they actually have them or where they keep them or how potent they may be."

"We did that. Or rather the administration preceding mine."

I cough and then clear my throat.

"I see," says President Stone. "Going in too soon without knowledge of the terrain can create a backlash of unintended results."

"Precisely, Mr. President."

"What does one do in the meantime?" asks Hampstead.

"Having a grief buddy is a real good thing to do. Does the president have a best friend he can talk to, someone who can be there for him whenever he needs to talk about his feelings?"

The president pauses. "They're dead."

I say nothing. The sadness in his voice along with the truth of his statement overwhelms me. What do you say to someone who's lost both his wife and his best friend within weeks of one another?

"Madison. I'd like you to be my grief buddy. Can you do that for me?" asks the president.

"Of course, if it will help, Mr. President."

"Let's hope so."

"I think it would be a good idea if you could come to the White House right now," adds Hampstead.

"I'm on my way." I hang up. My brows furrow with concern. He didn't sound good. Heavy. Weighted down from grief. It was too familiar. I lift my head and look at the dismayed expressions around me. "Excuse me, I have to go to work."

I pick up my bag, suddenly aware that I feel valuable and

worthwhile again. As I'm about to walk out I turn to everyone. "Um, this is an anonymous meeting, right? Even though I'm no longer anonymous? Which means whatever you heard stays here, right? Otherwise, I could see the secret police sending you all away from your jobs to a remote island in Tahiti with no Internet and no phones and no papers or pens, just sandy beaches with lounge chairs and sailboats."

They all quickly nod their heads, panicked by the mere thought of vacation and relaxation.

I sigh with relief. "Okay, thanks. I'm really sorry for the interruption. I promise it won't happen a second time."

The White House again

Pennsylvania Avenue glitters under the streetlights as the taxicab slows to a soft stop. The White House glows in the night. My phone rings again. The caller ID informs me that it's Sierra D'Asanti, my right hand in charge of digital productions at Lights Out Enterprises. I answer.

"Hi! Are you here yet?" I ask.

"I just checked in to the Hay-Adams. Where are you?"

"I have an emergency meeting with the president."

"Now? I thought you were going to curb your midnight hours."

"That's impossible."

"Only if you make it so, Maddy. Anyway, I couldn't be more proud of you."

"Thanks. I couldn't have gotten this far without *you,* though. Richard is in room 622 and Eve is in 620 in case you need any more updates before the morning. Otherwise, get some rest and I'll see you then. And I'm so glad you're here."

"Oh, I wouldn't miss being a part of your team for the world, Madison. I always knew you'd go global."

"I'm not global. I'm national."

"I wouldn't be so sure of that, Madison," she laughs. "Good night."

White House—Library

It takes me a few minutes to take in the fact that I am sitting on a couch in the library of the White House next to a warm fire, while the president of the United States pours himself a Scotch.

"Would you like one?"

"I'm not a big drinker."

"You sure? I thought you were supposed to be my grief buddy," he says. "How are you supposed to commiserate with someone if you're not participating in the same activity?"

"You have a point. Okay, I'll have mine on ice," I reply.

He pours me a drink and hands it to me. He holds his glass up. The rims clink together and I break beverage with the president.

"To life," says the president.

"*L'chaim*," I add.

"So how does this work?"

"It's like a story my mother once told me, which I believe she heard from Rabbi Harold Kushner."

"What's the story?" he asks.

"One day, Mrs. Berman turns to her son Billy who's about

eight years old and she says, 'Billy, will you please take this cake down the street to Mrs. Johnson?'

"Billy leaves the house with the cake in his hand. He's gone a long time. His mom can't understand what's taking so long and she starts to worry. She walks outside and looks down the street. She sees Billy coming home with his head down.

"'Billy, are you okay?' she asks. 'You were gone for a very long time. What took you so long?' Billy looks up at his mom. His face is full of sadness. 'Billy, what happened?' asks his mother.

"'I gave the cake to Mrs. Johnson and then I saw Timmy with his tricycle.'

"'Timmy has a tricycle? That's wonderful. Did you both get to play with it?'

"'No,' answers Billy. 'His tricycle was broken. And he was sitting on the curb crying. So I helped him.'

"'You helped fix his tricycle? That's nice, Billy. I didn't know you knew how to fix a tricycle.'

"'I don't,' admits Billy. 'I sat on the curb with him and helped him cry.'"

The president looks at me and nods his approval. "To tricycles." He takes another sip of his drink.

"So…you can talk to me," I try to cajole. "Share with me whatever memories or feelings come up. Show me photographs of Haley and Jonathon. Tell me stories about them. Or say nothing at all. We can sit here and be quiet and just think about them, too, whatever is most comfortable for you."

He quietly agrees while pacing in slow motion in front of the fireplace. I reach into my bag and pull out the grief guidebooks that Richard and I wrote back at The Eagle's Nest Restaurant on Clark Lake in Michigan.

"I don't know if you'll find these helpful, Mr. President, but you can have them to refer to if you need to." I place the books on the coffee table.

He glances at them. "*Grief Wellness: The Definitive Guide to*

Dealing with Loss and *Grief Tributes: The Definitive Guide to Life Celebrations.* Thank you, Madison." He stares at the fire. "I don't know where to begin." He remains silent for a long time.

"Mr. President? Can I ask you something?"

He nods.

"How did you meet Haley?"

Traces of a smile appear on his face. "We met at a debate tournament in college. She was the most articulate, beautiful, happy person I'd ever met. She was like…champagne." He takes his time remembering her.

"What was the subject of the debate?" I ask.

He looks over at me, and shakes his head. "I don't remember," the president replies. He stands there, thinking, trying to pull the memories back to the present. Moments pass. The fire crackles, cueing him to speak again. "She challenged me, though, every time I looked at her. She made me want to be a better person."

"How?"

"Oh, I think it was in the way she looked at me. It was in the way she spoke to me…and everybody else. Hmph, I think it was even in the way she brushed her hair." He looks at me harder. "Have you ever met someone who made you want to be better than you thought you were?"

I smile, thinking of Victor. "Yes, I have. I think it's something in their DNA."

"Yes," says the president. "Let me show you some photos of Haley in college. No one's ever seen these." He brings out a thick album of photographs and for the next few hours, the president reminisces with me about his early years with Haley Stone.

After a while, my eyes start to flutter from exhaustion. The president looks at me with gratitude. "I can't thank you enough for coming here under these circumstances."

"It's no problem, really. I've been there."

"Did you have a grief buddy?"

Sierra's pretty face quickly comes to mind. "Yes, I did."

"I've kept you up long enough, Ms. Banks. We should both try to get some rest. I'll see you tomorrow."

A return to the Hay-Adams Hotel

I reach the hotel lobby at two o'clock in the morning. The doorman opens the thick glass door for me. "Careful, ma'am," he says.

I notice I'm walking slightly on the crooked side and that the three Scotches I managed to drink during the course of the evening have taken hold of me through my bloodstream. "Um, thanks," I say to the doorman as I search for a dollar or two in my purse.

"There's no need for that. You just get on up to your room safely."

I nod. There's that sadness in his face; the same sadness that Victor spoke about, the same sadness that permeated everyone's demeanor. It was everywhere. You could even feel it between the lines of print in every newspaper story. Words embedded with insinuations toward grief. At the elevator I calculate the odds whether Victor might have surprised me and is sleeping in my room.

A thud hits the door. I wake up. I'm alone in bed. No Victor. But I do have a hangover. I roll over, stop myself, roll back and start saying the Serenity Prayer. But there's no room for it in between the pounding blood vessels in my head. I try to get up, but I'm overcome with sadness. I curl up in a ball and fall back to sleep.

The next time I wake up I glance at the clock. 10:00 a.m.? That can't be right. Light peeks from behind the heavy curtains. Maybe that is right. Shit. I leap out of bed and scramble to get dressed for Mr. Darcy's funeral.

Before I grab my toothpaste, I turn on my laptop. As my computer boots up, I hop in the shower, praying that a warm stream of running water will wash away the weighty residue of alcohol still treading through my veins. No such luck. My body is cleansed, but my brain remains somewhat…muddy. I gulp three glasses of water with some aspirin and run to my laptop for Eve's specific directions on my attire. Only the Hay-Adams Hotel has a friendly announcement. Their Internet connectivity is temporarily down. Apologies follow for any inconvenience it may cause. It should only take a minute or two. I don't have a minute or two. Now, there's no reason to panic. I'll just call her. After several rings Eve finally picks up.

"Where are you?" Eve demands to know. "There are some people, other than the press, who actually think it's okay to arrive *early*. And the paparazzi actually camped out here last night. Hold on. Excuse me, Mr. Paparazzi, but you might want to go across the street to that little pharmacy over there and get yourself some deodorant. Please. No. I am not Reese's younger sister. Okay, Maddy, what were you saying?"

"Eve. Listen to me. I'm on my way. Just tell me what I'm supposed to wear."

"You broke up. Did you say something's in your hair?"

"No, what should I wear?"

"Someone's having an affair? Who?"

And then, the inevitable happens. The line drops. I call again only to receive an all points bulletin that all circuits are busy now. There's no time to waste. I'm going to have to wing it. I throw open my closet and take a deep breath. I try to block out my brain throbbing, but the colors make me dizzy. Why did Eve have to add so many colors to my wardrobe? I was perfectly happy with a monochromatic scheme. It made the choices less complicated, which meant less time having to put an outfit together and more time for my obsessive work habits. Okay. I think to myself, what would Eve wear. Euew. Okay, what's appropriate? Black. Oh, but that's morbid. I know. Pink. She said that was a good color. But there's no shade of pastel. I grab a hot pink silk blouse and pair it with a brown linen skirt and gray wool jacket with the Messiah pumps.

The funeral service of Jonathon Darcy

Thirty-five minutes later I reach Gawler's Funeral Home with thirty minutes to spare before kickoff. Richard Wright has alerted security and I breeze inside through the loading dock into the back room.

Richard looks me over and offers a paternally-toned question, "You all right?"

"I will be. Can you pass me a headset and a walkie-talkie?"

He hands them over. "Channel Two," he says. "The secret service is finishing their inspection now."

I nod, glance at my watch, and then speak into the headset, "First and ten. First and ten." Within moments, Sierra arrives.

"Thank God you're here. I was about to have a helicopter take me back to the hotel to find you. You okay?"

"Fine, but there's no time for explanations. Are we ready to launch?" I ask.

Sierra sounds positive, adding, "Everything's set. We're ready to shoot for multimedia platforms on 1080p at 29.97."

Eve looks at Sierra confused and annoyed. "What language are you speaking?"

Sierra gives Eve a look.

"Is the disaster management team in place?" I ask.

"The tech guy is in position ready to activate on signal with backup tech for double protection. The glasses are ready to be distributed as mourners enter, and we checked every single one to make sure there were no lemons. Here's one for each of us." Sierra hands me a pair of white glossy glasses, and another to Eve.

It can't be helped. Sierra, Eve and I look like triplets in our matching headsets, holstered cell phones, and dressed to the funeral nines. I fear we've taken on a sheen reminiscent of Charlie's Angels and Richard is our soft-spoken version of Bosley. But then Eve takes one glance at me and the image vanishes.

"*What* are you wearing?" she asks, her mouth agape.

"Clothes. I couldn't get online and…"

"OMG! You need something to tie it all together, Maddy. It's nice that you're planting the seed for MGD with pink, even though we agreed upon pastel, not the gaudy hot version you have on, but once again, you have no C and C."

Sierra asks innocently, "What's OMG and C and C?"

"Oh My Gods. Color and Coordination." Eve answers as if this is obvious. She glances at Sierra's sleek fashion outfit and nods approvingly. "Some people have a natural knack for C and C, like you, and me. And some," she lifts her chin at me. "Don't have a clue."

"What about me?" asks Richard.

"It's optional on males, mandatory on females," replies Eve.

Richard smiles. "Good to know."

I glance at the clock on the wall. "Eve, there are more important things to implement right now."

"Fine, I'll take care of it myself," she mutters.

"Those are your glasses, Eve." Sierra points to her pair of the white glossy glasses. Eve stares at them as if they're a foreign object from another solar system infected with a fashion virus.

"What are these…things?" asks Eve, repulsed.

Sierra replies, "These are the stereo LCD shutter glasses we'll be giving out to everyone as they enter. They create the illusion of immersion, more commonly known as VR for virtual reality. This particular version is derivative of the CAVE system. That stands for Cave Automatic Virtual Environment, for *sensualized* interfaces and—"

"Stop!" blurts Eve. "You had me on VR." Eve gingerly holds her glasses. "I still think they're…disgusting."

"Well, maybe you can talk to the product designers when this is all over and ask them to make it pink." I notice Eve's eyes light up. "Can we get back to the funeral now?" I ask.

Eve holds the glasses as if they have cooties. I notice Richard gently smile to himself. I wonder where he gets his never-ending patience. Now wouldn't it be nice if patience was a product you could buy, or even drink or eat every day so you could replenish it whenever it was wearing thin.

"What's the keyword for this again?" asks Eve.

"Mountain view," I reply. "Okay. Remember, it's just like the rehearsal, except for the one that you missed, Eve. Only there are real people in the scene now and they have no idea what to expect. If anyone gets dizzy or faints, the registered nurse will be on site at the north end of the room. If anyone becomes emotionally distraught, escort them to the Grief Counselor Tent outside the east-side door. It's heated and private. Richard will be on call for that. Here are compasses with clips attached for all of us in case we lose our sense of direction." I pass them out and they become one more piece of technology we hook to our waistlines. "I'll do a walkthrough and signal the okay to open the doors. See you at your posts."

Everyone takes a deep breath. Richard quietly adds, "To the last public expression of Jonathon Darcy's soul. Let's do him proud."

We all take a moment to take that one in. Even Eve remains silent. I look at each of my friends and whisper, "Thanks for being on my team. Okay. Let's turn the lights on at Lights Out."

We part ways and I enter the main chapel that will comfortably seat the one thousand mourners who have come to pay their respects. All is in order as I review my checklist. In forty-eight hours, my team and I have transformed the main chapel into a combination real-life simulation and a virtual reality set of Mount Mansfield in the Green Mountain ranges of Vermont. Real trees line the perimeter of seats. Real green grass covers the flooring. Real logs are strategically placed in the front and back of the room. Portions of faux mountains flank the stage. An unlit campfire adorns the west side of the stage. Two dimensional murals depict green mountains, lush rivers, partially cloudy skies, and sun rays streaming through layered branches of leaves in full bloom. I raise my eyes to the ceiling. That, too, has been adorned with white sheets undulating in wavelike formation. A series of compact projectors fit neatly inside the seams of the sheets. The seating has been arranged in a large semi-circle around the room facing stage center where lies a top-of-the-line Batesville mahogany casket with Jonathon Darcy inside.

I look at Mr. Darcy's remaining vessel and flip the audio off my headset to address him. "I hope you like this, Mr. Darcy...and I hope you're back with Mrs. Darcy again and that you're...happy." I wait in silence for a moment and then flip the audio back on and whisper into my headset, "Sierra, Eve, Richard. Do you read me?" I hear a union of *yesses*. "Project Darcy has a green light."

Mourners begin to enter. First up is President Stone accompanied by Hampstead, his political advisor Tyler Simmons and press secretary James Damon. He is led to a seat up front. He glances my way and offers a small wave from across the room. One national news crew and two local news crews enter the hall jockeying for space to position their cameras and tripods.

As Eve escorts an older woman to her seat, she passes the news crew and I hear a faint snickering in my headset as one of the broadcasters mutters, "Well, now we know, the grief czar is either color blind or she can't dress worth a damn."

I hear Eve's voice chime in, "Au contraire. Talk about avant-garde. Those, ladies, are the new hot colors and fabric combinations for next spring, says Paris, as in France."

The broadcaster stops in her tracks and stares at Eve. "Really? Pink, brown and gold? You're kidding, right?"

Eve's smile is peppered with irony. "Oh, I wish I was."

I smile as the seats are now halfway filled with mourners and more are coming through the door with their white glossy eyeglasses in hand. I then turn around to face the stage. The two podiums on either side of the stage are empty. No clergy had been selected to lead the funeral because Mr. Darcy had once told President Stone that when his time came he wanted a bipartisan funeral. Mr. Darcy felt that was the most appropriate choice given his role in the Middle East peace negotiations and his public stature as secretary of state. We still needed an emcee, someone to act as master of ceremonies. I had suggested a civil celebrant, but President Stone asked his political advisor Tyler Simmons to take care of that one detail, thinking I had enough on my plate. I had called Mr. Simmons' office several times in the last four days requesting the name of that person so that I could brief him or her on the events of the ceremony. But Tyler Simmons was either avoiding me or simply too busy to respond. I chose not to take his rebuffs personally, except for the little voice in my head that suggested otherwise. My only chance to confront him…is now. I watch him mingle with other politicians, offering one consoling pat after another. There's something disingenuous about his actions. They remind me of someone, but I can't place who. He nears the end of the front row VIP aisle, leaning over to address a woman in a dark green felt hat when I make my move.

"Mr. Simmons. Hello. Madison Banks." Out of the corner of my eye, I catch the look coming from the stately woman's eyes beneath the lip of the dark green hat, and it isn't pretty. She glowers at me. Even Tyler appears to be upset. "Excuse me, I didn't mean to interrupt it's just that, well, I need to talk to you." Tyler stares at me. I put my hand over my mouth and mumble, "We have a funeral to put on."

"Yes. And he had his respects to finish paying," says the coiffed hat-woman, as her eyes narrow at me. "You must be from California."

"Actually, Michigan…followed by twelve years in California."

"It shows," she says.

Tyler clears his throat. "Pardon me, Mrs. Anderson." He turns to me, "So…you're Madison Banks. If your skills at interrupting are as good as your funeral planning, we should be just fine," he mutters, and then adds under his breath, "Don't ever interrupt me when I'm talking to Elizabeth Anderson again. Got that?"

I stare at him. "Nice meeting you, too," I whisper back.

He politely apologizes and excuses himself to the woman named Mrs. Anderson in the green felt hat, then takes a step away from her and motions for me to follow. He glances around the room as people walk by within earshot of us. "Nice trees you've imported here," he compliments, looking at me with the smirk of a Cheshire cat. "It's a pleasure to finally meet you, though it's unfortunate it's under these circumstances."

"Yes, it is. I was wondering if you might tell me *who* is leading the ceremonies."

He takes in a deep breath, looks me in the eye and says flatly, "Me."

I maintain my best poker face. How far off-base can you

possibly get from bipartisan? "Well, in that case, you're going to need this." I hand him some index cards. "Guidelines for the opening and intros for all the speakers are right here. I suggest incorporating dialogue about it being too hard to bring everyone to the Green Mountains, so we brought the Green Mountains to you. It's always good to begin with a little humor."

He gives me a snide look at my suggestion. "Humor? At a funeral?"

I press on, "Yes…humor. The renowned storyteller, Donald Davis, a national treasure I might add, said it best, 'Laughter and tears are not opposites, but twins of one another, and we often can't cry until *after* we've laughed.'"

He sniffs at me but somehow, quoting someone else on the matter appears to make it more palatable to him. I continue, "Please remember to discreetly remind everyone they have a ten-minute time limit." I glance at my watch. "Program starts in eight minutes." I turn to go, pivoting on my Messiahs when I hear, "Wait." I twist back.

Tyler Simmons takes another deep breath. "I'd like to suggest we volley on this." He shoots a quick glance toward the stage.

"I'm not following you."

"I'm not here to fumble on intros, Madison. I'm here for matters of the heart. You do them."

I wanted to ask him if he had perhaps confused ego with heart, but I held my tongue. Then it hit me. He was asking me to stand on the pulpit in front of Mr. Darcy's one thousand friends, family and colleagues. I couldn't begin to fathom the thought and I was starting to wonder why these people in the highest positions of public office were asking me to do things that were outside of my realm. "I don't belong up there," I quietly protest.

Tyler insists, "I think you do. This is your show…sort of like the ones on television where the hosts take turns introducing the talent. I think as a citizen of the United States, it's your duty to handle the introductions…except for Mr. Darcy's cousin. I'll handle his intro."

"Excuse me. There's another speaker? Someone mentioned this earlier, but no one confirmed for me specifically that Mr. Darcy has a cousin who is speaking. This has been carefully orchestrated. Where am I supposed to put him in the lineup?"

"It's a, uh, special situation. And it's fine if he goes last."

"Okay, okay. Just make sure he knows the time limit."

Tyler nods. "Good. It's settled then. Now excuse me, I have six minutes left to console John's friends and family." He walks away. I notice Mrs. Anderson paying her condolences to President Stone.

I turn and head for some respite behind a tree when I hear a chorus run through my headset and into my ears, "Are you okay?"

I hold the mic close to my lips. "Nice to have witnesses on the co-hosting idea. Obviously, I won't be at my post."

"No worries," whispers Sierra in my ear. "We've got it covered."

"Have Victor and Arthur arrived yet?" I ask.

"They just got here. Arthur's jet had mechanical problems and was late. They're trying to edge their way toward you."

I smile, happy and relieved. I look for Victor and Arthur in the crowd when Eve appears in front of my face holding a rose in full bloom cast in copper and 24 karat gold plating. A gold embossed logo on its stem reads Jonathon Darcy. Man of Peace. Remembered Forever.

"What are you doing with the funeral favors?" I ask. "We're not passing those out until Phase II in the Rose Garden when we serve John's favorite campfire food and s'mores."

"I am not letting you get in front of a worldwide audience without a flower. This is going in the lapel of your jacket."

"I don't have a lapel."

"Well, you will in one minute. And next time, leave the multiple colors for Mardi Gras, will you?"

As Eve tampers with my accessories and attire, I realize it's not one thousand people I'll be in front of, but millions. Eve finishes her task at hand and checks me over one more time, then repeats some words I've heard before. "You're golden."

By now the crowd has settled. People dab their eyes with tissues. Some sniffle through tears. Tyler Simmons gives me a look of summons. Why me? Why not Billy Crystal for God's sake? He was so good in *700 Sundays,* and that was all about grief, and he's always so good when he hosts the Academy Awards that you wish the Academy would just give him a blanket contract, or at least alternate between him and Ellen DeGeneres, because she did a really good job, too, and…

"Showtime," whispers Eve, as she pushes me forward, jolting me from my train of thinking. I nearly stumble but my Messiah pumps stabilize me as I quickly join Tyler on the pulpit to volley the intros.

Tyler begins with a beautiful and tasteful description of Jonathon Darcy and what his life represented to the world, to the American people, to his friends and family, and ultimately to Darcy himself. He comments on the astounding surroundings as a testament to the manner in which Jonathon Darcy lived and uses my line which gets a small laugh from the crowd. Then he pauses and starts referring to the guidelines I provided on the index cards, adding that Jonathon Darcy's greatest inspiration was Henry David Thoreau and the lessons to be learned in *Walden Woods.*

"Experiencing the world of nature is paramount to understanding ourselves and our fellow man. That's what Jonathon believed," says Tyler. "And that's why we have brought the world he admired and cherished so deeply to you here today. To present the view he cherished most, the view he shared with his wife Dorothy when they made their yearly sojourn to the top of Mount Mansfield. The mountain view…"

Suddenly, a lot of technical sounds come to life as projectors start blinking and glowing. Birds start chirping, and the campfire on stage lights up. I raise the white glossy glasses in Tyler's direction and place them on my face.

Tyler turns to the mourners. "Ladies and gentlemen, please place these glasses on to uh, share the mountain view Jonathon was so deeply humbled by."

Within moments, the entire congregation is wearing them. Several "oohs" and "aahs" float through the room. Although I notice Elizabeth Anderson sample the view and then quietly tuck the virtual reality glasses on her lap, seemingly unimpressed.

Someone in the front row blurts out, "I feel like I'm actually inside a forest."

Even Tyler Simmons is struck. "This is extraordinary," he says. Then he gestures to me. "Our newly appointed grief czar, Ms. Madison Banks, will introduce to you our next uh…" He looks at an index card and then back at me. I nod. He finishes, "eulogizer."

"Thank you, Mr. Simmons," I say. "Please feel free to keep the glasses on to experience the rest of this ceremony. Our next guest eulogizer is Jonathon Darcy's best friend and confidant. Not only in political affairs, but they have shared the same values that have been the moral compass in their life's work to lead our country. Please welcome President Andrew Stone."

The president rises and takes the podium from Tyler, shaking his hand in the process. He faces the crowd and begins, "This is exactly the environment in which John Darcy would have liked to have been remembered." He looks at me. "Thank you, Madison." Then he addresses the crowd again. "John Darcy was my best friend. We not only experienced the joys of life together, but the despair accompanied by the loss of a spouse. John Darcy died of a broken heart. And I understand that. But what he brought us during his time on earth has been nothing short of astounding. He has reminded us of the gentle gift of humility and of thinking about the other person, not of ourselves, in order to create win-win situations. Almost every night, John and I would sit in the library and share a Scotch as we discussed the events of the day and the events of the future. Once in a while, John would recite his favorite poem, 'The Vantage Point,' by Robert Frost. I think it best represents the man he was, and I'd like to share it with all of you."

After reciting the poem, the president continues, "To honor John's life, I promise to finish his work on earth for him and for all of us." He faces the casket and says, "It's not that I *will* miss you, John. I already do."

The president returns to his seat. I face the tearful audience again. I finally spot Victor and Arthur in the crowd, sitting in the center of the room. They have their glasses on so I can't see their eyes to make contact. Before I glance around the room though, Victor removes his glasses and gives me a quick wink and a thumbs-up sign.

I continue, "Our next guest eulogizer is John Darcy's childhood friend…"

And so it goes. Until we come to the sixth and last guest speaker. I nod at Tyler and step down from the podium to stand behind a tree off to the side. I put the glasses on. Everything seems so real. It even smells like gardenias and pine. But then there's this other smell I can't define, although it seems vaguely familiar, and carries a trace of something eerily negative that I feel in my bones.

I focus on Tyler's words. "John fought for many causes and he never gave up believing in the inherent goodness of all people. He believed in change from without *and* from within, so when his one remaining relative carried on a sustaining correspondence from prison with John, as pen pals and more, John decided to support the Prison Reform Bill…"

I look up at Tyler, wondering where he is going with this, when a simulated bird flutters past me. I look again and witness a 3-D Bambi dash through the main aisle. Eerily, I hear heavy breathing down my neck. I'm praying it's not a bear, a fox or an anaconda. I remind myself that they don't have anacondas in the Green Mountains. I'm about to turn around when I hear Tyler say, "Derek Rogers." My heart skips several beats. That's just not possible.

And then the breath behind my neck speaks, "You're in my way, Banks." And before I can move, Derek Rogers delicately shoves me aside to take center stage, grabbing one of the mics along the way, bypassing anything between himself, the audience and the camera crews.

"Holy shit, he's out on parole," whispers Sierra into my headset. "Mad, are you breathing?"

"Barely," I mutter.

Derek confidently faces the crowd of mourners. Prison hasn't changed him in the least. I see right through the faux sheen of humility he displays for the cameras. How he's come to stand here today is something only someone as slick and sly as Derek Rogers could pull off.

I had good reason to believe he was underhanded, having gone three rounds with him stealing my creative ideas and beating me to market. The shenanigans over his scamming the Tributes in a Box idea was his ultimate downfall. I had implanted a copyright code into the literature and proved beyond a doubt that he had stolen my intellectual property. I'd put an end to his nefarious activities, but one thing I knew for sure, a fourth round was something I didn't want to experience.

"It humbles me to hear how well loved a man John Darcy was and is and that I never had a chance to get to know him until recently," says Derek Rogers to the thick crowd. "Though he was a relative of mine, I unfortunately grew up without knowing that until two years ago. But I can tell you that the man I came to know through correspondence, phone calls and visitations, had a profound effect on me. He inspired me to explore what I could do for our great country. With the gross national product at an all-time low…"

"I don't believe it, he's promoting a personal agenda," I whisper into the mic.

"It's to be expected from a snake like him," comes Sierra's voice inside my headset.

"He's lying. Darcy could never have a relative like that," whispers Richard.

"I say we drop the projector on his head," offers Sierra.

"I say we block his play," Eve murmurs. "I'm going for it."

I glance at the back of the room and see Eve shift her post to purposely stand in front of the camera lenses, playing innocent and dumb, which I never knew had such incredible advantages until this moment. Eve actually succeeds for several minutes until the news crews insist that she move.

"Per my meetings and discussions with John, my plan," continues Derek, "is to help bring our government's deficit down. That's why I created the Insider Think Tank. ITT is a compilation of some of our country's greatest financial minds who have been incarcerated either for just reasons or because they were part of a trend in history…being in the wrong place at the wrong time. It's my great honor to have known John Darcy, to have been transformed by his very being…"

"I think I'm going to puke," says Sierra through my headset.

"Ditto that," I whisper back.

"…and to carry on his last wishes under the Prison Reform Bill," concludes Derek, as he wraps up his act an additional ten minutes over the time limit. He looks at the casket and vows, "On my life, John, I won't let you down." Then he hands the microphone over to Tyler and exits the pulpit. From my peripheral view, I see a subtle nod of approval pass from Elizabeth Anderson to Tyler Simmons and wonder what that was about.

Tyler glances at my index cards and then informs everyone of the procession to the White House and the after-ceremony gathering in the Rose Garden. "In addition, Jonathon Darcy's casket will lie in state, in the center of the U.S. Senate Rotunda for the next two days for those who wish to pay their respects. We recognize that the protocol here has been reversed. It was President Stone's request that we do so, so the public may have the opportunity to see videotaped excerpts of the memorial that has taken place today. The excerpts will also be on display at the Rotunda. Following two days of viewing at the Rotunda, Jonathon Darcy's body will be cremated to join his wife's ashes on Mount Mansfield."

Tyler solemnly steps down from the podium. There are several beats of silence. I notice the front row doesn't move until Mrs. Anderson does. I had no idea who she was, except that without one word spoken, I could see her tacit understated leadership was omnipresent. My brief encounter had obviously rubbed her the wrong way and I hoped never to come face-to-face with her formidable nature again.

Little did I know that my wishful thinking was the most benign defense of all.

3

The newspapers hit the bottom of my hotel room door. My first instinct is to jump up and devour whatever they have to say. But I am trapped. Only in a good way…lying on top of the sensual and chiseled frame of Victor Winston with his arms wrapped around my waist. He senses the twitch in my body, then smiles at me. "Was that for me or the newspapers?" he asks.

"You." And lower my face to kiss him.

"You're a terrible liar," he says.

I continue to kiss him, placing my lips on his mouth and then dipping down to kiss the nape of his neck. I murmur, "Well, aren't you the least bit curious about what's going on in the world?"

Victor smiles. "You mean aren't I the least bit curious about what the reporters have to say about Mr. Darcy's funeral?"

"Well, that is part of what's going on in the world, wouldn't you agree?" I smile back.

Victor flips me over and holds me tightly in his arms. I've missed his touch. I've missed his skin. He gently strokes the hair away from my eyes, all the better to see his delicious green eyes.

"It doesn't really matter what they think. We both know it went off perfectly…except for Derek Rogers' disingenuous, self-serving speech."

"Yes, but do you think the press will pick up on that?"

"Why do you care? Does it really matter if they're perceptive or not? There's a reason for the saying 'people's true colors always shine through.' You know what, Maddy?"

"What?" I ask, stroking his soft olive-tone skin and sneaking a quick glance at the door, wondering if some rogue hotel guest might snatch my papers before I have a chance to read them.

"When you actually get that you don't need to be validated by anyone else but yourself, you are going to be unstoppable."

I sit up and look at him. "So you think I'm stoppable now?"

"Absolutely not." He grins.

"If this is another one of your blessed conundrums I'm going to the door right now. Just what do you mean, Victor?"

"I mean that everything changes when you own your actions without the concern of others."

"So you think I'm flawed?"

"We're all flawed."

"I don't think you're flawed."

"Believe me, Maddy. I'm flawed."

"Well, I don't see it. But you obviously see mine…and you still love me?"

Victor nods. "Of course I love you. Really loving someone comes down to accepting them for everything they are and everything they are not."

"You know what, Victor? You should have been a rabbi or a minister."

"You think? How about a modern-day prophet?"

"That works." I climb inside his warm arms again. "So what did you think of the president?"

"I told you five times already. He's great. His entire staff is great, though I have deep concerns about Tyler Simmons. I'd watch out for him if I were you." He touches my shoulder and softly says, "You did good, Maddy."

"Thanks…can I go get the newspapers now?"

He rolls over, pulling the sheets and blanket off of us. I leap to the door and drag the papers inside. The headline on one paper reads, "A True Tribute for John Darcy." I flip over to the front page of another. The headline reads, "How Grief Turns to Mockery: An inside look at the funeral of Jonathon Darcy." Ouch.

"One good, one not so good," says Victor.

"How'd you know?"

"It's always that way. All anyone has to do is simply remember the story about the Chinese farmer."

"I'm listening." I tell him, as I continue to read both articles at the same time. "It's amazing how these reporters experienced the same event and came away with completely different opinions." I hear Victor get out of bed and start to make coffee.

"Chinese farmer," Victor repeats, as if that's the answer to everything.

"Okay. I'm listening. For real." I put down the papers and stare at him.

He goes on preparing the coffee. "Chinese farmer finds a wild mustang and brings him home. It's a bad thing, he's wild, what good is he? Until the farmer tames the horse. The horse helps with the farming and it's a good thing, right? Until the farmer's son rides the horse and breaks his leg. One would consider that a bad thing. But then soldiers come to the village to recruit young boys into the army. The Chinese farmer's son is exempt because of his broken leg, so…then it's a good thing…and so forth and so on. When we think something's bad, it just might be good and vice versa."

"Hmmph. Good story. By the way, who's Elizabeth Anderson?"

"A Washington socialite, descendant of one of the *Mayflower* families and a very wealthy widow," replies Victor. "Her husband used to own steel mills. That's all I know."

"I'll bet you anything she's got something devious to do with that Insider Think Tank program."

"I'm not making that bet." He hands me a cup of coffee.

"Why not," I ask, taking a sip from my mug. The caffeine gives me just the jolt I need to start thinking and scheming. But Victor reads my mind before I have the chance to. He leans in and looks me square in the eye.

"May I remind you…a grief czar doesn't have time to play investigative journalist."

I really hate that his sense of priorities can cause mine to dim in comparison. "Yes. You may have a point there. But I know someone who does."

Victor stares at me and I can feel another one of his mini-prophetic sermons coming on about time management or minding your own business. I've never ignored his storied soliloquies because, well, usually he's right, and it's much more fun and meaningful to receive a truth in the context of a story than didactically. But right about now, I'd prefer not to be enlightened on these issues and pursue my instincts my way. I had a feeling something was amiss between ITT, the Insiders Think Tank, and the spheres of political influence. But aside from my curiosity on that front, there was something else more pressing I had to do.

"Victor, I have to resign from The Tribute Network. Temporarily," I announce.

"But it's your baby."

"Yes. Yet, I think it's a conflict of interest while I'm in the White House."

"You don't think there's synergy between your company and My Grief Day?"

"I do. But I don't want the press or anyone else misconstruing my involvement and jeopardizing My Grief Day or The Tribute Network. Of course, as head of the House Bereavement Specialists Committee, I can still offer my opinion. I just think I should resign and refrain from receiving any financial remuneration related to TTN."

Victor looks me over. "Okay. I'll take you off the books. For now. Whenever you want back in, it's yours. And in the meantime," he says, leaning over to kiss me gently on the cheek, "I'll be the steward of your baby."

"You always know the perfect thing to say, Victor. Thanks." I kiss him on the lips and let my lips linger over his. "Mmm," I murmur. He reaches for my breast and I start to melt, but the conversation is far from finished.

"Now that I'm off the books, I'd like to create a strategic partnership with TTN to cross-promote My Grief Day. It's the only company that has any type of experience with this sort of venture."

"What do you have in mind?"

"The usual. Banner ads, hyperlinks."

"That's all?"

"I'll let you know the rest when I come up with it." I smile.

"Done deal." He smiles, going for my breast again, but then I remember all of the work that awaits me. I whisper in his ear, "So…can I order you some breakfast in bed?"

He offers a salacious grin. "Only if it comes on the side, with Madison Banks as the entrée. Is that possible?"

I glance at the clock. "Uh. No. I have to go now. I'm already going to be late as it is." I sift through my wardrobe and start throwing on some clothes while Victor turns the shower on. I follow him to the bathroom.

"Where are you off to?" he asks.

"Um. It's sort of personal."

Victor looks me over. "Is it health related?"

"No. Well, sort of."

"Is it a checkup?"

"More like a tune-up."

Victor quietly moves to give me space at the sink. "You'll let me know if and when there's anything to know. Right?"

"Right."

"Okay…well, good luck with it."

It is one of his more impressive qualities, knowing when to press and when not to. He and I both know each other well enough to know that when I feel comfortable, I will share my secrets with him. For now, revealing my new and latest task to attend work addiction meetings isn't something I'm ready to share with him. Of course, as I bolt from the bathroom, I wonder why I'm compelled to go to a meeting the one morning Victor is in town to be with me.

"Are we still on for dinner with Arthur Pintock at the Lafayette Room downstairs?"

"Yes. We have reservations for eight. But we're meeting at Off the Record first for cocktails at 7:30 pm. See you then." He comes up behind me to give me a kiss. I throw on a blouse, grab a suit jacket and I'm out the door.

Work Addiction Meeting #2

I slip inside the room. I'm twenty-two minutes late. I recognize the forty-something woman named Rachel and the young twenty-something man named Brian. But the pale man in his fifties in charge of the plastic folder is missing. Instead, a fifty-something woman now handles the literature coming from the same plastic case and appears to be the new leader of this small posse.

She smiles warmly at me, as if she knows me. "Welcome back," she says. "We finished reading the Twelve Steps and the Twelve Traditions. Let's welcome each other. I'm Stephen Stephanie, recovering workaholic."

I wonder if she has dyslexia. Isn't her name supposed to be Stephanie Stephens? And how does she know me if she wasn't here last time?

"I'm Brian. Workaholic," says Brian.

"Rachel. Workaholic," says Rachel.

"Madison. Um…hmm…workaholic." I'm trying to relax, but I haven't checked my BlackBerry in the twenty minutes it took me to get here, and I didn't even do my action plan this morning. Workaholic!

Stephen Stephanie or Stephanie Stephens asks, "Would anyone like to lead the sharing today?"

Everyone sits silently, with their heads bowed down. They appear to be a rather shy group. If that's a trait of workaholics then maybe I do not belong here. No one's ever accused me of being shy. I just happen to have a high-pressure job. Who wouldn't have to work long incessant hours under these conditions? Look at the president. Look at all presidents. If leaders of free nations and the people in Congress aren't workaholics, then I would think something is terribly wrong with them. How can you work in government serving the people, who have infinite needs, and not be a workaholic? And why, if one is serving the people, which requires working round the clock, do workaholics get a bad rap?

The room remains silent. I'm not sure how long I can stay, so I raise my hand figuring I might as well dive in and get it over with. Stephen or Stephanie smiles and nods at me to begin. Then she hits a timer and I hear the tick tock start.

"Well, um, my fiancé and my best friend think I need

some...uh, guidance. So I'm trying to find a way to create some balance in my life. But when the president asks you to lead the nation out of grief, what are you supposed to do? Say, 'Gee, I'm sorry, but it just doesn't fit into my new work less, play more program.' Then there's the actual work itself. I mean, does my work really help people? Of what value am I? To myself, to others, to the nation? How do I fulfill my purpose on earth and is what I'm doing my purpose? I work so hard to make a difference, but am I really doing that? I think that's one reason why I keep working so hard. How do you measure the value of your work? Because..." The timer sends a loud ding through the room. I stop speaking. No one says a word.

"The ding means you have one more minute to talk," Stephen or Stephanie informs me.

"Oh. Okay. Well, I was just trying to find some correlation between the value of my work and the measurement of its effectiveness. Because I think if you could see or feel the results of your work and you knew that you were being recognized and valued for your work then um, you might not have to work so hard. Does that make sense?"

The timer dings again. Everyone looks at me with a knowing expression. A long silence follows. Stephen or Stephanie or whatever her name is raises her hand and then sets the timer.

"Stephen Stephanie, recovering workaholic. Thank you for sharing, Madison," she says. "I appreciate what you told us because I've often felt the same way but have found it very hard to articulate. I feel like my own feelings have been masked by my identity issues to the point that I lost the ability to identify the value of my work. My work didn't have any value for years, or I guess it had a false value, because I used work as a cover, like an alcoholic who uses liquor...to bury my feelings and hide my true nature. I was afraid my wife might find out who I really was, so staying late at the office was not only a great refuge for me, but I thought I could repress my urges by burying them under enormous amounts of work."

I look at her again. Did she say wife?

"I always knew I was different than the other little boys in the neighborhood. And I tried to make those intuitive feelings go away by studying, doing chores, keeping my room clean, making my bed every day. When I finally came out as a transgender person, it was a very large part of my recovery from work addiction. Once I didn't have to hide my true nature, I could start to peel away the false pretenses in my work. I've been in this program for twelve years now and I know I'm making a great deal of progress because for one thing, I've stopped sneaking into the office in the middle of the night to work. This is a very hard disease to define and by running the program, I get better every day." The timer dings. "That's all."

I look at Stephen Stephanie with clarity now and tremendous respect for her or his courage, as silence reigns once again. Finally, Rachel raises her hand. The timer is reset.

"Rachel, workaholic," she says. "Thanks for your share, Madison. I totally understand what you're saying. I don't know the value of my work anymore…or if I ever did. I think it's worse when you're in the research end of your field. You collect data, you do all this hypothesizing, you discover new theories, and you have no idea if, or how, they are being implemented, or if they have any positive results. I feel like I can't stop trying to solve the problem until I really help someone… And the problem is huge and always multiplying. There are all these dysfunctional children out there. I can't help thinking that if they don't get healed in their infant stages with early prevention methods that their entire lives will be one big mess, not just for themselves, but in how they affect the rest of the world. When you consider how a child develops a sense of moral reasoning and whether they lean toward a descriptive ethic or a normative ethic, and how the gradual accumulation of their knowledge is acquired through experience and social context, let alone genetic dispositions, in order to avoid child psychopathologies, which in my opinion is the root cause of dictatorship, well, that kind of cognitive development can create rampant cases of ODD and…"

"Excuse me, what's ODD?" I ask. I can't help it. I'm utterly fascinated by the intellectual theories flowing out of Rachel's mouth.

"There's no cross-talking," blurts Stephen Stephanie.

"ODD is Oppositional Defiant Disorder," explains Rachel. "The Wikipedia definition is an ongoing pattern of disobedient, hostile and defiant behavior toward an authority figure that goes beyond the bounds of normal childhood behavior. As a child psychologist I've developed what I believe are solutions to the root cause. I even have a thesis that demonstrates some of these theories in an analysis of the Middle East. It's a clearcut case of ODD resulting from sibling rivalry and abandonment that has developed into national dysfunctional co-dependency and low self-esteem finding its outlet in aggression and violence. But I have no idea if my work means anything at all to anyone…so I just keep working…." She takes a deep breath and adds, "I don't have anything more to say."

I want to applaud her for her work, but no one else lifts their hands, so I quietly follow the assumed protocol where all eyes now turn to Brian who slumps in his chair.

Brian remains in his depressed position as he takes his turn. "I'm Brian. Complete workaholic. Madison and Rachel are right. I've been working on this genealogy software program and I know it's dope. I've worked out intricate logarithms with data warehousing using keywords in correspondences to match and trace family relations in worldwide genealogy pools. People can input DNA tests with scans of letters about family histories to identify their great ancestors all the way back to the Middle Ages. But until I sell it, I can't stop working. And there's always this looming fear that someone else is going to beat me to it. I feel like this rat running around inside a fucking maze all the time, chasing dreams I totally see but can't seem to get others to see them. Everyone keeps telling me to give up and go get some normal job. But what good does that do? You get a job and the corporation gets swallowed by some other corp and you're history, or they outsource to India and you're dust. It's the death of job culture and runaway industries. One after the other. So what the fuck, man. I think I'm obsessed with my program because it's all about finding out where we come from and if we know where we come from, maybe we'll know what the fuck we're supposed to do with our fucking lives." He stops talking and stares at his navel.

We all look at him and nod. Stephen Stephanie looks at the clock. "Thank you for sharing, Brian. Let's all hold hands for the Serenity Prayer."

Our small group stands up and holds hands reciting the prayer out loud. But an extra line is added which I don't know and I find myself mumbling, "Keep coming back. It works if you work it." Two "works" in one sentence. Sounds good to me.

I'm about to take off when Stephen Stephanie approaches me. "I'd like to give you some literature to read about the disease along with a meeting schedule and a contact sheet with our phone numbers in case you're in a crisis situation, and/or you just need to talk. And when you're ready for a sponsor to help you work through the steps, let me know. I'm available or I can find you someone else."

She loads me up with packets of information. Oh, good, more homework, I think, just what a workaholic needs to justify going to workaholics anonymous meetings.

"So will we see you at the next meeting?" she asks.

"When is the next meeting?"

"Tomorrow evening at seven o'clock."

"Oh. I'll try," I say, careful not to make a commitment I

can't keep while folding the paperwork and shoving it inside my tote bag.

Inside the Rotunda

The following morning, I'm standing inside the lobby of the Senate building waiting for my team. I wonder how Brian's genealogy software works and what kind of groundbreaking insights Rachel has developed in her field. And if those theories combined with the intricate knowledge of one's ancestral roots might not play a significant part in the development of well-adjusted children, which in turn would make happier societies, which in turn would make happier nations. Could the trickle down theory, where top management sets the tone and attitude of a corporation analogous to that of a nation, be reversed to a bottoms-up theory where the collective society of well-adjusted individuals could naturally override and dictate the manner in which a country was run. Hmm. I don't think so. I take a sip of coffee and meditate on My Grief Day. I imagine the plan inside my head and as more ideas grow, I grow in confidence, envisioning each detail and every component.

"There she is." It's Eve's voice. I turn around to find Richard Wright, Sierra D'Asanti and Eve Gardner approaching me.

"Good morning." I smile. "How is everyone?"

"We're all good," answers Richard. "Gawler's Funeral Home did an outstanding job. Plus, they bought a thousand of the grief guidebooks, five hundred each of *Grief Wellness* and *Grief Tributes* as part of their After Care Program."

"That's great," I say. Instead of funeral homes passing out light flimsy pamphlets on grief that could easily blow away in the wind, they were buying the grief guidebooks at wholesale, and distributing a solid palatable hundred pages on the etiquette of grief and how to create personalized life celebrations.

Sierra tells us, "Hampstead said the equipment is all set up in the Rotunda."

Eve scans my wardrobe and rolls her eyes.

Sierra holds up a DVD and smiles. "You just need to slip this into the DVD player and push play. An automatic loop of the edited soundbytes exactly like you wanted. Here you go." She hands it to me.

"Wow. You're good. And fast." Eve starts coughing and clearing her throat. We all turn to face her. "Are you okay?" I ask.

"No. I'm not okay," Eve replies. "How can you wear a stripe suit with a plaid shirt?" She hands me a notebook. "Here."

"What's this?"

"A backup presentation design database. I copied all the Polaroids I've taken of your wardrobe and put together a visual list of options for you. So you won't have to *think* about what to put on. Not that you're capable of that anyway."

"Thanks, Eve." I smile. "Here's something for you." I hand her a CD. "It's a rough draft of the itinerary for My Grief Day. I've also included an executive summary describing our purpose and expectations."

"Isn't it obvious?" asks Eve. "We're manifesting a cause celeb."

"I would modify that," says Richard. "Our purpose is to create a national holiday to celebrate our personal and collective grief."

"Yes. And our expectation is to heal as many people as we can…on budget," adds Sierra.

"Well put! I'd like you guys to start going over the production logistics. We'll have to take into account risk management, too. Richard, please figure out how we can integrate traditional funeral rituals into the program. Sierra, think about how you want to stage the video displays and who you think would be best to host the streaming media online. Eve, let me know what kind of concepts you come up with for the grief attire. Please add any ideas or suggestions you have for the experience design and public awareness campaign. I'll meet you guys back at the Roosevelt Room. Oh, and Eve, do me a favor and find out how Derek Rogers is related to John Darcy."

Richard and Eve start walking. Sierra steps in front of me, looks me in the eye and nods her head. I get the feeling she knows something I don't know.

"Waiting long?" she asks.

"A few minutes," I reply.

"What were you thinking about?"

I look at her, oddly. "Why are you asking me that?"

"Because you're standing on the gold dot."

"What gold dot?" I look down. There's a gold dot under my feet. "So?"

"So. That's the center of the capital. It's considered the axis of political power."

"Okay. Nice useless knowledge." I start to move but she blocks me and stares, waiting. "And your point is?" I ask.

"Folklore says that when one stands on this gold dot, it's possible to draw in the energy of the capital to achieve one's goals. Apparently, many politicians have stood here looking for a source of strength and power."

"Did they get what they came for?"

"I have no idea," says Sierra. "That's not the point."

"Then what is?"

"That they tried. I suppose."

I nod. "There's trying to touch a wall and then there's stepping forward and touching the God blessed wall. We're touching the wall." And with that I step off the gold dot and start walking toward the Rotunda.

Sierra follows. "That's what I love about you. You don't quit."

"Is there really a choice?"

"For some, Maddy."

But I can't begin to sort out the concept. And for once, I am glad there is something I cannot do. I turn the corner, heading for my next mission, aware that I have taken a last glance behind me at the gold dot where I had stood thinking about theories on ODD, genealogy and the execution of My Grief Day. None of which seemed to have anything in common. Folklore. Hmmph.

A long line of mourners gathers outside the Senate Rotunda. Friends, family, members of Congress and ardent admirers politely and silently wait their turn to pay their respects to John Darcy. Their heads hang low and their eyes slowly glance from one nondescript place on the floor to another. I search their tired faces, seeking a connection. As I approach the throng, I can feel the weight of their malaise. I can smell the scent of collective grief. Collective grief has its own peculiar energy; it is thick, and labored, and it has a way of sucking you inside a vortex of darkness. Once inside, you are blinded by pain and all you can feel is an intense alchemy of sadness, guilt, regret, shame and doom that offers no other choice but the express single conscious desire to lie down, to quit living, and ask if the unbearable ache in your heart will ever slip away.

I step toward the mass of depressed energy lined up before me. Someone staring at the floor hears the click of my heels. There's a momentary glance upward and a slow, methodical step to the side. Another person follows suit. Suddenly, the mass of depressed energy appears to part way and in my Messiah pumps I step through with an ease and lightness I have never known before.

John Darcy's casket lies in the middle of the Rotunda, as is the customary ritual for politicians of his stature. A security guard unleashes a rope for me to pass through to where the casket lies. I am alone and the public viewing has yet to begin. I move toward the DVD player which lies on top of a desk near a large flat-screen monitor on the wall. A box of wireless headsets is on the other side of the desk. Mourners can pay their respects to John Darcy and tune in for a private viewing of an abridged version of yesterday's funeral service. I place the DVD inside the player and hit the play button. The monitor comes to life and the images roll. I turn around and take one last look at the hollow shell of John Darcy. I recall the words of Thomas Lynch, a renowned funeral director hyphen poet, who, in his book *The Undertaking,* hammered his observations based on his life's work into four words; *the dead don't care.* I stare at Darcy. He can't possibly care because he's not there, to care. Where he is, is the great mystery. His soul, like all others upon death, has pulled a Houdini. The display of his body is for one reason only, for the living. Only the spirit of the living has died with him, and with his wife, and with Haley Stone and with the hope that our country can survive its collective grief.

"If you don't mind, I'd like a moment alone with my cousin."

My stomach aches. I look up to see Derek Rogers, wearing his trademark smirk. My eyes narrow. And instead of stepping to the side, I quietly and confidently step in front of him. "Exactly how are you related to John Darcy, Derek?"

"My family tree hardly deserves your scrutiny, Madison. Now, if you don't mind." He clears his throat. "Besides, don't you have better things to do, like plan a country's pity party?"

"Right. While you use the incarcerated minds of white collar criminals to cure the nation of its budget deficit."

"Madison. Let me remind you. Without a budget, you can't have a party, no matter how frivolous it may be. Now. I'd like some time alone with my cousin, without getting dizzy from your…whatever you have on."

I glance at my clothes, and undeterred, counter, "I thought criminals on furlough weren't allowed to be out alone…and unsupervised."

"Who said I'm alone, Madison. The whole country's watching."

I turn around to witness the arrival of all the major news crews as they set up shop. Other members of the press snap photos. Having the whole country's eyes upon him was exactly what Derek wanted. He couldn't give a damn about paying his last respects to the man he claimed to be his cousin. Derek Rogers had something else up his sleeve and he was using Darcy's death as the stage to unveil it.

My BlackBerry sends a shiver through my hip. I answer it as I exit the curtain on what's become the Darcy Death Show. "This is Madison."

"Hampstead here. The president would like to see you."

"I thought he was at his lake retreat."

"I'm aware of that. The whole country is aware of that. Your point is?"

"Um. Logistics."

"Exit the building, Ms. Banks, and leave the details to me. It's what I do best."

"Hampstead. I'm not prepared to report to the president any new details regarding My Grief Day."

Hampstead pauses. "This is about *his* grief day, Ms. Banks. And I believe you accepted the offer to be the president's grief buddy."

"I'm exiting the building now."

Two hours and one helicopter ride later, I'm sitting in a row boat with President Stone. We're casting fishing lines into a body of cold water on an Indian summer day in the middle of October. The trees surrounding the lake form a perimeter of fall colors that dot the horizon with a beauty befitting nature. I can't help but think of Uncle Sam. He would have loved to have been here or at least hear about how his niece, the funeral planner, went fishing with the president. I glance between the ripples in the water and the slow-moving clouds in the sky and wonder if Uncle Sam is nearby.

"I really appreciate your coming out here today," says President Stone.

He looks like he hasn't slept much and he appears to have lost some weight. The pain in his eyes is hurtful to witness. I want to make it go away. I want to look at the president and know that he is leading our nation. But all I can see is a man lost inside the grief cloud. I need a gentle way to coax him into conversation.

"I didn't know this lake had rainbow trout."

He looks at me for a long time, then, "How do you know your fish?"

"I thought I saw you put a Spinnerbait on your hook, sir. Style N. Green Monkey Shine."

He gently nods, revealing a faint gesture of unexpected approval. "How long have you been fishing?" he asks.

"Since I was able to sit in a boat." I smile.

"Who taught you?" he asks.

"My uncle Sam. He owned Banks Baits and collected antique lures."

"Me, too," he whispers, and then retreats into silence. Even the discovery of a shared passion does little to break the bonds of grief.

"Please, tell me what I can do to help you, sir."

He looks at me and drops his head, depleted of his life force. Grief was sucking on his energy like a leech. A fish nibbles on his line, but the president does nothing about it. After several moments pass, he whispers, "John was a good fisherman…until two years ago."

"Would you like to tell me what happened?"

It's several minutes before the president is able to talk again. When he does speak, his words roll out in a measured manner. "He caught a thirty-inch bass. That fish fought hard for its life. John. He was patient. He kept negotiating with the fish, giving him slack, then reeling him in, giving him some slack again, and reeling him in. They took turns. Giving and taking. For hours. John finally wore the poor fellow out. When the fish surrendered, John took the lure out of its gills, placed the fish back in the water, and set him free."

The president pauses and then looks at me, and his words begin to pick up some speed. "I asked John why he did that. He said, 'Freedom comes when we surrender to our choices, but I tricked that poor fish into surrendering. I won't do it again.' After that, he'd sit with me in the boat, but he wouldn't fish. And every time I caught one, I'd look at John and slip it back in the water. Eighteen months ago, I told John, 'Let's not cast any bait. Those who choose to negotiate can.' That's how we started the Middle East peace negotiations."

"That's a wonderful story, Mr. President. Thank you for sharing that."

He nods. "It was working until he…" He looks out at the water, past the secret service men in nearby rowboats, to the canvas of colorful trees lining the shore. Conviction returns to the underbelly of his words. "Out of respect for John, I won't resort to using any bait to resume peace negotiations. Oil or no oil. At some point, the Middle East needs to grow up. It might as well be now."

Talking politics is bringing the president back to life. I only hoped it wouldn't become a bandage to dealing with his loss. But I was a grief buddy, not a grief counselor. My job in this situation is to be the best listener I can.

"By the way, Madison, I admire your political strategy."

"My political strategy? I'm not sure I understand you, sir."

He smiles. It's the first time I've seen the president smile in days. "You're good," he says. "You're very, very good." He wags his finger at me like Robert De Niro in the films *Analyze This* and *Analyze That*.

"Mr. President." I lean in and whisper, "Could you please tell me what I'm good at?" He laughs. I am baffled yet thankful that whatever I'm doing seems to amuse him.

"Deflecting the media," he explains. "You've got them so focused on the odd manner in which you dress that they're not even paying attention to what you're doing. Interesting psychology, Madison."

"Thank you, sir." I wondered how Eve might take this news. I wasn't sure if I should tell the president the strategy was purely unintentional. But I decide against it. If it brought him one bright moment in his day, I could afford the laughter at my expense.

"Speaking of My Grief Day, Madison. What's the projected budget?" asks the president.

"I estimate approximately five million dollars, sir. That's including venues for two live performances from both coasts with online simulcasts. We'll continue to try to cut that budget number down, but we haven't approached the television networks yet and that doesn't include the public awareness campaign."

The president reels in his line. "The psychological healing of our nation is important, Madison. Go to twenty million if you need it."

"Thank you, Mr. President. That's very kind of you."

On my way back to the White House, it occurs to me that the president of the United States is no longer sharing his feelings about grief, but including me in his own political strategies. He had used an interesting choice of words. The Middle East needs to "grow up," implying that their behavior is similar to that of undisciplined children. Sibling rivalries, I think, stemming from Isaac and Ishmael. I consider whether their respective nations really were suffering from ODD, as Rachel had suggested. I'd have to ask her more about that, before or after the meeting, of course. But when on earth would I ever find time to go to another WAA meeting. Between planning the events around My Grief Day and my extracurricular activities as the president's grief buddy, let alone carrying on a relationship with Victor, I didn't see how I could possibly make it to the meetings. And then it occurs to me. Perhaps the meetings could make it to me. I pull out the contact sheet that Stephen Stephanie gave me and start dialing.

The Roosevelt Room reprise

Sierra draws two large diagrams side by side on a giant whiteboard. "This is the east coast venue, the Kennedy Center—and over here is the west coast venue, the Disney Concert Hall."

Richard, Eve and I watch as Sierra paces around the whiteboard.

"The program will stream live on MyGriefDay.com and The Tribute Network," adds Sierra. "We can use The Tribute Network's terms of service agreement for copyright protected material with respect to UGC."

Richard raises his hand. "UGC?"

"User-generated content," replies Sierra.

"User what?" asks Richard.

"It's another way of saying, 'programming for the people by the people,'" I say.

Sierra hands me the marker. "Why don't you take it from here?"

Sierra and I switch places. I stand at the whiteboard and face my team when a ding sound goes off.

Eve looks at her phone, then at me. "Gotta go." She immediately pulls lipstick from her purse and generously applies it to her lips.

"Now?" I ask.

"Yes, now. It's for you. And I already know what these acronyms mean."

"Well, can you at least wait five minutes?" I plead.

Eve sighs and glances at her watch. "Two tops," she agrees, and puts her makeup away.

"Okay, so…I'm thinking we need to create a call to action for the user-generated content. That will be one source of programming along with our own original content, interviews with bereavement professionals and with celebrities on their own personal grief stories, what process they went through and how they dealt with their feelings, etc."

"How are you going to get people to send in their stories?" asks Richard.

"Good question," I reply. "We're going to launch the Tribute Film Festival."

Eve rolls her eyes. "Just what the world needs, another film festival. What are you going to do? Offer the winners a Golden Tear Award?"

Sierra, Richard and I start to giggle.

"That's funny," says Sierra. "Maybe we should do it."

Eve stands up and grabs her purse. "While you guys figure out if golden tears are enough of a draw for a brand that doesn't even exist yet, I've got an appointment to keep."

She leaves. I turn to my remaining pair. Sierra looks at me, "Well, she does have a point, about the brand thing."

"Brand shmand. We're addressing a national grief crisis. People need to know it's okay to grieve in any way they need to. This is about opening up a dialogue for grief. Why is it always shoved under the rug? Just like conversations about sex and money. The more we talk about it, the less isolated we feel and the better equipped we are to deal with it."

"I agree with you, but how do people identify with something so intangible and painful? I think Eve's right. We need to think of our event as a product and brand it."

"Fine. Then we'll build it and they will come," I reply.

"So the product is grief?" asks Richard, dubiously.

"It's not a product. It's life, it's a part of life. Look at Martha Stewart. She turned living into a brand. We'll do the same thing with death."

Sierra shakes her head. "So we're going to be the Martha Stewart of dying?"

"That's right," I reply. "Only a not-for-profit version. And My Grief Day is just one part of it."

"Are we going to call it 'Maddy Banks Dying'?" asks Richard.

"No, because it's not about dying. It's what Lights Out Enterprises stands for. It's about life celebration."

There's a knock on the door. "Come in," I say. Press secretary James Damon enters the room.

"Ms. Banks. We have a situation." James frowns.

Richard, Sierra and I stare at him. From the tone in his voice, it's clear we need to brace ourselves.

"A bomb exploded at Reagan National Airport. Ten people are dead." James turns to me. "The president is on his way. In the meantime, he'd like you to say something inspirational to the media until he gets here."

Shocked and shaken, I look at Sierra. She squeezes my hand.

I swallow hard, trying to shore up my resources of strength and stamina; wondering why me again? There were all kinds of agencies for this, like CHS, the Center of Hazard Studies, and ICC, the Institute of Catastrophe and Crisis. There were plenty of acronyms to choose from.

I slip on my Messiah shoes and head out the door and down the hall with new resolve. "Excuse me, James. Where's the head of Home Security?" I ask.

"In the hospital, recuperating from a kidney stone."

I nod, keeping pace with him. "And the vice president?"

"At a global warming summit in Beijing," he answers.

"What about Tyler Simmons?"

"On his way to a budget deficit conference in South Dakota."

"Don't tell me. The 'conference' is being held at Yankton Federal Prison."

"That information wasn't publicly released. How did you know that?"

I shrug. James seems to read my mind. "The president feels you're best as well as readily available to address the situation at this time." He hands me a piece of paper as we round a corner. "You can read over the speech I've prepared for you while we walk to the Rose Garden."

"Anyone take responsibility for this?"

"We have every reason to believe it's terrorist activity… the obvious. But the president wants you to avoid those questions."

The Rose Garden is packed with reporters in a feeding frenzy, vying for answers. James takes the podium and addresses the crowd. "The president is on his way. I've already given you the facts as far as we know them. In the interim, President Stone has asked the Head of our House Bereavement Specialists Committee, Ms. Madison Banks, to say a few words. There will be no questions at this time."

James looks at me and steps down. I step up and clear my throat. Everyone settles into silence. I scan the piece of text James prepared for me, but I can't see it because tears of grief and sorrow have begun to stream down my face and cloud my vision. I start to speak but no words come forth. Instead, I stand there. And then I cry. A long involuntary cry. Everyone stares at me. My tears keep flowing. My voice appears to have gone on hiatus. I think how embarrassing this is and try to get a grip. I lift my hands up, hoping to unlock my chest cavity, increase my oxygen flow and find my voice again. "It's okay to cry," I say, my voice finally coming home. "It hurts to see innocent lives taken. It hurts to see the lives of survivors destroyed. It hurts to be the victim of angry, violent people. It hurts because we are a nation of those who are capable of empathy. It hurts because in the back of our hearts is the added fear that one day, it might be one of us, or someone we know, if we don't already." I pause to collect my breath and notice that the reporters remain unusually silent. "So it's okay to be hurt. It's okay to be sad. It's okay to cry."

I glance at James, ready to leave the podium now. But he taps his watch and gives me the "keep rolling" sign. So I continue, "Crying. Crying is not a sign of weakness. Crying is a sign of strength. Whoever hurt us wanted to…hurt us. Why should we hide from the success of their goal?" I look into the lens of the news camera and I cry. "I hurt. Your actions and the consequences of your actions have hurt me. Physically. Emotionally. Psychically. Collectively. Is this what makes you happy? Do you want me to be angry? You don't deserve my anger. Anger is what we show children when they misbehave and inside of that anger is guidance and they know deep down they are loved. But for you, I shall show no anger. For you, I shall show only pity. I feel sorry for you. And I pity you."

I'm about to walk off again but James signals me to keep going. I turn back to the crowd. I don't know what to say anymore. I stand there, silently looking at the expectant eyes in the faces before me and blurt out, "I…I suspect that whoever did this, must suffer from ODD. That's uh, Oppositional Defiant Disorder. This person must be in terrible psychological pain to lash out in such a destructive manner. To the person behind this all I can say is that I wish your wounds heal…until then…I pity you." I step back, ready to leave this time. "Oh, I would just like to add that not all of these ideas are mine. I was recently influenced by a child psychologist whose theories on ODD I find to be fascinating and highly applicable in this situation."

The reporters all simultaneously raise their hands. Julie Waters from BBS News shouts out, "Who?"

I'm about to reply, but I remember the oath of anonymity. Besides, I only know the woman's first name. But if I tell them, "I don't know," or "I can't say," then it could appear as though I have no credibility, and what if Rachel got mad at me for not mentioning her name, especially after she shared her frustration over the lack of validation and recognition she's received for her work in her field to date. I'm in the middle of another God blessed conundrum.

I decide to solve the problem with a combination answer. "Rachel A., uh, Nominos." I try to hide the word behind a mask of syllables with switched accents to make it sound Spanish and Greek.

James holds up his hand to signal the end of the press conference. As he walks me out of the Rose Garden, he smiles. "I liked your speech better than mine."

"Thanks," I say.

"Just don't do it again."

Off the Record is the name of the bar at the Hay-Adams Hotel and it is packed with the who's who in Washington D.C. I maneuver past politicians, key staffers and lobbyists searching for my party. I find Victor and Arthur Pintock sitting at the bar nursing their drinks. Victor greets me with a kiss and takes my coat. Arthur gives me a warm hug.

"You okay?" Victor whispers in my ear.

I nod.

"You did good, Maddy. I think you opened things up," adds Victor, as he gently caresses my shoulder. I rub my hand across his back, in gratitude for his words and touch.

"I'll say," Arthur points out. "Your words were moving and dare I say, unusual." He glances around the room. People are sniffling, holding tissues to their faces and watching the news on the flat screen monitor above the bar for the latest update in the crisis.

"Has anyone taken responsibility yet?" I ask.

"Not yet," replies Victor.

Broadcaster Bill Sutter's face fills the TV screen. He shouts, "Well, she can't dress, but she certainly can cry!" A photograph from today's press conference flashes on the screen highlighting my outfit. The one I'm still wearing.

Arthur shakes his head in disgust at the TV screen.

"Ignore him," says Victor.

I look at Bill Sutter huffing and puffing like the big bad wolf, who is forever trying to blow other people's houses down. "What is wrong with him? People are dead and he's commenting on me."

"What do you expect from what some call the unfair and unbalanced channel?" Victor quips, rhetorically.

"I pity him," I say, "off the record."

Arthur smiles. "That's the ticket. Let's go eat, shall we?"

We sit down at a nice booth inside the Lafayette Restaurant. Victor and Arthur read over their menus. But I'm not hungry. I've lost my appetite. The waiter comes and goes, and for the sake of appearances I order a large salad.

"How's Grace?" I ask Arthur. Since Tara's death, I had developed a special fondness for Grace. I was always taken by her quiet strength. I admired the way she dealt with Tara's death and I hoped that she and Arthur would repair their wounds and find a way to stay united after their loss.

"She's good, Maddy. We're good. It hasn't been easy. But ever since Richard Wright gave us a framework for how to communicate we've been talking…every day. We get together and we remember Tara…together."

"I'm so glad."

"Me, too," says Arthur. "Congratulations on Jonathon Darcy's funeral service. It was a wonderful way for him to be remembered."

"Thanks. Of course, I had a lot of help." Victor smiles at me, ever so proud. "So...did Victor tell you, Richard? I've resigned from The Tribute Network."

"So I've heard. Until you leave your post in the White House. Meanwhile, you'll be an unpaid, bipartisan advisor, which leads me to my next question. How can we push the user-generated content?"

"You think it needs to be pushed more than the current plan?"

Victor produces a stack of papers. "We've done some research and a lot of thinking. We feel strongly that Americans who create and upload their personal stories and Americans who watch it would be better served in a different viewing format. Not just for economic reasons...but to help with your goals for My Grief Day."

"Different viewing format?" I ask. "What are you getting at?"

"We want people to be able to watch the events of My Grief Day *together*," Arthur outlines. "Not alone in their offices or bedrooms with just themselves and a computer monitor. That only feeds into the whole zeitgeist of solitude in the world of grief and technology. We want to break out of that."

"So you want people to be able to grieve together?"

Arthur leans in closer to me. "We want collective transformation," he says.

I hadn't thought of The Tribute Network or My Grief Day in that way before. But as soon as Arthur said those words, I knew it was the bottom line to everything we were doing together and apart. I felt an immediate awareness to my purpose. That I was sharing it with two men whom I admired enriched it even more so. Collective transformation was the next frontier. Pine & Gilmore had mentioned it in their breakout book, *The Experience Economy.* They had outlined the evolution of economic growth from commodities, to products, to services, to experiences; the next step they predicted would be transformation. And Victor, Arthur and I were now at one of its epicenters.

"My Grief Day has a terrific message," Arthur enthuses. "To lay our grief bare, to acknowledge our pain, together."

"The value of the experience is totally there," says Victor.

"We think if we modify the intake of the experience, we can do better. We can transform and heal. But that requires more than solitary viewing."

"Any ideas?" asks Victor.

"Two. And they fit perfectly with the Tribute Film Festival."

"The Tribute Film Festival? What's that?"

"The call to action for people to send in their trib vids. The Tribute Network and My Grief Day will co-launch the online Tribute Film Festival. People send in their two- or three-minute trib vids and over the course of three months, viewers log on and rate the films."

"Did you just think of this?" asks Victor.

"It's been brewing," I reply.

"What's going to compel people to send in tribute films or go to the trouble of making one? Some sort of cash prize?" asks Arthur. "I hate to see this turn into a contest for money."

"Well, we did kick around the Golden Tear Award," I say. "But more than some cash prize, this is about recognizing our grief, while honoring and commemorating the people, and pets, that help us on our life journeys. So, here's how I see it. The top ten highest viewer-rated films will be judged by an elite Hollywood jury. And the winning films will be exhibited at a national movie theatre chain as a short before the feature film—tying in with our goal of collective transformation."

"How are you going to get a national movie chain theatre to do this?"

"Create a strategic partnership based on goodwill."

"Unfortunately, goodwill doesn't cover the cost of that kind of prime real estate."

"Well, the president gave me carte blanche on the budget, so it shouldn't be an issue."

"What about people who don't live near movie theatres?" asks Victor.

"They can see it in mobile cinemas, across the country, so no small rural town is spared. What do you think?"

Victor sits back and smiles.

"How many people can fit in a mobile cinema van in the dead of winter?" asks Arthur.

"Not vans. Semi-trucks," Victor points out. "When they park they use hydraulics to spread the sides of the truck out creating a space measuring a thousand square feet. I've seen them used as traveling tradeshows for conventioneers who can't get to a convention. So they bring the exhibit to them. They can comfortably fit a hundred people."

Arthur nods. "How many do you think we need to cover fifty states and how many can we get?"

"I'll look into it," offers Victor, then he smiles at me. "Did I ever tell you how brilliant you are?"

"No, I'm not." The blood courses through my veins—I'm so excited over all the concepts I've laid out. I didn't see how what was so obvious and apparent to me could be construed as brilliant. I only knew I could hardly wait to get back to my room and start putting it all together. A thought suddenly appeared that joined my excitement and an adrenaline fix for work addiction. The thought lingered for a moment, then dropped out of sight, as I realized an online Tribute Film Festival didn't have national borders. The prospects were global. My adrenaline reached a new high. Grief was not just a national affliction. It was global. So why stop at healing grief in the U.S.? International tribute films could play in movie theatres everywhere… One antidote to grief was to stop dwelling. And honoring another person, or pet, in the format of a trib vid, was one way to stop dwelling and start healing.

"So, Madison," says Arthur. "I want you to use my private jet for any traveling you have to do. Understood?"

"Excuse me? My mind wandered. What did you say?"

"I want you to use my private jet for any traveling you have to do."

"That's hardly necessary, Arthur. You don't have to—"

"Oh, yes, I do, Madison. Yes, I do."

Ever since Tara died, Arthur was prone to fall into bouts of paternal protection for me. There was no arguing with him whenever these moods struck. I understand it was what he needed to do more for himself than for me. My acquiescence gave him respite from his loss, and it had become my pleasure to do so. This was one of those times. I look at him and graciously reply, "Thank you."

Our dinner talk soon turns to the politics of the day. We discuss the terrorist attack, the government subsidized tax breaks in affordable housing projects to help rebuild the Midwest and New Orleans, what will happen to the Middle East peace negotiations, and the general malaise of the public at large.

Victor and Arthur believed in the value of The Tribute Network as a Web site for all things tribute related, including information and entertainment on everything from celebrity roasts to pet memorial videos, to the latest updates on green burials and designer caskets. And they believed in My Grief Day and what it could do to help heal the nation. I was glad, because I knew there would be days where I wouldn't be so sure, where I would continue to question myself, doubting the purpose of my work, and I would need to rely on their unwavering faith to float me. I didn't think that others might question me. Or that I could be so naïve as to not realize that they would, and with a vengeance.

4

"I love you, Maddy," Victor whispers in my ear.

We are in bed. His arms are wrapped around my waist. My legs are wrapped around his hips. I smile at him. I don't think I've ever felt so loved. But the more Victor loves me, the more foreign the whole relationship feels to me and I can't figure out why.

"I know you do," I whisper back. What a weak reply, I think. It's the best I can do in this moment. But he doesn't seem to mind my answer.

Victor's breathing intensifies. His grip tightens. The rhythm of our conjoined arms and limbs gains momentum and then he climaxes and sweetly moans at the same time. When the lovemaking is over, Victor doesn't let go. He hangs on to me. It's the only time I feel as though I am his raft in whatever seas he's sailing through. He gently kisses me.

"Did you come?"

I pause. "It's not you. I think all the grief is getting to me."

"Do you want to talk about it?"

"Not really."

"A release would be good for you. What if I go down on you?"

"Why don't we both get some sleep, Victor. You've got that follow-up meeting in Austin tomorrow morning. I'm exhausted, and I know you are, too."

Victor yawns. "You got that right." He kisses me on the cheek. "Hey. Don't forget to let me know about New Zealand. I can still get a good deal on tickets for January. And we could both use a good long vacation."

"Okay…I'll think about it."

He closes the gap between his stomach and my back, spoons me in his arms, and is fast asleep. I count to ten and then slowly unwind myself from our cuddle. I slip out of bed and tiptoe over to my laptop. I hit the mute button, turning the computer on so it awakens in silence and then I hoard in three hours of work. I shift between writing down ideas, collecting data online, researching national and international movie chain theatres and mobile cinema exhibits and developing more content and implementation plans for My Grief Day. Plus, I have to figure out how to get Hollywood's elite filmmakers on board to participate in the Tribute Film Festival jury.

I'm in the middle of crunching numbers for several proposals when an Instant Message pops up on my screen. It's from Eve. It reads, Got what you wanted. I look at the clock. It's four-thirty in the morning. She's up. I'm up. So I e-mail back, Can I get it now? She replies, If you must. Meet me in my room in ten minutes.

I quietly put my computer to sleep, throw on the white terry-cloth hotel bathrobe, a pair of cozy slippers and stealthily slip out the door. I tiptoe down the hotel corridor to the elevator and head for Eve's floor. I reach her room and quietly knock. Thirty seconds pass. I knock again. The door opens a crack. She peeks out and animatedly whispers, "I said ten minutes, not three. Come back in seven."

"Why?" I ask.

"Everything okay?" inquires a male voice from beyond the door.

"Oh. That's why. See ya in seven," I say. I turn around and start pacing. A loud robotic thud repeats itself. I walk down the hallway and turn a corner to investigate the noise. A bellman methodically drops newspapers off at the foot of each door. I wait for him to disappear then quietly snatch newspapers and start reading the headlines.

The first reads, "Grief Czar Madison Banks Releases Ineffective Tears as Weapons of Revenge." Who said anything about revenge? The reporter completely missed the point. The second reads, "She Can't Dress, But She Can Cry," repeating the slogan of broadcaster Bill Sutter. I skim the articles, reading false claims about me. One reporter suggests my tears are nothing more than a cop-out and challenges the real Rachel A. Nominos to stand up and come forth with her theories on child psychology. A columnist purports unethical behavior on my part because of my relationship to The Tribute Network, accusing me of corrupt and illicit behavior. There's not one kind word among any of them. Each reporter concludes with comments on the frivolity of My Grief Day, calling it nothing more than a pity party, using the same words Derek Rogers used, and citing more important ways for our government to spend resources it doesn't have.

I take a deep breath. I know that what I said at yesterday's press conference came from my heart. If I felt it, surely others must have felt it, too. But a balance of opinions was absent here and I wondered why. My challenge: not to take any of it personally. Yeah, right. Still, where was the fair and balanced reporting?

I return the newspapers and despondently tiptoe back to Eve's room. A cute young man exits her room and nods as he passes by me for the elevator. Eve opens the door and lets me in.

"Who was that?" I ask.

"Isn't he dreamy?" Eve asks, rhetorically. She flops down on her bed. "He's the cute senator's aide I met the other night...who happens to be roommates with Jonathon Darcy's secretary...who happened to get me this." She holds up a small blue memory stick hard drive and waves it in my face. "These are the letters of correspondence between Jonathon Darcy and Derek Rogers."

I perk up, and then quickly sag. "I can't accept that. That's private correspondence obtained under false means."

"Who said anything about false means?" She smiles. "I told them you wanted to verify Mr. Rogers' familial relationship with Mr. Darcy. The office even signed off on it. There's the paperwork." She glances at the nightstand with a manila envelope on it.

"And did they ask why I would want to do that?"

"Of course they did, silly." She then pauses for a dramatic reveal. "Because you're interested in having Mr. Rogers speak about the value of family legacies and the unexpected joys that can be found in tracing long lost relatives during My Grief Day."

"But that's not true."

"It is if he's really related...isn't it? And you won't know that until you look at this." She wags the blue mini-hard drive in front of me.

"Nice work," I tell her and reach for the mini-memory stick, but Eve quickly folds it back in her hand like a magician performing a disappearing trick.

"Not so fast," she says. "We need to work out an arrangement."

"Eve, don't be ridiculous. I can't be bribed."

"Who said anything about bribery?"

"No one...I've just become sensitive to implications of it. The newspapers seem to be launching a smear campaign with me as their target."

"Gee. I wonder why."

"Come on, Eve. It can't be because of the way I dress."

"Well, it doesn't help. Did anyone ever attempt to smear Jacqueline Kennedy Onassis? Or Haley Stone for that matter? No. Why? The way they dressed. But don't worry. I have a plan to fix it."

I shudder. "What's the arrangement?"

Eve starts tidying the room. "No more ridiculous outfits. From now on, everything is tailored, even your T-shirts, and you promise to wear the designs I've chosen for you. If you get stuck, you call me, day or night, cocktail party or black tie affair, breakfast meeting or walking the dog. Are we clear?"

"Very."

"Good." She turns on her heels. "One more thing."

I tap my foot, eyeing the little hard drive in her hand. "What?"

"You grant me exclusive rights to trademark the content of your little speech yesterday in the Rose Garden."

"Why?"

"I have an idea."

"Care to share it?"

"It's a work in progress. You'll just have to trust me."

"Fine. I trust you." I hold out my hand.

She drops the mini-hard drive in it, then smiles at me. "So what are you wearing today?"

I look at her, once again clueless. "I don't know. How about Page Two in the booklet you gave me."

She beams. "Perfect." Then she grabs her suitcase and starts packing. "I'll be in New York the next couple of days in case you need me."

"But we have meetings and..."

Eve yawns. "Right. And I have wardrobes to create for My Grief Day...among other things. Celebrities, speakers, performers...they all need styling. And if you want the rest of the country to participate, they need...uniforms, if you will."

"Uniforms? This isn't a marching band."

"Okay, costumes...whatever."

"It's not Halloween," I object.

"Maddy, events are made special by what we wear. We need affordable fashion that defines this holiday."

By now, I've learned not to argue with Eve, and "affordable fashion" was more than acceptable, so I head back to my room. I leave the newspapers outside on the floor and tiptoe back inside my room. At 5:30 a.m., I climb into bed with Victor, who is still asleep. I quietly slither inside his arms to capture an hour of sleep beside him.

When I wake up, Victor is long gone, on his way to Austin. He's left behind a pot of hot coffee, a rose on top of the *Financial Street Journal* and a note telling me not to bother reading the other papers, unaware that I've already read them in the wee morning hours. I stand up and look out the window. A flat pewter-colored sky highlights the landscape of buildings, domes and treetops that are still standing, and so am I. And on this morning, I remember to say the Serenity Prayer with one hundred percent accuracy on the second try.

At 0900 hours, Hampstead leads Sierra and me through several hallways. I try to walk lightly with my Messiah pumps whenever we cross marble floors. He finally stops and points to our new more permanent office complete with desks, chairs, computers, phones, faxes and office supplies. A TV monitor plays in the background with round-the-clock news coverage. The sign on the door reads, "House Bereavement Specialists Committee."

"Will this do?" he asks.

"This is perfect," I say. "Thank you. Except that we should probably add 'My Grief Day,' too." He raises one brow at me. "No hurry or anything."

Hampstead nods, then looks me over and offers an approving glance. "Nice outfit, Ms. Banks." I nod in return, thinking to myself how Eve's new mission statement for me is already working. "I see your fashion advisor is back on the job," he mumbles.

"Um…how did you know I have a fashion advisor?"

He looks at me. "I don't answer rhetorical questions. Please let me know if there's anything else you need," he adds, and starts to leave.

Sierra raises her hand. "Would it be possible to order lunch in? We're behind schedule."

"The number for the kitchen is in your top left drawer," replies Hampstead.

"Thanks," says Sierra. He turns to go.

"Oh, uh, Hampstead, I forgot to ask, did you by any chance get approval on those socials and DOBs I gave you?"

"Yes. All three have been approved," he says. "Security has been notified."

"Thanks." He leaves. I turn to Sierra who's checking her e-mails. She glances up at me.

"Our production insurance has been approved. Are Richard and Eve coming in?"

"Richard's helping the forensic specialists today and Eve's working in New York. Where are we on the TTN produced content?"

"I finished the scripts for the host. Now we need to get one…and line up celebrities willing to share their personal grief stories…on camera…in front of millions of people…in order to attract more eyeballs so that others will be willing to share their stories…any ideas?"

I'm about to respond when in between breaths I hear the distinct voice of Derek Rogers coming from the television set. Sierra and I turn around. Sierra increases the volume. We watch Derek Rogers stand next to Tyler Simmons outside the Yankton Federal Prison in South Dakota.

Derek speaks into a reporter's microphone, "Following the footsteps of John Darcy's vision with prison reform, we've been able to use ITT, the Insider Think Tank, to harness these brilliant minds…"

"He left out 'criminal'," interjects Sierra.

Next to Derek stands his cohort Johnny Bright.

Derek continues, "…To solve our nation's deficit problems which will provide the United States with greater autonomy and less dependence on other nations."

Tyler Simmons chimes in, "Through correspondence with John Darcy, Derek Rogers, a long-lost relative of Mr. Darcy's, was able to put this unique and extraordinary program together."

Roger Duke from the *New York Chronicle* asks, "What does the program entail?"

"We'll be announcing our findings to Congress shortly," replies Tyler. "But we believe the result will immediately stimulate the economy and raise the gross national product."

Sierra looks at me and shakes her head in disbelief. "How does slime like that rise to the top?" she asks.

"Derek's got a special talent for failing upwards," I reply.

Dramatic music blares from the set. "BBS Breaking News…Ali-Shi-Ali-Ali has claimed responsibility for yesterday's attack at Reagan National Airport where eleven people are now dead," claims the announcer. A photograph of a striking young man in full beard and a turban appears on screen. "Ali-Shi-Ali-Ali is leader of a new sect of terrorists with ties to the Middle East. He told reporters in a language called Katunie that he was pleased with the results of the attack. Although, the originally suspected terrorist group is claiming that they are responsible and that Ali-Shi-Ali-Ali is stealing their limelight in order to wedge his way into the Middle East peace talks, if they ever resume…"

"How can this be happening?" I ask.

"It's just sad," says Sierra.

"Stay tuned tonight for the biography of former First Lady Haley Stone. We turn now to the thousands of people left homeless from the tri-State tornado…" blares the voice again.

"Let's turn it off," I suggest.

Sierra hits the remote and all the incoming grief momentarily disappears. "How are you holding up?" she asks. "I haven't wanted to bring it up, but is the media getting to you?"

"A bit," I reply. "Victor helps me keep things in perspective. What about you? How are you holding up?"

"I don't need holding up. I'm not the one on center stage," she says. "I like being in the background. If you ever need more backup, I'm right here for you."

There's a knock on the door. "Come in," I say.

President Stone enters. Sierra and I jump to our feet.

"Hello, Mr. President," we both say.

"Sit, please. Good morning, Madison. Good morning, Sierra."

We sit back down. "Can we get you anything, Mr. President?" asks Sierra. "A cup of coffee?"

"I'm fine, thank you. In fact, I'm doing much better, today, at least." He pauses. "I just wanted to personally tell you not to pay attention to the press. I liked what you said in the Rose Garden, Madison. For what it's worth, I thought your approach to the situation was…interesting, and, well, unprecedented."

"Thank you, Mr. President."

"I'd also like to ask you if you'd be interested in attending a reception this evening at eight o'clock."

"Um…I'd love to, Mr. President," I reply, on automatic.

Sierra looks at me. "Don't you remember? You told me you have a *meeting* tonight?"

"Oh, yeah. I forgot, Mr. President. I have a seven o'clock meeting. I don't think I could make it before 8:30."

The president pauses for a moment. "Then join me when you finish. I think you'll find it interesting. I'll ask Hampstead to get you the address." He starts to leave, then glances back at me. "I'd be interested in knowing more about those theories stemming from child psychology."

"Yes, Mr. President," I reply.

"Oh, and thank you for those books on grief. They've been

most helpful. I especially liked that story about the organ donor. It really touched me."

"You're welcome."

"Where can I get a few more copies? I'd like to give them away as gifts."

"Oh, well, they're available online. Or you can just tell me how many you need and I'll get them for you. On the house."

"Thank you, but I'd like a hundred of each, so I'd have to insist on paying."

Then it occurs to me; an endorsement from the president would increase sales of the grief guidebooks. I decide to put my patriotic capitalistic tendencies on the table. "Mr. President. Um...that would come to quite a bit of money; however, if you would consider endorsing the books with a quote on the cover, I'd say that's more than worth the cost of all those books."

The president smiles at me and nods. "I heard you were good, Madison. Reminiscent of EA. Glad you're on my team. It's a deal." He grins and leaves.

"Who's EA?" I ask Sierra.

She turns to me. "I don't know. But I do know that was one hell of a ballsy request. Asking the president to endorse your guidebooks!"

"I have to think of the future. What happens when this job is over?"

"Will you please stop future tripping? Grief never goes away. You could be here forever. Ever think about that?"

"I'm not here to milk the system. I'm going to do the best job I can and then move on to my next endeavor. I think that's what anyone in this position would do."

"Only those who are capable of living in interstices."

"Interstices?"

"The in-betweens."

I look at her, requiring further explanation.

"You live in between here and there. In between this idea

and that idea, in between this place and that place…you live between the connections of things. It's why you always feel so unsettled. But it's also why you're always able to see other opportunities and reinvent yourself if you have to."

"You make that sound like a positive thing."

"It is. Your problem is that you put yourself down for it because most people don't live there. So you judge yourself, which is part of the whole interstices dilemma. But it's because you live in that space that you're able to think the way you think, and to have the perspectives you do in order to make the connections that you make. You think it's bad. But it's really a gift, living in the interstices."

"Thanks. I'll remember that when I'm between here and there," I say.

"And when you're at receptions with the president!" she exclaims.

Two hours later, after Sierra has left for the day, I'm lost in my work when Hampstead knocks and enters.

"Ms. Banks. It's seven fifteen and your seven o'clock meeting is here." Behind Hampstead is Stephen Stephanie, posing as Stephanie today. He or she carries the plastic folder.

"Thank you, Hampstead." He leaves, giving Stephen Stephanie a curious glance on his way out the door.

I turn to my guest. "Thank you so much for moving the meeting here."

"Oh, I think it's a good idea to change locations now and then. Plus, your offer to let us use your office space at no charge is very generous of you," Stephanie says.

"It's no problem. Here, let's move the desks together and create a conference table."

As we shuffle tables and chairs around, Hampstead reappears with Rachel and an animated Brian in tow.

"So that's how the software works," explains Brian. "Where did you say were from again? Somewhere in the UK?"

"Cordwainer Ward, to be precise," answers Hampstead.

"I could input your family data and find out if there are cross-pollinations of nationalities in your ancestry."

"Wonderful," drones Hampstead, handing them over to me. "It's now seven thirty-two and I have two more arrivals for your seven o'clock meeting."

"Thank you, Hampstead. I really appreciate it." He lingers for a moment. "We're good. Thanks." I walk him out the door.

Hampstead quietly comments, "One day, Ms. Banks, you'll have to inform me on what genealogy, child psychology and food service have to do with bereavement, in particular with helping the president through his."

Hampstead may have had access to everyone's name and social security number, but he didn't know the purpose of our gathering and in order to protect that, I chummily guide him into the hallway and reply, "Well, Hampstead, it comes down to the importance of knowing and remembering our origins in order to maintain our legacy when facing death and dying. It's about the value that children bring when sifting tough concepts down to their basics, and, finally, it's that…food, is comfort. By the way, what's the president's favorite meal?"

Hampstead offers a dubious look. "He likes a club sandwich, Ms. Banks."

"Good to know, thanks." I leave Hampstead and go back inside my office. Our small group settles around the makeshift conference table. Stephen Stephanie leads the meeting. I take comfort in the routine as we alternate reading from the Twelve Steps and the Twelve Traditions.

I curiously watch Stephen Stephanie unveil a bag of colorful poker chips and address the group. "Has anyone had one year of sobriety?" No one raises a hand. "One month?" No takers. "One week?" Silence. "One day?" Brian raises his hand.

Stephen Stephanie smiles and hands him a blue chip. "Congratulations," he/she says. "Would you like to share now?"

Brian shrugs. "I'm Brian. Workaholic."

"Hi Brian," the rest of us say in unison.

Brian sits up and begins, "I finally left my office yesterday at about nine. I kept telling myself I didn't have anything to feel guilty about, even though there was a ton of stuff to do. There's always a ton of stuff to do. So I just kept repeating that what I don't do today I can do tomorrow, and that I shouldn't worry about competition that I don't even know exists. I tried making it into a mantra because I kept feeling this tug to run back to the office. But I forced myself not to. When it got really bad, I ducked inside a movie theatre. I hadn't seen a movie in three years. Most of the time, I was able to get caught up in the story and forget about work. When I did think about work, I made a conscious effort to stop myself. The whole time I sat there in the theatre I had a really weird feeling. But I got through it and I told myself I just have to keep doing this kind of thing until I get used to it. Anyway, this chip means a lot to me. So, thanks for letting me share."

Everyone offers solemn nods of understanding and acceptance.

Stephen Stephanie looks around the room. "I think we should make this meeting about recovery with a ten-minute speaking period."

"Um, excuse me," I interject. "Can we make that five minutes? I have to meet the president at eight thirty."

Everyone shares a glance and smiles in agreement. Stephen Stephanie continues, "Does anyone have anything to share about something they've done or experienced that felt like they were making progress?" No one says a word. Moments pass. I raise my hand. I receive a go-ahead group glance.

"Hi. Madison. Workaholic."

"Hi, Madison," says the group. Stephen Stephanie starts the timer.

I clear my throat. "I got up in the middle of the night and did three hours of work, which I kept a secret from my fiancé." Everyone gives me an offbeat look. "Um…that's not the progress. I think the progress came in a moment of awareness. I had this epiphany where it occurred to me that I'm using work to hide from being intimate with Victor. Only I don't know why. He's the greatest guy. Kind. Loving. Sweet. Thoughtful. Smart. Handsome. But I'm petrified to be with him when I don't have work around. I think I would have a complete identity crisis. So I'm always working. He wants to take me on vacation to New Zealand and I can't justify going unless there's something for me to do that relates to work, like studying foreign customs and rituals around funeral service. Work gives me something to do, something to feel purposeful about, or at least try to. I don't feel valuable otherwise. And if I stop working, if I stop moving in order to relax or rest, I'm afraid…I'm afraid…well, I'm afraid…I'll die…"

Everyone stares at me. The funeral planner has spoken. Silence follows. I feel a sense of relief. Then I feel a sense of fear because I have no idea if what I shared was understood or accepted. I am beginning to see a pattern. No one validates you in these meetings. I guess the healing lies in the free fall. I have a funny feeling that this is where one's faith is tested, in the interstices, the in-between moments where no person outside yourself is there to validate you. You get to hold up the mirror on yourself…all by yourself…and learn to trust yourself.

Stephen Stephanie speaks up. "Thank you for sharing, Madison. Rachel, would you like to share?"

Rachel looks at the small group. "No progress here."

Stephen Stephanie mouths "okay," then sets the timer for him/herself. "I'm Stephen Stephanie. Recovering workaholic."

"Hi Stephen Stephanie," we say.

"I'm thankful for all your shares. I'm thankful for this program. Madison, I hear what you're saying and I used to feel the same way. Twelve years ago I thought this disease would kill me. But I practiced being, and not doing, and convinced myself that I wasn't going to die from not working, that rest and relaxation were not going to kill me. If anything was going to kill me, it would be the consequences of work addiction. Today, I feel a sense of balance I never knew as a child or working adult. Through practice, by putting myself in uncomfortable situations and forcing myself to be conscious of what I was doing and feeling in the moment, I have been able to create balance in my life. One day at a time." He pauses, and then turns the timer off. "This brings us to our seventh tradition. Since Madison has provided us with a free office, I suggest we donate a dollar to fun night."

I raise my hand. "What's fun night?"

"Sometimes we turn a meeting into something fun, like putt-putt golf, so we practice how to have fun," answers Stephanie.

"Oh," I say as everyone reaches in their pockets for a dollar donation.

"Let's hold hands for the Serenity Prayer." Stephen Stephanie leads. Our motley group huddles together and recites the prayer out loud.

When it's over, I announce to the small assembly with five minutes to spare that, "I have a nonmeeting work agenda item I wish to discuss." They all look at me. I seem to have broken tradition. "I'm sorry to bring up work, but these are rather important matters." I pull out the blue mini-hard drive and hold it up to Brian. "Do you think you could use your software program to look into the genealogy pool mentioned in the contents of this hard drive and determine its veracity?"

"Sure," he agrees, willingly.

"Okay, here, just sign this NDA stating that you won't disclose any of the information in this blue thingy."

"Blue thingy?"

"Short for miniature memory stick hard drive." I hand him

an NDA form. He immediately signs it and grabs the device like an alcoholic who's been offered free booze.

"Do you want an MRCA?" he asks.

"Excuse me?"

"Most recent common ancestor," he explains. "The progress can go back two to four thousand years. I can also trace the migration patterns of family histories."

"Sounds great," I say. "Go for all you've got."

"Okay. What format is it in?" he asks.

"It's a word document," I reply.

"I'll need more than words though. My database operates on a gene pool. I'll need a DNA report."

I nod. "Okay, I'll see what I can do." Then I turn to Rachel. "Since yesterday's talk in the Rose Garden, I'd like to make sure you're okay with getting credit for some of the ideas you proposed about ODD during your last share."

"What talk in the Rose Garden?" she asks.

"You haven't seen the news? Or read the paper?" I ask.

The whole group shakes their heads. Rachel stares at me. "I've been working."

"Right…well, your theories are sort of out there now and the president would like to discuss them further with you."

"The president of what?"

"The president of the United States."

Rachel swallows the visible lump in her throat and stares at me. "Are you shitting me?"

"No, I'm not. I sort of put some of what you said the other day in the context of the terrorist situation and well, now the press wants to know who Rachel A. Nominos is, and the president would like to know more about your theories. Do you think you could prepare a report for him? I know it's extra work but—"

"I'll get right on it," says Rachel, twittering like a junkie.

Stephanie shakes her head. "This is not healthy."

The rest of us look at her and shrug our shoulders.

"I think she feels left out," Brian suggests.

"Classic projection of a pseudo sibling rivalry," offers Rachel.

I turn to Stephanie. "You know, the House Bereavement Specialists Committee will be requiring food services for My Grief Day. Would you like that account? I'd have to see your references, of course."

"I'm not sure of the protocol of—"

"Stephanie, let me ask you this. Is there anything in the Twelve Traditions that would counter the opportunity for opportunities generated by, uh…."

"Fellowship," says Brian. "We call it fellowship."

"By fellowship," I say. "Thanks, Brian."

Stephanie Stephen thinks it over. "I don't believe there's anything of that sort. But still, we're talking about generating work for each other. And the whole point of workaholics anonymous is to…"

"Excuse me. But we're talking about work with a national purpose," interjects Rachel. "And isn't valuing ourselves ultimately what we're after? This could be an opportunity for us to explore the relationship between work and self-love."

"And self-fulfillment," adds Brian.

"Not to mention self-approval," I add.

"In fact," Rachel argues, "this could be a group experiment. Will work that services the greater good, the nation, perhaps the world at large, satisfy the empty pit inside our souls, which might feel empty because we've been too wrapped up in work as an addiction, as a means of hiding out, as work for work's sake, as opposed to work for the sake of others? Actually, the more I think about it, this is a very interesting paradigm."

I glance at Rachel. I'm not sure if she meant everything she said, or if it was work addiction brilliantly masked in the guise of a group experiment that was fooling everyone and no one.

"Okay," says Stephanie, mulling it over. "I propose that we

wholeheartedly explore Madison's opportunities, but with an eye on the progress of our healing."

"Amen," says Brian.

Everyone smiles and walks out the door excited to get to work. I check my watch. It's 8:32 p.m. I wonder how fashionable it is to be late in Washington.

Twelve minutes later, a cab drops me off in front of a large immaculate brownstone in Georgetown. I gently knock on the door. No answer. Muffled conversation from inside drowns out the sound of my knock. I knock louder. Nothing. I try the door. It's open. I quietly enter and am about to pass through the foyer into an expansive living room filled with Washingtonians when a large-bodied security guard blocks me with a clipboard and pen in hand. "And you are?"

"Madison Banks," I reply.

"Sorry, but you're not on Mrs. Anderson's list."

"I'm a guest of President Stone's," I reply.

I glance around him in search of the president. Small clusters of well-known politicians and reporters gather around one another as waiters in white attire serve wine and hors d'oeuvres. I don't see President Stone, but I do see the stately Elizabeth Anderson bearing down on me. She glances at the guard who immediately backs off.

"Ms. Banks, I presume. You are…*un*fashionably late, nor do I recall sending you an invitation to my home."

"Oh, hi…I'm terribly sorry I'm late, Mrs. Anderson. I had no idea the reception was at your home. But I did mention that I'd be late to—"

"There you are," says President Stone. "I see, Madison, that you've already met our gracious hostess. Madison, this is Elizabeth Anderson, one of Haley's oldest and dearest friends. Elizabeth, this is Madison Banks. As you know, she's helping solve our nation's grief dilemmas and on an informal basis she's generously taken on the role of my grief buddy."

Mrs. Anderson politely extends her hand and with a mock grin accompanied by a monotone delivery, states, "Welcome. What does a grief buddy actually do, Ms. Banks?"

"Mostly listen. And provide support."

"Did you have a grief buddy, Elizabeth, when Alexander died?" asks President Stone.

Elizabeth's face immediately tightens up. She takes a deep breath and replies, "I had no one. I didn't find it necessary."

"No one?" asks President Stone.

Elizabeth reflects momentarily, then replies instead, "I had Haley."

President Stone's face falls. The memory of his wife clearly overcomes him.

"Are you all right?" I ask.

Elizabeth straightens her shoulders, pulling back, uncomfortable with the pain on the president's face.

"I'll be fine. May I get you a glass of wine?" asks the president.

"Oh, sure. Red is fine."

"I only serve white," huffs Mrs. Anderson. "Everyone knows that."

"Okay, then…white is perfect," I say. The president excuses himself and leaves. I nervously smile at Mrs. Anderson. "I think we got off on the wrong foot. I'm really not a bad person…."

"Excuse me, Ms. Banks. I must tend to my guest of honor," she murmurs, heading toward a group of people next to the fireplace.

The president returns with a glass of wine and a sense of having recomposed himself. He gingerly hands the glass to me. "Here you go."

"Thanks." I carefully take the glass from him. "Who's the guest of honor?" I ask, taking a sip of wine.

"They're always a surprise. It's part of Elizabeth's modus operandi."

"Oh. Does she always get big turnouts for mystery guests?"

"Always," says the president. "You might say she's the E.F. Hutton of Washington." He pauses, and then adds, "When Anderson *hosts,* Congress swings *votes.*"

"Does she know she carries a slogan like that?" I ask.

President Stone smiles. "I'm sure she does."

"How does one woman wield so much influence?"

"Like everything else. Years of quiet practice," says the president. "Although with Elizabeth, I tend to think she was a born prodigy of persuasion."

Tyler Simmons appears from the throng. "Mr. President. There are a few people I need to introduce you to." Ignoring me, he whispers, "Manny Milot, campaign manager, in the southwest corner."

"Excuse me, Madison," says President Stone. He leaves. Tyler starts to follow the president when I tap his shoulder.

"Wait a second," I say, baffled. "I saw you on television this morning. How did you get from Yankton, South Dakota, to Washington, D.C. in a New York minute?"

Tyler stops and cocks his head at me. "Haven't you ever heard of green screen, Ms. Banks?"

"You faked a newscast? Is that ethical?" I stare at him, incredulously.

"Probably not. But private jets are," he tells me, with a Cheshire grin and he stalks away. But I don't believe him. I watch him introduce President Stone around the room. I don't recognize a single face in the crowd. I guess that's what I get for not watching C-Span more often. I was clearly out of my domain.

Uncomfortable, I wander through the halls looking for the guest bathroom. The hallways are lined with historical references to Mrs. Anderson. I become mesmerized by the traditional black-and-white photos of her life, of her wedding to the late Mr. Anderson, photos of people who appear to be her parents and grandparents. All of her presumed relatives are elegantly dressed beset by beautiful settings that include turn-of-the-century mansions and automobiles. There are photographs marking the opening of one railroad, stadium and skyscraper, after another. And there are photos of her with Haley Stone in college together. I travel the length of one wall, then the next, leading me through a maze of hallways as I follow the trail of her biography. I notice one thing for sure. There is not one photograph of Mrs. Anderson that appears to have been taken in the last ten years, not one. The last framed photograph of her husband is the one inside a *New York Times* obituary from eleven years ago. After that, the trail ends. I bet if I showed these walls to Richard, he'd whisper in my ear, "S.I.M.," his acronym for stuck in mourning. Richard believed a telltale sign of S.I.M. was the lack of any photographs following the death of a loved one. If that were true, and Mrs. Anderson was really stuck in mourning, how could she have the strength and focus to be such a persuasive character in Washington circles…unless it was all a part of grief avoidance. But my thinking was pure conjecture, and always tended to—

"You shouldn't be here," orders a voice from behind me. At first startled, I'm then relieved to see Hampstead. "It's bad manners to go where you're uninvited," he says.

"I was just looking at…"

"The foundation of our country's industrial power," he says.

"No," I claim. "I was looking at the biographical timeline of Mrs. Anderson."

"The two are synonymous," he says, offering his first genuine grin to me.

"Except it stops here." I point to the framed obituary. "Just curious, Hampstead, but what kind of funeral did Mr. Anderson have?"

"He didn't actually have one," replies Hampstead. "He died

overseas in a remote part of Senegal. By the time they brought the body back to the States, it was too late for an open casket. There was a short, private memorial, formal, nothing more."

"Is there anything you don't know?" I ask him.

"If there was, I wouldn't be doing my job," he answers.

"What exactly is your job?"

"My job, Ms. Banks, is to know everything about anyone who steps foot into the White House," he declares, glancing at the Messiah pumps on my feet.

Speaking of footsteps, the sound of sharp high heels approach us followed by the voice of Mrs. Anderson calling out Hampstead's name. She rounds the corner and stares at me. "What may I ask are you doing here?"

I gulp, frozen in place. Hampstead quietly responds, "I accompanied Ms. Banks to the second guest bathroom as the first one was occupied," he says, adding, "and am seeing to it that she makes her way safely and unobtrusively back to the dining area."

Mrs. Anderson nods. "Fine. Please come now. We're introducing our guest of honor."

Hampstead leads the way as we approach the assembled guests, then he silently disappears. I stand on the periphery of the crowd. A server takes my empty glass and I have nothing to hold on to. President Stone is wrapped up in conversation across the room. Next to me are two well-dressed gentlemen chatting among themselves.

"She's persuasive all right," says one man. "To the tune of ten million."

"That's nothing," his drinking companion retorts. "Our corporation put in fifty."

"So, we're basically funding a government equity firm," comments the first gentleman.

"That's right, but in return, we get a percentage of the profits and we're protected against Sarbanes Oxley, so we should be able to more than make up for it."

"I hope these fellows don't screw it up," wishes the first man.

"They're too crooked to do that," replies the second fellow.

Elizabeth Anderson takes center stage and all other voices in the room become mute. "Our guest of honor tonight is a man with a vision that I unreservedly embrace," says Mrs. Anderson. "I view his program as a necessary and vital step to our country's economic growth and stability. I, for one, would like you all to hear more about what he has to say. Please welcome Jonathon Darcy's cousin and founder of the Insider Think Tank…Mr. Derek Rogers."

I nearly choke. Amidst the instantaneous applause, I stare at Derek as he thanks Mrs. Anderson. Manners or no manners, I simply refuse to clap on his behalf. The whole thing is an atrocity. But now it's all clear to me. Derek Rogers infiltrated the powers of Washington through its top-rated influencers, and masterfully pulled the wool over their eyes to create a well-funded equity firm for himself. Did they really think Derek would take their money to help reduce the deficit, while generating big profits for them, too? If Washington could be this easily duped, we were a country in trouble.

"Are you okay?" asks President Stone, now standing next to me.

I shake my head and whisper between breaths of hyperventilation, "Some hot air went down the wrong pipe. I don't feel so well. In fact, I think I should go."

"You don't look too good."

"It's just an anxiety attack. I'll be fine," I say.

"You look very pale, like you've seen a ghost."

"No, more like the future," I blurt.

"I'd better get you back to your hotel."

"You can't leave! Mrs. Anderson will kill me," I whisper.

"I don't feel so hot myself, Madison. If you don't mind, I'll exit with you. Hampstead will cover for us."

As we make our way through a side door, accompanied by

secret service agents, I glance back to see Derek Rogers casting his spell upon everyone while Mrs. Anderson shoots me an admonishing stare.

My breathing returns to normal once I'm finally back at the Hay-Adams.

★ ★ ★

I'm dreaming that newspapers keep piling up outside my hotel room door. Mounds and mounds of papers from all over the world disseminating news in the form of a small mountain, calling for my attention one announcing thud at a time. The thud is soon accompanied by the sound of my name. I think that seems odd, and then I realize it is no longer part of the dream. The noise is not the thud of newspapers, but an urgent pounding on the door. I wake up from pulling an all-nighter and look at the clock. It's 7:00 a.m. and the knock is real. I answer it to find Sierra standing there in her hotel bathrobe.

"Are you watching the news?" she asks.

I shake my head no.

"Well, you should be." She storms inside and turns the television on to one of the news channels, then sits on my bed. I join her. On television, we watch crowds of people mill around the morning news crews. They all look alike in white T-shirts with pink lettering.

"What is this?" I ask.

"Read," Sierra insists.

I zero in on the T-shirts. They read, I Pity You, ALI-SHI-ALI-ALI.

"Oh, my God," I cry out, covering my mouth.

"In the last two days, somebody mass produced the T-shirts and distributed them. It looks like the whole country is wearing them," says Sierra. She flips to other news channels and sure enough, everyone in the crowd is wearing the T-shirts.

The news anchor, Mike Piper, speaks to the camera. "It looks like the American people are taking the words of grief czar Madison Banks to heart and speaking out, and not with rage, but with pity for Ali-Shi-Ali-Ali…"

Sierra squints at the television set bewildered. "Why pink?"

I look at Sierra and shake my head. "I have a funny feeling Eve is behind this."

"Ah. That would explain it. What are you going to do about it?"

"Nothing. I need to stay on point."

There's a ding notifying me of an e-mail. I immediately check it, of course. It's an e-mail from Rachel with an attachment of her theories on child psychology as it pertains to terrorism and the issues in the Middle East. Apparently, I was not the only one up all night working. I hit the print button.

Sierra stares at the flashing image of Ali-Shi-Ali-Ali. "Wonder what he'll do."

The image on the screen switches back to Mike Piper. "According to reports from a lone Katunie television station, Ali-Shi-Ali-Ali is demanding to be part of the Middle East peace talks and threatens more attacks unless he is included, even though other well-known terrorist groups claim Ali-Shi-Ali-Ali is stealing the attention from them. Since the death of Jonathon Darcy the peace talks have disintegrated and…"

Sierra turns the set off. "Good grief. What next?"

What next, indeed. Being a news junkie is like being addicted to depression. Sometimes, it is imperative to put your head in the sand and take a break. And that's what I feel like doing in that moment. But that isn't an option. Not even for a minute. I have so much work to do, work that is fueling my soul. Call it passion. Call it addiction. Call it fulfilling my purpose on earth. Call it a twisted set of priorities. Oh, fuck, for Chrissakes, it's work. Someone has to get it done. Maybe workaholics are people who really care about getting the job done, people who aren't afraid to roll up their sleeves and dive in, people who are responsible and dependable, okay, maybe they're perfectionists, too. But is that a bad thing? In fact, for those who delegate, the smartest thing one can do is hire a workaholic. They'll get the job done. And then I remember. They'll get the job done, all right; at the expense of their health, their family, their friends, their pets, their past, their present and their future. And with that, I put on my jogging clothes and decide it's time for a good long healthy run around Washington, D.C. I do, however, slip Rachel's printout of theories into my jogger's backpack, just in case I have time to read it during my run because you never know when you might get held up and regret not bringing along something to do.

I run by the Mall, passing the Smithsonian and the Washington Monument, through Foggy Bottom, around George Washington University, across a sliver of the Potomac River and into quaint Georgetown. I run across Rock Creek and along Embassy Row, into funky Adams Morgan and then down to the melting pot of Dupont Circle. My legs ache, but it's a good ache as I feel my muscles activate in motion. I stop to take a small break and stretch my hamstrings outside an electronics store.

In the window I catch clips of news anchors promoting the latest stories: "Special Report on people crying helplessly, not eating or sleeping...the effect on our gross domestic product...and how to fight the battle on grief...tonight at 11:00!" Oy, I think. They've got it all wrong. Grief is not an enemy. You don't fight it on the Fields of Loss & Pain. You don't suit up in armor and Hummers and go looking for it in dark urban alleys. No, grief is not an enemy. The whole point is to make grief your friend, to become familiar with it. In fact, sometimes, grief is a gift. For the greater we grieve, the greater we have loved. Hopefully, MGD will set the record straight.

I shake my legs and start running again. The jog helps me get out of my head and I start to feel my body again. While I run, I silently repeat the Serenity Prayer. Of course, other thoughts creep in and out, causing the prayer to become a medley of disjointed ideas and expressions that go something like this: *God grant me the courage to accept the things I cannot change... I wonder why I seem unable to appreciate the position I'm in. To change the things I can... Why am I playing the reluctant hero? In both my profession and my personal life. Why can't I embrace my present? Shoot, I forgot the word courage. The courage to change the things I can. What do I need to change inside myself and do I have the courage to do it? And why can't I remember this prayer? Can I really make a difference? Will My Grief Day work? Can my team and I "transform" a nation? Why does the insidious Derek Rogers keep popping up in my life? What's that about? And the knowledge...no, the wisdom, that's it, the wisdom, to know the difference.*

I stop to catch my breath in front of the Golden Triangle Business Improvement District. A black-and-white mural on the wall of a building depicts the memory of Haley Stone. Sitting on a bench, facing the mural, is a thin, neatly-dressed, elderly Asian woman. She's got that dismal, grief-stricken look in her eye that has been plaguing so many Americans. She puts a tissue to her face and wipes some tears away.

"Are you okay?" I ask.

She turns and peers at me with indifference. That's what the grief does. It makes you indifferent to your surroundings because the pain is too thick and too heavy to cut through, to really see anything or anyone.

"My husband passed away," she says quietly.

"I'm so sorry. When?"

"Five years ago. The same day, the same month, as Haley Stone." She sighs. "I can't seem to do anything anymore. I can't work. I'm not up for seeing friends. It's hard to eat."

"Do you have family?"

She nods. "I missed my grandson's wedding because I couldn't get out of my home. I got all dressed up. Then I sat on the edge of the bed and I never got up. I just couldn't do it."

"Have you tried a grief support group?" I gently ask.

She shakes her head no. "I feel guilty," she confesses. "He was sick for a long time. I took care of him for years and when he passed, well, I was, in a way…relieved." She watches me with long sad eyes. "I feel so bad about myself for that. How is that possible?" Tears fall down her face.

I sit next to her on the bench. "It's possible, because it's normal. Guilt is part of grief. We all feel guilty. We all have regrets. It comes with the territory. You don't have to beat yourself up for that."

"I don't?" she cries.

"No, you don't," I state.

She offers a small smile of gratitude and nods her head. I see a flicker of brightness shine in her eyes as if the pilot light had been turned back on.

"Thank you," she says, and squeezes my hand.

"It's okay to be part of the living again."

As I say those words, three things dawn on me; first, that My Grief Day could in fact be truly valuable and that to second-guess the path I'm on is to do a great disservice to those whom this program can touch and help, that there's a reason I'm here, in this place now, and to embrace it and stop the inner conflict. The second thing I grasp with more meaning than ever before is the sheer power of storytelling, the act of sharing *our stories* with each other. Whether sharing our story is for the sake of creating a legacy, telling a good story, or revealing a value or morality, it helps not only the listener, but even the teller on their journey. And as far as the third thought, I need to heed my own words and stop denying that I have a work addiction problem. Then my phone rings.

"Excuse me," I tell the Asian woman and answer my Black-Berry. "This is Madison Banks."

"Hampstead here. I'm afraid the president is in need of his

grief buddy…so that he can make the meeting with his cabinet, in the next hour."

"I'm all sweaty."

"I have plenty of towels, Ms. Banks."

"Right." I hang up, bid adieu to my new friend, and let the addiction kick in all over again.

The bedroom of the president

"I'm tired," murmurs the president. "How am I supposed to go on without Haley?" He rolls over on his side, burying his head in the pillow. "And John," the president mumbles. "He was so integral to the peace process. What's the use?" He rolls over again with no strength to look at me standing next to the bed, in my sweaty running clothes.

I wonder what I can say or do to motivate our leader, who lies prone, unshaven and approaching an increasingly gaunt appearance. I glance at Hampstead tucked away in the corner of the room. He points to his watch with a sense of urgency. The cabinet is waiting. I draw strength from my earlier words this morning and how they seemed to help the elderly Asian woman. Surely, I can repeat their effectiveness once more…I think.

I lean down. "President Stone," I say quietly. "I know you're hurting terribly right now and that your heart needs time to heal. The bad news about grief is that the rest of the world keeps moving even when we're in pain. There's no right or wrong on our time frame for getting used to our losses and the adjustment they have on us in our lives…and that's what makes it so hard. The rest of the world has a different time construct for grief than the griever does. The rest of the world wants us to get over it and move on. That kind of pressure only makes it worse."

I hear a clearing of the throat and turn to see Hampstead roll his hand in a circle giving me the "speed-it-up" sign.

I take a deep breath and continue, coating my words with compassion. "Mr. President. I think it's important for you to take dominion over your emotional being right now. Part of the journey in life is to stay present, Mr. President. That would mean letting go of the pain right now, for a little while, you know, long enough to attend your cabinet meeting. Sometimes, when you're the leader of the free world, you have to uh, well, you have to go on with the show because there are no understudies and there are no dress rehearsals. Actually, I suppose you could call the vice president an understudy, but the vice president is in China anyway so it doesn't really matter. What matters is that you make an appearance on behalf of the United States. Because your cabinet members are counting on you, because the world is counting on you, because, Mr. President—Haley and John are counting on you."

At this, the president raises his brows, consideration brewing at the thought that they still exist in some form or another and that his actions could matter to them now.

"Mr. President," I continue. "What do you think Haley and John would want you to do right now?"

He closes his eyes for several minutes and when he reopens them he shouts, "Hampstead, bring me a suit and tie. We're going to the meeting." Then he looks at me and adds, "The 'we' I'm referring to includes you."

"Me?"

"Yes, you," indicates the president. "It's what Haley and John would want."

I consider my attire and swallow that reluctant feeling yet again. I'm thrilled that President Stone is getting back on his feet, at least for the moment, but I'm awestruck and disinclined to be included in this meeting that I have no business being in, and worst of all, I'm utterly petrified at what Eve Gardner will do to me. In my opinion, this is not about being a reluctant participant; it is simply not part of the protocol.

"Mr. President. With all due respect, I'm not at all dressed appropriately for this."

The president examines me. "You're right." He glances over at Hampstead. "Hampstead, bring me a jogging suit." He turns back to me. "We'll dress alike." He takes in a deep breath, adding, "Strength in numbers."

Oh, geez, I think, nothing like a little pressure to communicate. "Really, Mr. President, I'm not the head of an executive department and therefore—"

"You are head of the House Bereavement Specialists Committee. Close enough." Hampstead hands the president a neatly pressed navy-blue jogging suit. "Excuse me, Ms. Banks, I need to change." He disappears inside the bathroom.

I look at my wrinkled sweaty clothes and then at Hampstead, who hands me a towel and grins. "At least there's nothing inauthentic about you, Ms. Banks."

"That doesn't help, Hampstead." I stare at my dry bare legs, my scrappy socks and my tattered running shoes. Without my Messiah pumps on, I have a bad premonition about this meeting. And for once, I am hoping my instincts couldn't be more wrong.

"Short of turning into the fairy godmother right now, is there anything I can do for you, Ms. Banks?" asks Hampstead.

"Yes." It's one thing to be seen in running clothes with the president and quite another to be wearing them to a cabinet meeting. Even beyond the bad manners and the anticipated wrath of Eve is the thought that I might break the promise I made to her about the clothes thing. And breaking promises is something I loath doing. But it is hardly possible to call or text message Eve right now. And besides, what could she possibly do about it? Advance warning however would have to beget forgiveness under the circumstances.

I jot down a phone number and hand it over to Hampstead. "Please call this number and explain where I'm going and what I'm wearing and that I'm terribly, terribly sorry."

Of course, I had no idea that underestimating Eve was beginning to seem like a bad habit.

5

The de facto job of organizing cabinet meetings typically falls upon the spouse of the chief of staff. And originally, that person decided that the participants in the cabinet meetings as a whole should expand their horizons and have the meetings take place at a variety of locations that might otherwise be unfamiliar to the cabinet members. That's why President Stone and I are walking briskly toward the Textile Museum on S Street for the president's seventh cabinet meeting since he took office. Trotting secret service men flank our fast-paced stroll.

"It was a good idea to get out of the car and walk for ten minutes to the meeting," says the president.

"Exercise is a good antidote for grief, sir. It's crucial to keep the body moving so the endorphins can help minimize the grief and act as a natural antidepressant. It's also important for you to drink lots of fluids, and I would suggest avoiding sugar, caffeine and alcohol. Deep breathing with guided imagery and meditation are also helpful. And when you feel sad, let the tears go."

The president winks, "I'm beginning to feel better already."

"Would you like to try some more deep breathing?" I ask.

He gives me a thumbs up, and together we simultaneously suck in some oxygen and climb the steps of the museum. Outside its doors, the press corps snaps shots of us in our respective jogging clothes.

A lone male reporter steps in front of me with a snarl. His press tag is covered keeping his identity hidden. "Ms. Banks, what business does the grief czar have in attending today's cabinet meeting?"

I'm thrown off by the animosity in his voice, and feeling like a fool in my shorts and running shoes, I stutter for a reply.

The president turns around and calmly glares at the reporter. In a low-key voice he declares, "Ms. Banks is my grief buddy. And as president of the United States I have every right to invite whomever I wish to attend a cabinet meeting. We have a grief crisis in this nation and Ms. Banks holds an important position in helping alleviate that problem. Are we clear?"

The reporter nods and retreats behind the pack of other journalists. I look at the president and smile. He's back…for now.

Inside the museum, we pass the gift shop and several exhibits with samples of textiles from around the world. There are Persian rugs, and Indian shawls, Japanese kimonos, Chinese ties, and tote bags bearing Navajo, Peruvian, Laotian and Congolese designs. I can hardly focus on the art. I feel utterly naked, even more so because of the air-conditioning blasting through the cavernous halls, causing goose bumps to attack my arms and legs.

Other cabinet members enter the building in their best suits. I apprehensively fall behind the president. We enter the main exhibit hall which has been transformed into a conference room spacious enough for the president, all of his cabinet members and his political advisor Tyler Simmons.

Simmons approaches the president. "Mr. President. How are you today?"

President Stone takes in a deep breath and exhales. "I'm fine, Tyler. Thank you for asking. And you?"

"Good, sir." Then he whispers, "Mr. President, I wasn't sure you were going to make it today. Hampstead said you left early last night because you weren't feeling too well and so the agenda was modified to primarily focus on the budget."

President Stone rubs his jaw. "That's fine. But I still want to hear suggestions for the appointment of a new secretary of state."

Tyler agrees, "Yes, Mr. President." Other cabinet members approach the president to greet him. Then Tyler notices me and stops to gradually look me over in my current attire. There's a long pause. He leans toward me and says, "You're very odd." Then he walks away.

"Welcome to the Textile Museum," announces a flamboyantly robust gentleman in his fifties. "I'm Lowell Frazen, president of the museum. Before you take your seats, it's my pleasure to bestow upon each and every one of you a gift from the museum." He stops to refer to some notes in his hand, and then continues, "…which you may begin *wearing* right now." He checks the notes in his hand again. "It is in the spirit of recognizing the importance textiles play in our everyday life that we grant you this opportunity and appreciate your participation with the deepest sincerity."

The entire cabinet stares at him, utterly dumbfounded. Not one of them is able to speak up, the speech having been delivered in such an elegant fashion. They look to the president, seeking guidance.

Mr. Frazen turns to the president and bestows upon him his gift. "Mr. President, may I present you with the Dragon Tie from China. Its symbol represents decisiveness, boldness and imagination."

President Stone looks the tie over. "Thank you, Mr. Frazen. We can all use a little of that. Perhaps this meeting will take on some new creative dimensions." He puts the tie on over his jogging suit.

With the president's acceptance, Lowell Frazen starts passing out kimonos to the men and shawls to the women, including me. Suddenly, with respect to one's outer appearance, I am about to be an equal again among my peers.

When Mr. Frazen reaches me, he glances at my running clothes, leans down, and says quietly, "I believe you are the one who is supposed to receive the *pink* shawl. Here you go." He hands me an Indian shawl laden with pink hues.

I offer my thanks, and wrap the shawl around me, wondering how he knew to give me a pink one…and then it occurs to me. I whisper to him, "This doesn't have anything to do with an Eve Gardner, does it?"

He smiles and whispers back, "Indeed, it does."

"Let me guess. There'll be a group photo afterwards that you can hang in the lobby?"

"The photographer is on his way," he whispers, and moves on to the next cabinet member with a bright red kimono.

I smile. Leave it to Eve. Within the past twenty-five minutes she had gotten to the head of the museum and convinced him of my plight, or the fact that it would be a great post-cabinet meeting photo opportunity to market and popularize the museum by having the cabinet members wear the museum's apparel. As long as they were having a cabinet meeting there, they might as well participate all the way.

I spot Tyler Simmons squirming uncomfortably in his kimono and smile to myself.

The cabinet meeting begins with secretaries from the different departments taking turns standing up in front of the president to brief him on the status of their departments as well as propose emerging issues and solutions as they see them. The secretary from the Department of Agriculture speaks about increasing subsidies for farmers and the threat of lower productivity based on the malaise of the nation; the Department of Education addresses needs for increased revenues to subsidize smaller classrooms and concerns around a general sense of apathy among grief-depressed educators; the Department of Commerce discusses a dearth of entrepreneurs generating new businesses and competition resulting in the low status quo of the gross national product; and so on and so forth. No one seems to have any clear solutions for the president. The secretaries themselves appear depressed and of low energy. The only bright spot to them are the colors they wear from the kimonos and shawls on their backs. Finally, the Office of Management and Budget is asked to give its report. A diminutive man in glasses named Stuart Provost stands before the group in a blue and white kimono.

"Mr. President," he says in a squeaky voice, "as part of my presentation today, I'd like to invite an individual introduced to me by your political advisor, Mr. Simmons. This individual has what I believe are some sound solutions to raise our GNP and stimulate the economy out of its protracted recession. Please welcome Mr. Derek Rogers."

My face drops as Derek Rogers enters from the hallway. How is this possible? And furthermore, he's the only one in the room not wearing a kimono or shawl.

Derek smiles at everyone as he adeptly whips out a series of large posters with colorful graphs, charts and tables.

"Mr. President. Cabinet members," he begins by addressing the group. "This is a crucial time in our history. It's imperative to bring the deficit down and with it our country's debt reliance on other nations. Please look carefully at these charts and the handouts which identify solid solutions brought to you by the Insider Think Tank."

The charts indicate drastic cuts from other programs to finance ITT's development and implementation of investments in growth sectors.

"We need to tighten our belts and be extremely disciplined concerning expenditures of every kind if we are to save this country without further taxing the taxpayer. ITT members will not receive any compensation for their service, creating a substantially greater savings to the government," says Derek.

"How incredibly considerate of you," I sarcastically mumble to myself, wondering if anyone else in the room is on the same page as me.

"Eventually creating funds for social services, the kind that Haley Stone would have been proud to support."

I quickly glance at the president. The mention of Haley's name has induced another wave of grief. His posture starts to slump and his eyes glaze over; a clear indication that he's zoning out into grief land again. I look back at Derek, who notices the president's depressed demeanor with a faint air of accomplishment. I'm sick to my stomach over the psychological sabotaging of the president.

Tyler sits straight up, clearing his throat, proud of his protégé's presentation. Derek is the spore cell in a room infected by the grief virus. The rest of the cabinet members stare hopefully at Derek, clearly wanting to rely on his boundless charismatic energy for their personal and professional salvation.

"Any questions?" asks Derek.

The president pretends to peruse Derek's handout, but he's no longer fully present.

"Mr. Rogers," asks Tyler Simmons, "what are examples of ITT's proposed budget cuts?"

"Frivolous social programs and pork bellies for starters," answers Derek. "And this uh, My Grief Day business, is another obvious example," he declares.

Once more, my mouth drops open. I know I've been a somewhat reluctant player on this front, but in the past week I had become passionate about My Grief Day and the prospects of co-launching the Tribute Film Festival, with a firm belief as of this morning that it is a valuable national and international event with or without my involvement. Here, once again, smack in the middle of my career, Derek Rogers has appeared as the devil of good deeds and the thorn in my professional ventures and my personal well-being. I glance at President Stone, trapped in a reverie of grief.

"With all due respect to the parties involved in this," continues Derek, "it is not something that deserves the millions it will take to launch it, when that money, as a clear example, under the direction of ITT's intellectual capital could multiply fiftyfold. Furthermore, as a national holiday it means yet another calendar day of the year where people are not working which continues to negatively affect our GNP. Yes, loss is painful, but I propose it remain a solitary experience, not a grief fest."

I raise my hand. Derek ignores me. I stand up. "Excuse me, Derek, but on behalf of the virtues of My Grief Day, a national holiday has no bearing on the GNP since polls show that people are not working anyway due to the documented high levels of grief the country is presently experiencing. Part of MGD's mission is to celebrate our grief together so that everyone can get back to work. Not only that, but your plan fails to recognize compassion as a valuable human emotion and resource. Without compassion, we might as well cash in on being human and become robots of finance. It's not always about the bottom line. Besides, when you do the right thing, the bottom line always works out, at least spiritually speaking. Furthermore, MGD involves disaster-preparedness awareness so that future catastrophes can be, at the very least, minimized, saving billions of dollars as well as emotional and physical aftermath."

Derek looks at me as if I've punctured his favorite colored balloon. "Have you finished?" he asks.

"No. I'm not done. I don't see why you need to cut any programs at all."

"Why is that?" he asks, smirking, as if I'm a fool.

"Well, isn't it true that multinational corporations are investing tens of millions of dollars into your little rumination tank for a piece of the profits and protection from Sarbanes Oxley?"

Derek's eyes turn steely gray and narrow with constrained hostility. He quickly checks the cabinet members, who've perked up at the possibility of a scandal. "Members of the cabinet, this is how ugly rumors begin." Then he turns back to me, his eyes glaring with animosity. "I'm sorry. What is your name again?"

"You know full well what my name is, Derek. We went to school together. With your criminal activities, you have managed to undo every business I've ever developed. Don't make me stand here and waste my time or the cabinet's time with your pseudo-Alzheimer's of convenience for the purposes of getting a rise...out...of...me!" I stall to a stop, suspecting I have just fallen hook, line and sinker for his little ploy.

Derek looks at me and smiles. It was exactly what he hoped for from me; an emotional reaction that would make me look silly, and cause any concern of a scandal to become fleeting at best.

He calmly turns to the group. "Ladies and gentlemen, it seems as though our grief czar is also the czar of anger and resentment and perhaps the czar of big ego wishing to push her agenda when other issues are clearly more relevant, such as terrorism, global warming, identity theft and drugs...to name a few. May I remind all of you that in order to effectively deal with these issues, there need to be capable-sized budgets in place with a surplus of capital...and that's what ITT will deliver. And then," he says, referring to me with sarcasm, "you can have your national grief party."

Tyler Simmons jumps in. "Mr. President, with all due respect to this uh, My Grief Day event, a recent poll demonstrates that a budget surplus will have a far greater influence on voters when your second term options come around."

I focus on the president, who slowly considers Tyler's words, then looks at me, his energy waning, I assume, from a wave of overwhelming sadness. "I like what My Grief Day stands for and I do believe in it. Ms. Banks, do you think you can salvage the program with funds from the private sector?"

"I can certainly check into it, Mr. President." I sit back down. I look at Derek who just stole my budget…but not my program. For his part, he simply ignores me, as if I no longer exist. I maintain a steady gaze at him. I want to look into his eyes and stare through to his soul. But he refuses to as much as glance in my direction. He takes a sip of water and then my attention shifts; from Derek's eyes to Derek's glass…the one with his fingerprints now on it, and to his neatly trimmed head of hair, with all that lovely DNA inside it. Derek may refuse to deal with me now, but once I get my hands on that glass or a lock of his hair, in due time, Derek will have to deal with me later. I was willing to bet on it.

"Mr. President, we understand that replacing Jonathon Darcy is impossible," states Tyler. His words capture the president's undivided interest. He continues, "but we have come up with a list of suggestions for a new secretary of state, who we hope will come close to filling his shoes." Tyler rattles off a number of names and credentials of people with backgrounds in foreign affairs.

The president tugs the fabric of the Dragon Tie around his neck, takes a deep breath and responds, "I'm thinking of an entirely new approach to an old problem." He pauses and turns to me. "Ms. Banks, what about that child psychologist you referred to the other day?"

I'm stunned that he's brought it up in the context of a cabinet meeting. And then I remember. "Yes, Mr. President, sir. I happen to have her theory presentation with me." I reach into my backpack and take out the printout of Rachel's work. Instead of having it passed to the president, I stand up and walk around the massive table to hand it directly to him.

"Wonderful," exclaims the president. "I'm looking forward to reviewing this. Thank you, Madison."

"You're welcome, Mr. President," I reply. I walk back toward my seat, and as I pass Derek Rogers, seated next to Tyler Simmons, I just so happen to trip over my lengthy shawl, falling into his back, causing his water glass to tip over.

"Woah! Ahh!" I shout, trying to look as if I'm in need of regaining my balance.

Derek quickly saves the glass from tipping over and sending ice cold water onto his crotch as I surreptitiously pluck a few strands of his hair.

"Ow!" he hollers and turns around to rub the back of his neck as I maneuver to my seat, hair in hand.

The cabinet meeting comes to an end, but not before group photos are taken of its members in kimonos and shawls, compliments of Eve. I realize she is a resource I need to tap into with more frequency.

As I jog back to the Hay-Adams with Derek's lock of hair secure in my backpack, my mind races with ideas on how to reorganize and raise funds to keep My Grief Day and the Tribute Film Festival afloat. I know what we need…a mere six or seven million dollars, or I could kiss my mission and the healing of America goodbye. I just have to figure out how to get it.

I'm exhausted when I reach my hotel room. Slid under my door is an expensive parchment envelope with wax sealer on it, bearing the initials E.A. I put Derek's lock of hair in a safe place and then open the envelope. There's a fancy invitation from Elizabeth Anderson to attend a charity event she's hosting at the Kennedy Center. Wow, she works fast, I think.

There's a knock on my door. "Who is it?" I ask.

"It's me," calls Sierra. I open up. She stares at me in shock.

"You went to the cabinet meeting like that? Eve's gonna kill you."

"On the contrary, Eve managed to save my ass and get the entire cabinet to wear textiles from the museum."

Sierra nods her head, impressed, while I slip out of my jogging things.

"You could stand to update your workout clothes," she says.

"If I had time to actually work out, I would."

"That's another conversation. But for now, how'd the meeting go?" asks Sierra.

"Surprise, surprise. Derek Rogers appeared and managed to kill the entire budget for MGD."

"What?"

"Don't worry. President Stone saved the program. We just have to raise the financing."

"Maddy, we're talking about millions of dollars. Do you have any idea how much it costs just to execute your little tribute film festival idea in nationwide movie theatres for one month on sixteen thousand screens to forty million viewers?"

"No, but I'm sure I'll find out in ten seconds," I tell her, standing naked, running the bath.

"Try two million," yells Sierra. "That bumps this project to twelve million for hard costs, production insurance, labor and Internet servers. We're not even into the cost of mobile cinemas and advertising and promotion."

"Why can't we just go viral on all that? And put out a PSA? Can we cut the theatrical exhibition from one month to a week?" I ask, pulling a towel from the rack.

"I asked. It's a package deal, otherwise they stand to lose too much revenue."

"You are seriously deflating my hopes, Sierra."

"I'm sorry, Maddy. I'm trying to be realistic here. And it's not a pretty picture."

I sigh and adjust the water temperature as the tub rapidly fills up. "Can we change the subject? I'd like a moment of avoidance if you don't mind." Sierra chuckles. "So…are you going to the Kennedy Center tonight?" I ask.

"To do what? *Crash* the hottest charity do on the east coast that's been all over the news for the last seventy-two hours?"

"It has? Elizabeth Anderson invited me an hour ago. But I'm not going."

"Are you crazy? Why not?"

"She hates me," I reply, climbing into the tub.

"Then why the hell would she invite you?"

"I think it's to humiliate me," I say, submerging my body underwater. "She's got a real knack for it."

"You have to go. That's a huge deal."

"I don't care. I refuse to be humiliated by her. She's intimidating and…she scares the shit out of me." The phone in my room rings. I holler to Sierra, "Can you get that for me?"

Maybe Sierra was right. I'm too idealistic to think we can do this on our own. Who's going to give us that kind of money? I could ask Arthur Pintock, but he's already helped me so much as it is. I could ask Victor for advice, but hadn't I bothered him enough with my work issues? My lack of success was getting to be embarrassing. I should just resign. No one would notice anyway. The headlines would have a heyday. *"Grief Czar Grieves Under Pressure." "My Grief Day Turns Into One Big Miscarriage."* Thoughts of giving up play in my mind, becoming more and more a viable option, as I hear Sierra's voice in the background.

"Now?" asks Sierra. "Are you sure you have the right room number? I see… Well, he'll have to wait a few minutes… Thanks. Bye." She hangs up the phone. A moment later, she enters the bathroom. She takes one look at the disappointment on my face and softens. "Elizabeth Anderson has a limo waiting downstairs to take the grief czar to the Kennedy Center."

"Too bad, I just resigned."

"In your head?"

"Uh-huh."

"That doesn't count."

"Why not?"

Sierra sits on the edge of the tub next to me. She knows me too well. "Listen, Maddy. I'm not letting you fall into a depression over another attempt by Derek Rogers to ruin you plans. You've prevailed before. You'll prevail again."

"No, you were right before, Sierra. I should listen to you. This is ridiculous and impossible to pull off."

"When have you ever listened to me? Except when it's technical mumbo-jumbo. Now come on, I'll help you pick out the right outfit. We'll make Eve proud. You'll hold your head high and prove to everyone the show is going on."

"That's just it, though. I don't want to put on a show. My Grief Day is about creating an open dialogue for grief and the Tribute Film Festival is about paying tribute to someone other than ourselves. Isn't that what ultimately helps us heal? And isn't everyone sick and tired of all the me-ism, anyway? Isn't it time we honor someone else other than ourselves?"

"Do you hear yourself, Maddy? That's the underlying message. And it's beautiful and worthy of coming to life. So trust your instincts. They never fail you."

I stare at her, coming to a hundred realizations at once. "Neither do you, Sierra. Thanks. Can you help me put on makeup, too?"

The Kennedy Center

The building is packed with the who's who of Washington and a cadre of Hollywood celebrities. A number of noted speakers take the stage to talk about autism in America today. I cautiously stand behind a post, watching the room. Every time I see Elizabeth Anderson I duck for cover. I spot the president being smothered by Tyler Simmons, James Damon and Derek Rogers, as members of the press snap their photos. I see Lowell Frazen and Stuart Provost in another corner. At one point, I watch the popular and beloved talk-show host, Torah Grant chatting with a movie star. If we could get Torah Grant to endorse My Grief Day, all of our troubles would be over. Elizabeth Anderson walks by followed by two female aides holding clipboards and walkie-talkies. I duck out of sight again. A moment later I hear one aide say to the other, "Think the grief czar will show up?"

"She better. Anderson sent a limo for her."

"Maybe she'll come in jogging clothes and kimonos."

I catch my reflection in a mirror and shake my head. Their derisive banter stings. So who am I kidding? I don't belong here. I'm heading for the exit when Hampstead appears in my path.

"Whoever dressed you did a remarkable job, Ms. Banks," he says, looking at me as if I had stumbled upon the magic Cinderella shoe.

"Oh, thanks, Hampstead." His comment does little to bolster my self-worth. "Do you know which way is best to catch a cab?"

"It's not midnight yet, is it?" he asks, smiling. "I believe you've got another three hours before turning into a pumpkin."

"Feels like I already am one. Look, can you do me a favor and tell Elizabeth Anderson I showed up?"

"You're asking me to lie?"

"No, I showed up and now I'm leaving."

"Ms. Banks, there's showing up and then there's showing up. Hiding behind pillars and curtains is far from showing up. And it's not like you're still in jogging wear. You did receive an invitation, did you not?"

"I'm sure it was a vanity invitation because I'm the president's grief pal. Not because Elizabeth Anderson gives a damn about me."

"Maybe because you are the president's grief buddy, she does give a damn about you. I certainly wouldn't waste your time making assumptions. Washington is far too complicated for that."

"Well, it's far too complicated for me. Do you ever see things that seem so obvious and wonder why others don't? Things that damage democracy, compromise ethics and hurt the direction of the country?"

"All the time," answers Hampstead.

"So what do you do?"

"What every American should do," he says. "If you can't work the stage from front and center, you work it from behind."

I stare at him. "Did you know that I hate conundrums?"

"I did not know that. But that wasn't one."

"What was it then?"

"Politics, Ms. Banks. It's part of life. You can let it work you or, you can work it. It's really a matter of choice. Have a nice evening."

Hampstead takes his leave. I stop in the bathroom before reaching the exit, only to bump right into Elizabeth Anderson.

"Maddy Banks, there you are," she comments, reaching into her purse for some lipstick. "I was wondering when you were going to say hello. I should have guessed it would be in the bathroom." She applies her lipstick, and keeping her eyes trained on the mirror, practices a pucker in front of me.

I want to tell Mrs. Anderson to take her sarcasm and stick it up her nose. I want her lipstick to suddenly glue her mouth shut. But then, what I really want is for Elizabeth Anderson to be nice to me. So I make a choice, like Hampstead said, and decide to be nice to her. Super nice.

"That's because it's much more private here," I reply. "And I wanted to personally tell you how impressed I am with what you've managed to put together tonight. In fact, I'm so impressed that I was curious to know if you would mentor me?" Mrs. Anderson freezes. I go on, "It's obvious I don't know my way around Washington and well, I thought if you had any spare time I'd love to learn from the master."

Mrs. Anderson unfreezes and looks me over. "I'm flattered but I couldn't possibly afford to have you cramp my style."

"I understand," I say. "A student's only as good as their teacher, anyway." She bristles at this as she puts her lipstick away. "Well, if mentoring is out, will you consider joining the advisory board of The Tribute Network? Arthur Pintock is on the board."

"Arthur Pintock…of Pintock International?" she asks.

I nod. "Yes, and he's an active board member, too."

"I'll have to think about it."

"Sure. We meet all over the country, so it might not suit you."

She studies her watch. "Time to go, I have a bill to pass."

I stare at her, perplexed. "A bill to pass?"

She smirks. "Surely, you don't think they get passed on the floor of Congress, do you?"

"Mrs. Anderson, why did you invite me here?"

"Because you have become an important part of President Stone's life…for now…and to tell you not to meddle in ITT, which can help this country, if people like you don't get in the way."

"Is that a threat?"

"Not at all," she says theatrically. "More like an order. Good evening, Maddy."

She walks out the door. I smile at myself in the mirror. "She did say 'Good evening.' That's progress."

A new approach

Arthur's private jet is clean and cozy. Sierra and I are the only passengers on board. As we fly through friendly skies, I discover it's a great place to get a lot of work done.

Sierra sits next to me catching up on all the newspapers I've already scoured. She points to an article in the *Dupont Circle Times* on top of stacks of other papers.

"I've now read through ten papers…and I'd say someone's out to get you. Got any enemies?"

"Mrs. Anderson. I'm on her list of bad-mannered sinners."

"Bad enough for her to go to the trouble of paying a bunch of journalists to write this stuff?" asks Sierra.

I stop typing on my laptop and look at her, thinking. "That's an interesting concept…is it possible Derek Rogers paid off journalists to say he was related to Jonathon Darcy?"

"First you have to prove that he isn't, before you go down that road."

"I'm already on it," I tell her, returning to my laptop.

Sierra stares at me and raises her brow. "Really?"

"Really," I reply. I can feel her lingering stare upon me. "I'll tell you when I've got something real."

"Meanwhile, how are you managing to let this bad PR slide off your back?" she asks.

"Oh. Chinese farmer," I say.

"That makes sense." Sierra seems quite satisfied as she opens her purse, searching for something or other.

"You know the Chinese farmer story?" I ask, shifting to face her.

"Everyone knows the Chinese farmer story. Where have you been?"

I watch her pull out a sleek thin leather case about five inches by seven inches. She opens it up and starts reading an e-book. "How do you have time to read?"

"I make time, Maddy."

"How? When?"

"I think part of it is that I'm not distracted by a lot of inner emotional turmoil." She gently smiles at me. "That's why I want you to go to those meetings."

I sigh. "I am."

"You have to work at it, Maddy."

"Work at work addiction. How apropos." I smile.

A stewardess informs us to prepare for landing. As we approach the ground, I close down my portable shop and look out the window at cloudy skies for Los Angeles.

Sierra turns to me. "Is Victor meeting us here?"

"He's going to try. But then he has to take a red-eye to Toronto tonight so it's doubtful."

"What's in Toronto?" asks Sierra.

"I don't know. He never goes into the details with me anymore. Probably some new start-up he thinks is worth investing in. Lately, we just keep crisscrossing the country and missing each other. What about you? Is Milton meeting you here from Chicago?"

Sierra smiles. "We're getting together after our powwow."

"So it's still good?"

She nods. "He still makes me laugh. How about you guys?"

"We laugh...until I have to work."

"You could always drop in on a meeting in L.A., you know? I'll go with you, if you want."

"I'll let you know. First, we have to raise money." I didn't see how I could possibly have time to drop in on a work addiction meeting. But I held on to her offer, anyway. I knew if Sierra went with me, I had a much better chance of going. Her reaction to a meeting, however, was something I could never have predicted.

The L.A. powwow

Eve, Sierra and I gather inside Caffe Pinguini in Playa del Rey. Victor and Arthur should be arriving any minute. I lift my glass of wine.

"To Eve, for saving the day," I toast. We clink glasses over several appetizers.

"Thank God you called Hampstead," Eve says, as she sips her wine. "While you're caught up in whatever you're caught up in…"

"It's called 'politics,' Eve," points out Sierra.

"Whatever," she mumbles.

I clear my throat. "Okay, quiet, please. I have an announcement."

They both stare at me. Eve breaks out into a huge smile. "You're pregnant!" she declares. "Oh, my God. That is so cool! Can I be your fashion stylist when you start busting out? Because you're going to need—"

I roll my eyes. "I am not pregnant, Eve." Eve slumps back down in her seat, disappointed. "I was going to announce a new plan for My Grief Day."

"Whoa. Hold it. Just wait a second," exclaims Eve, perking back up. "Because I have an announcement, too. I've secured MGD's fashion designer." Sierra and I quickly exchange *uh-oh* glances. "Ready?" asks Eve, excitedly.

Sierra and I look, expectantly. "Ready," we say in unison.

"Z Mas," announces Eve, with overwhelming pride.

Sierra's mouth drops. "He's the hottest designer there is—supposedly untouchable. How on earth did you get him?"

"Okay, wait, who's Z Mas?" I ask, feeling lost already, but they don't seem to hear me.

"I picked up the phone and dialed," Eve says.

Sierra stares at her. "That is not a good enough answer. I want to know how you got past his entourage," she insists.

"Who said anything about getting *past* them?" Eve smiles. "I befriended them."

"And how did you befriend them?" Sierra is relentless. I feel as if I'm watching a rerun of Perry Mason, master interrogator of the courtroom drama.

"I used a teaspoon of persuasion mixed with a dash of persistence and two cups of cleavage."

Sierra leans in. "Oh come on, Eve. I'm not buying it. He's notorious for being impossible to reach. So how did you get to Z Mas and how did you convince him to design the attire for My Grief Day?"

"Who is Z Mas?" I ask again, only to be ignored again.

"Okay," admits Eve. "I outbid him."

"Oh, no," sighs Sierra.

"You outbid him?" I ask. "What are we paying this guy?"

"He's not a guy. He's a fashion god," says Eve.

"Good, then if he's a god, he won't need any money at all."

Eve shrugs. "You said the president increased our budget. So I offered Z Mas double to drop everything else he's doing and focus on this, exclusively, for the next four weeks. Plus, I sold him on all the press that will come from it, and the fact that it's a new national holiday, which he'll gain historical recognition for and..."

"How much?" ask Sierra and I.

"Two million," replies Eve.

"Oy," is all I can say. "That's taking advantage of the government."

"Excuse me," asserts Eve. "Remember the tiny nineteen cent washers the Pentagon had delivered from South Carolina to Texas for almost a hundred grand? You call that responsible government?"

"One wrong does not make a right. Did you ask if he might consider doing it for altruistic reasons, as in without pay?" I ask.

"Why? We have the budget. So what's the problem?"

I'm shaking my head in despair, unable to speak.

Sierra takes over. "The problem is that in yesterday's cabinet meeting, Derek Rogers shot down the whole program so there's no more government money. The president is still endorsing the project, but now we need to find financing from the private sector. Starting at zero."

"You're telling me we can't pay the fashion god!" screams Eve. The eyes of the restaurant patrons are all on us. Eve whispers fervently, "How can you do this to me?"

Sierra and I look at each other. "What did we do to *you?*"

"This is a total embarrassment to my reputation!"

"Uh, Eve," I interject, "did you ever think to call and discuss the matter or at least the fees before you went ahead and closed the deal? You can't just impulse buy a designer's design like you can impulse buy a pair of shoes? It's not like you get a receipt with an option to return the deal."

"What am I supposed to tell him?"

"Well, maybe he'd be willing to donate his time. After all, this is a good cause."

"After promising him two million?" she asks, dropping her jaw in disbelief.

"Look, I'm hoping to talk to Arthur tonight, maybe he'll make a donation. But even if he does, he'll want to see a budget, and based on the revised budget, the designer is at two thousand...not two million. Can't you get someone more reasonable? What about the designer of those shoes you got me?"

"The Messiah ones?" asks Sierra. "Those are hot."

"Impossible," Eve states. "No one knows who he or she is."

"A designer who seeks anonymity? I feel a conundrum coming on." I've twisted my cloth napkin into knots.

"No one gets it," says Eve. "He or she could have had an order for thousands of those shoes. But they dropped out. Poof. Gone. Not a trace..."

"*Okay*, we get it," mutters Sierra. "Sounds like John Galt," she adds.

"Who's John Galt?" asks Eve.

"'*Who is John Galt?*' is the first sentence, or question rather, in the novel *Atlas Shrugged,* by Ayn Rand," I explain. "The name represents a state of total helplessness and despair for capitalism."

"What are you talking about?" asks Eve, clearly frustrated by anything not self-evident.

"Never mind," I say. "Let me ask you something, Eve. How did you get the shoes?"

"I get samples sent to me all the time for my Fashion Therapy 101 label. When those pumps arrived, in your size no less, and with moments to spare before you were to meet the president, I knew what had to be done."

My BlackBerry dings. I check a text message. "Good, Victor is on his way but he didn't say if Arthur was with him. In the meantime, we need to find a really good charity to wrap this event around. I was thinking of a low profile charity before, but now we might need a high profile one to help with publicity."

Sierra offers, "How about both? People can donate online to whichever one they want to."

"Interesting," I comment. "Eve, what's this Z Mas guy's favorite charity?"

"You still didn't tell us how you got to Z Mas," Sierra reminds us.

"It was rather simple," replies Eve. She pauses, baiting us.

We stare at her. "Continue," says Sierra.

"Yes, please do," I add.

"Well, I happen to know his idiosyncrasies, like the fact that he loves scavenger hunts."

"How do you know that?" I ask. She offers a small scowl.

"I read, Maddy. I read."

"What?" I ask.

"*Cosmopolitan, Vogue, Fashion Planet,* etcetera, etcetera, etcetera," she says. "Sometimes I wonder how you get around."

"Okay. Okay. Please, go on," implores Sierra.

"I made sure I was sitting with George, one of his entourage, at a fashion show. I told George where to find the best limited editions of the most unique architecturally-sophisticated European designer blends that would put this fashion show to sleep. I promised he'd find something there that would blow Z Mas away. George took the bait, which I knew he would. Once he showed up at the store, I made sure the owner sewed my offer on top of the label in whatever George ended up buying. Once Z Mas saw the offer, he called me in for a one-on-one meeting. The rest is history."

"Clever," says Sierra. "What's the store?"

"Really Great Things," replies Eve.

"I know that store," I say. "It's on the Upper West Side, right?"

Eve stops sipping her wine and stares at me. "If you know that, then why don't you go there more often!"

"I'm busy working."

"What else is new?" she says.

Before I can defend myself further, Victor enters, spots me and waves as he crosses over to us. He greets me with a kiss, says hello to Sierra and Eve and sits down to join us.

"How was your flight?" I ask.

"Fine. I was able to move my meeting so I can stay until the morning."

"That's great. Can I get you a glass of wine?" I offer, noting the bottle is empty.

He grins. "In a minute. How is everyone?"

There's a mix of groans from all three of us.

"That's not good. Looks like an epidemic of bad days all around, which I think, calls for a bottle," Victor gathers, and then orders a bottle of Sangiovese, my favorite. We all put in our dinner orders as well.

"What happened to your day?" I ask.

"My day became the compilation of everyone else's, worst of all, Arthur's, which is why he's not here and why he's not coming. It will be in all the papers tomorrow, so I might as well tell you now," he says. "The SEC is coming down hard on him."

"For what?" I'm stunned.

"Lack of corporate compliance resulting in cooked books, overinflated stock prices, the works."

"That makes no sense," I exclaim. "He's got two full-time employees designated for corporate compliance alone! He even has monthly business ethics classes at every office so employees are up to speed. He's impeccable about every aspect of his business, most especially that one. In fact, he's one of Sarbanes Oxley's biggest supporters."

"They don't seem to be aware of any of that. In fact, they're scrutinizing his business like Nazis and treating him as if he's already a convicted felon. Needless to say, Pintock International's stock is plummeting. Arthur is completely tied up with resolving the issue and conducting damage control before it hits the papers tomorrow."

Sierra's eyes narrow with a contemplative stare. "Something's not right in Denmark," she quietly says.

Eve looks utterly confused now. "What does Denmark have to do with this?"

"It's a phrase for something's fishy," Sierra replies.

"Well, what's fish got to do with this?" she asks, more confused.

"Forget the fish," says Sierra.

"Then why did you say it's not right in Denmark?" asks Eve.

"It's just a saying, Eve. It comes from one of Shakespeare's plays," I explain.

"*Hamlet,*" Victor points out. "His father, a former king of Denmark, supposedly dies from a snake bite, but in fact was really murdered. The character, Marcellus, suspects foul play and makes the point that something isn't right in the state of Denmark, hence, the idiom."

I stare at Victor, in love with his mind and his memory.

"Thanks," replies Eve.

Victor looks around the table. "Where's Richard?"

"He's holding up the east coast office," I tell him.

The waitress appears with the bottle and soon Victor is pouring for us all. "So what's your plan now, given the she-nanigans of Derek Rogers at the cabinet meeting?"

"Plan A was to ask Arthur for help with funding," I answer.

"He's not going to want to touch his assets right now," says Victor. "What's Plan B?"

"There isn't one," adds Sierra.

"There's always a Plan B," I argue. "Plan B was to plan our own fund-raiser. But we don't have time for that right now. So we're on to Plan C, which is to find corporate sponsors and a high-profile celebrity." I pause to pull out several sheets of paper and pass them around. "This is a list of talent agents and corpo-rations in the area. I think if we divide we can conquer and—"

"And what? Raise two million overnight to get us out of the hole we're already in?" asks Eve.

Sierra shakes her head. "We need a lot more than that."

Victor reacts. "What's in the hole for two million?"

"Z Mas's fashion design budget," I say.

"Who got Z Mas? That's a coup," says Victor. He's clearly impressed. "That's actually not a bad price for him."

I'm shocked. "Hold it, did you say that's *not* a bad price?"

"Not for a fashion god like him," insists Victor.

I'm speechless. Sierra's smile lifts her brows.

"Ahem," Eve coughs, loudly clearing her throat. "I got Z Mas," she says, with pride.

Victor looks at her and smiles. "Nice."

"Except we can't pay him, so it's over," I chime in.

"I doubt that. Just appeal to him," says Victor. "Be totally honest about what's happened based on circumstances out of your control, and appeal for a revision in your agreement with him. It may sound like a story, but it's the truth you'll be telling. And everyone appreciates the truth, even if it hurts."

And then it hit me. Another keyword in Victor's tiny speech and more details around my plan quickly take shape. I grab pen and paper from my purse, and start making notes. I glance up to note Sierra watching me with a knowing look in her eyes.

"I think Plan D has arrived." She smiles. "We can all eat now."

"Good, cuz I'm starving," blurts Eve, as the waitress hands us our dinner plates.

Victor glances at me with an odd mixture of expressions. I can't tell if he's pleased or upset. "What's wrong, Victor?" I ask, furiously jotting down my ideas while everyone else begins eating.

"I have a feeling I'll be spending the rest of the night alone," he says. "*Bon appetit,*" he adds, piercing his salad with a fork.

"No, you won't. I promise. I'll just get the basics down and then we'll do whatever you want."

Victor sighs. He and I both know I'll be at the computer all night, trying to fit the rest of my life into one evening. Our exchange isn't lost on Sierra.

Victor looks around the table. "Anybody up for going to some clubs after dinner?" he asks.

"I am," agrees Eve.

"Good. How about you, Sierra?"

"I've got a date, thanks."

Victor smiles. "Okay, Eve, where are we going?"

"I know just the place!" she gushes. "And we won't have to stand in any lines either."

"Sounds good," says Victor. "That way we can save our feet for the dance floor." Victor pulls out some cash and drops it on the table, then glances at Eve. "You ready?" She nods eagerly, finished with dinner, and grabs her purse. They both stand up to leave. I'm still trying to finish a thought before it escapes me. Victor reaches down and kisses my cheek. "See ya, later, Maddy."

I didn't like the way he said that. There was an unfamiliar shade of sadness in his tone and because it was unfamiliar to me, I shied away from it like a xenophobe. "Okay. Have fun. And don't stay out late, Eve. We've got back-to-back meetings tomorrow," I remind her.

She and Victor exit.

"Maddy. This has to stop," implores Sierra.

"Hold on, I can't lose this thought," I reply. While I'm furiously writing I hear Sierra clicking on her BlackBerry. I finish getting my idea down and then pause to look up at her. "What?"

"We're going to a meeting," she states. "This is ridiculous."

"What are you talking about? And what about Milton?"

"I'll buy Milton a massage at the hotel until I get back. But right now, you need some serious intervention or you're going to lose what you don't even know you've got."

"First of all, you're overreacting. Second of all, there are no meetings at this hour and..."

"I just found one," she says, holding up her BlackBerry. "So...shut it down. We're going to Brentwood."

I stare at her.

"Now!" she orders.

There is one thing about Sierra. When she gets mad, which is almost never, the best and only thing to do is acquiesce, even if it's temporary and you're not fully committed. It's best to pretend you mean it, and wait for her rational side to reappear. This is one of those rare times. So I humor her and follow her into our rental car that would take us to the one and only work addiction meeting in all of Los Angeles County. Although neither of us could have anticipated how our arrival would open new doors, and one box—Pandora's.

6

The L.A. work addiction meeting

Sierra and I sit at an old conference table in a dingy room above a grocery store at a quarter past nine in the evening. No one else is there.

"Maybe this is the wrong location," Sierra mutters.

I pull out my computer. "No, this is right," I say. "They're always late."

"Everyone?"

I stop and stare at her. "Sierra. They're busy working."

Sierra makes a long face. "Obviously." She watches me boot up. "Do they all work during the meetings, too?"

"Well, sort of. Everyone's working on their work addiction. That's a form of work, isn't it?"

"What an insidious disease," remarks Sierra.

"No shit," I say. "Look, I think I've got a solution. We just need to find some celebrities who will endorse this thing. The way Elizabeth Anderson manages to do it…"

Sierra looks at me. "Can you talk to me about something else?"

I stare back at her, thinking, then reply, "No."

A door opens and a tall thin man with a buzz cut and sculpted muscles enters the room, nods his head, and sits down. A moment later, a large burly man in his fifties lumbers in and takes a seat. We all nod at each other. Then in straggles a young woman in her midthirties. She also nods and sits down. We all stare at each other. I sigh and stare back at my computer screen until a scurrying sound takes over. A short, hyperactive, wiry guy scoots in carrying the all-too-familiar plastic folder.

"Sorry I'm late," he apologizes. He opens up the plastic folder and starts dispensing laminated literature. Sierra clears her throat and stares me down. I get the hint, shut down shop and reluctantly face the group.

"Who would like to read the Characteristics of a Workaholic and the Tools of Recovery?" asks Hyper Boy.

"I would like to," offers Sierra.

I give her a look. It's one thing to observe my issue; it's another to watch your best friend dive right in along with you.

Sierra reads the twelve characteristics of a workaholic and I watch everyone else watch her speak. Her words mellifluously roll off her generous lips. Besides Sierra's rare expression of anger, she is also completely unaware of how exotic she is, which happens to make her even more beautiful. I consider whether this would affect a roomful of devout workaholics. Maybe it would work as an antidote? Beauty as distraction, enough to get the mind off of work, and with Sierra's newfound passion for solving the affliction, she could easily inspire her newfound congregants to make resolutions and stick to them. I was dreaming through this scenario as Sierra reaches the last two of the twelve characteristics.

"Waiting is painful for us," she reads. "We have no patience with process and instead focus on result-driven methodologies. Our inability to practice patience disrupts any possibility for working with a balanced pace." She stops and looks at me, clears her throat, and continues. "Number Twelve. We are preoccupied with how others perceive us. We think appearing busy produces an image of importance and will bring with it recognition. We are unaware of the fact that living in this manner disempowers us by giving over a sense of self-acceptance to the exterior world. We don't realize that this action actually hurts us, by leaving us distanced from knowing ourselves. If we don't know ourselves, we can't know what we want. If we don't know what we want, then we ultimately end up saying yes to everything, which in turn feeds the workaholic." Sierra stops and takes a deep breath. Everyone seems mesmerized by her tone and delivery. She looks up at her newfound admirers and smiles sweetly, and unbeknownst to her, insures their devotion.

"Please, continue," says our leader.

Sierra reads, "Tools of Recovery," from the other laminated sheet of paper. "Underscheduling. Listening. Prioritizing. Substituting. Playing. Concentrating. Pacing. Relaxing. Asking. Meetings. Telephoning. Balancing. Serving. Living in the now."

Our hyper leader, turned comatose from staring at her, finally regains consciousness and speaks. "Thank you. Let's introduce ourselves and then spend five minutes each on our shares. I'm Jay-Jay, recovering workaholic," he says.

"Hi, Jay-Jay," the group replies, in muttered undertones.

"I'm Smitty, workaholic," says the burly dude.

"Hi, Smitty," the group repeats, again in muted voices.

"Lana," says the woman. "Recovering workaholic," she adds.

"Hi, Lana," says the group, the energy waning.

"Eddie," says the tall, lanky fellow. "Anorexic workaholic."

"Hi, Eddie," the group mutters.

"Maddy, workaholic," I say.

"Hi, Maddy," they respond, with a welcoming lift.

"Sierra, friend of Maddy, here to support her and to intervene when necessary."

The group offers a resounding, energetic, "Hi, Sierra!"

And so the shares begin. The ritual timer is set. The speaker has five uninterrupted minutes to say whatever they want.

Sierra is fascinated by the stories that come out of all the shares. I watch her listen to their stories with riveted attention. I listen too, with a fascination to ascertain the professions of each member of the group from little clues in each of their talks.

Jay-Jay is a high-powered Hollywood agent driven by the need for approval. Smitty is a director of some sort of awards ceremonies for the television industry with manic fervors that swing between work and play and nowhere in between. Lana works for a major public relations firm and struggles in the boundary-making department, unable to say no to any request that is made of her. And Eddie, I'm not sure yet, but he has something to do with technology.

Eddie's still talking in the background when it occurs to me that the people sharing in this room could unknowingly take part in history. I just have to figure out how to pose the problem. I am so fortunate to be in a work addiction meeting in Los Angeles—what better place to solve your entertainment needs? Sierra has unwittingly walked us into a lion's den of work heaven.

My turn arrives. The timer starts and I begin my share.

"I'm a workaholic," I state. "My friend Sierra has helped me recognize this terrible problem. I know she wants the best for me. And so do I, but this is a really hard disease to crack. It creeps into every aspect of your life, especially when your job is twenty-four seven, like mine. After all, it's difficult to say no to the president of the United States when he needs you to solve the nation's grief crisis and to be his on-call grief buddy. And it's really hard to find downtime when your whole budget has been swiped out from under your feet by a nefarious thief known as Derek Rogers. I can say that, right?…because this meeting is about anonymity. So now I have seven weeks and counting to put on a national grief holiday and I'm in desperate need of funding from the private sector, which the president has endorsed by the way. The fact is, my team and I really believe in our work and the good that can come of it. A national grief holiday with everyday Americans as well as a few celebrities sharing their personal stories of grief together on television, online, in movie theatres and mobile cinemas around the country, would no doubt represent a feeling of solidarity and social acceptance that would promote collective healing. We're making it possible for users to upload their tribute videos to TTN, The Tribute Network, that's trademarked by the way, which is an online network for all things tribute related. So instead of *America's Funniest Home Videos* this will be like *America's Greatest Tribute Stories.* And there will be a Tribute Film Festival as well. In fact, the national holiday for this is called My Grief Day, that's trademarked, too, and it could launch an ongoing series, both online and on TV. Furthermore, celebrities would gain incredible PR from this and…"

Sierra's eyes start to narrow. She is so on to me. But I keep going. "Celebrities would get to wear clothes designed by Z Mas, the fashion god, in case no one happens to know who he is, because I didn't, and that's a clear indication of—"

Sierra clears her throat and speaks up, "Maddy, this isn't the forum for—"

"Excuse me," Jay-Jay interrupts. "But there's no cross talking here."

"Thank you," I say to Jay-Jay, and then give Sierra a look of triumph.

"Where was I? Oh, yeah. So, I'm trying to find a way to solve these problems, like whom from the private sector can help finance this very worthy tax-deductible event that offers unlimited media coverage. I suppose it could be a foundation or maybe a conglomerate of networks and studios or something like that. Anyway, as you can see, it's really hard for me to stop thinking about my work. It's affecting my relationships with my friends and family and most especially my fiancé, Victor, who also works and travels a lot, but he seems to have things in perspective. I believe there's something to the 'work-to-avoid-intimacy-thing.' But if I don't get the work done, then I'll feel like I failed not only myself, but the nation, and the president. And hasn't our president had enough grief already? His wife. His best friend. Haven't we all? The first lady. The secretary of state. Tornadoes, hurricanes, terrorism, nuclear threats and a Wall Street bailout. The grief is overwhelming. And it's weird because the only thing lifting me up is my work. And then there's this incredible feeling that you're not just working to work, you're working for something bigger than yourself, for something greater than your own problems, which makes your problems petty in comparison and in a way that's good because you get a larger, and therefore, more healthy view on the entire world and your purpose in it. Plus, there's working with Sierra, which is always so much fun. I mean how can you not want to work with someone who makes work fun? And I can't help but admit that the more time I spend working with her, the healthier I'll become because she's always there as an example of someone who knows how to balance her life. She paces herself, never overschedules, and listens. And um, what were some of those other things on the list of recovery? Anyway, so now all I have to do is find a way to save My Grief Day and…"

The timer dings. Jay-Jay looks at me. "You have one more minute."

I take a deep breath. "I just want to add that if anyone has any suggestions on how I can accomplish these objectives in a manner that is not prone to work addiction, I would greatly appreciate hearing your thoughts, including any ideas on strategic partnerships or celebrity appearances. Hearing your thoughts would also help me practice the tool of listening." I nod, summarizing, with heartfelt emotion, "So, um, thank you all for letting me share tonight. I feel like I've gotten a lot off my chest."

Time's up. Everyone stares at me, intrigued. I glance at Sierra. She's not staring; she's actually glowering at me.

"I'd like to thank everyone for sharing tonight," says Jay-Jay. "That wraps up our evening. If anybody wants to buy pamphlets or literature, please see me after we join together for the Serenity Prayer."

Jay-Jay stands up. Everyone follows. We join hands and recite out loud together the Serenity Prayer, which I still have trouble remembering as I trip over every third word.

The group breaks. Smitty makes a beeline for Sierra. Jay-Jay puts the paperwork back in the folder while glancing furtively between Sierra and me, trying to calculate which one of us he should talk to first. Eddie hangs back a moment, as Lana is first to approach me.

"Oh my gosh, that is so cool what you're doing. I'd love to help you in any way I can. I have a ton of celebrity clients and I'd be more than happy to arrange one-on-one meetings with you and to urge them all to do this. I lost my grandfather and I've never gotten over it. Actually, I never dealt with it. He was the one who really raised me and I don't think I ever grieved for him. I always ran away from that pain because it was ridiculously intolerable. I think having a national holiday to grieve our losses is wonderful. Here's my card, so please, call me, I'd love to help and I know my clients would, too."

I hold her card in my hand. "Wow. Thank you, Lana. This is really very kind of you. You know, Sierra and I are only in town for a few days. Do you think we could meet with you sometime tomorrow?"

"Oh, absolutely. Call my office first thing in the morning and we'll fit you in. I'm there by 7:00 a.m. See you then."

"Thanks so much, Lana!"

"No problem. Well, I've gotta go to work now. Thanks for your great share. It was really inspiring."

Lana leaves and Eddie approaches me. In the near distance, I can hear a snippet of Smitty's conversation with Sierra.

"So how do you do it?" Smitty asks, with sincerity. "I can't seem to find a balance. Especially when you're a freelancer like me and you never know when or where your next job is coming from…"

Eddie's standing right next to me. "Hi. I couldn't help but admire what you're trying to do."

"Thanks," I offer, turning to focus completely on him now.

"You mentioned you're open to hearing about strategic partnerships. Well, I think I've got something that can be beneficial for both of us."

"I'd love to hear about it."

"It's an online social-networking site for people to digitize and organize their life stories as well as a way to publish their stories, into books and CDs, or DVDs. I think you've got something with The Tribute Network where we could partner together on the storytelling angle."

"That sounds great. What's your company called?"

"StoriesMakeUs.com. We're in Marina del Rey. Here's my card."

I take a careful look at it. "Nice logo."

"Thanks," he replies.

"This is great. I'll call you in the morning and we'll set it up. I'm really looking forward to this, Eddie."

"Me, too," he says, and leaves.

I walk over to Sierra, who is now holding court with both Smitty and Jay-Jay.

"It's about looking forward to things," she says. "So you create opportunities to do those things that you love, like take a bike riding trip with friends through Acadia National Park, or going to a great new restaurant and making an adventure out of discovering new cuisines. Really, guys, I think the answer is in having other things to look forward to—even a friend's son's bar mitzvah party is something to look forward to." They stare at her, dumbstruck. "On the other hand," she adds, "maybe you have too many things to look forward to and you're overwhelmed. If you can't summon up the energy to look forward to something and plan for it, then you might have some sort of low-level depression going on, in which case I'm not qualified to advise you in that area. I make sure I always have something to look forward to that balances my life with work that I love, and nonwork activities that are equally pleasing to me."

"Amazing," says Smitty. "I'm going to think about that."

"I have something you can look forward to," I say. They all turn to me. "Smitty, we plan on having live performances on My Grief Day, would you be interested in co-directing them? Sierra is directing the east coast feed, but we need someone for the west coast. What do you think, Sierra?"

"I think having an acclaimed director such as Smitty Santos, who's directed the last four broadcasts of the biggest movie-award show would be an amazing coup…Madison."

"You…?" I ask Smitty. I had no idea.

"Yeah," replies Smitty. He pauses. "I'm interested. You can go over it with my agent."

"Your agent?"

"Yeah, Jay-Jay. He's right here."

I turn around and face Jay-Jay. "Hi," I say. I glance back at Smitty. "Um, as you know, we don't have financing anymore, so until we get some, that is if we get some, how would you feel about doing it for a charity, once we find one?"

"I'm not really into charities," says Smitty.

"What about doing it for the experience of working inside an architectural masterpiece designed by Frank Gehry?" I ask.

"I don't really care about architecture," replies Smitty.

"Okay, what about doing it for the cause itself, to help people face their grief head-on and heal?"

"Nah," says Smitty. "I'm too depressed in my own state of mind to help strangers heal their shit."

"Well, then…how about doing it for the fuck of it?" I ask. Smitty grins and nods. "Okay. For the fuck of it, I'll do it," he says.

"Great. You'll be working with Sierra, too."

"Even better," says Smitty. "I'm down for it. Jay-Jay, you cool with it?"

"Not particularly, but I can't stop you," says Jay-Jay. "I prefer that my clients earn an income, which means the agency earns an income. However, in this case, we're not going to worry about that and neither are you, Madison. I'm going to see to it that we get you the funding and the celebrities you need for My Grief Day. Why don't the two of you call me tomorrow and we'll discuss the details." He hands us his card. It reads Jay-Jay Lovenheim, Literary Agent, STA, Significant Talent Agency.

That was the end of my first work addiction meeting in Los Angeles. By the time we reached the car, Sierra had done a complete turnaround, though it came with deep vociferous misgivings, from which I knew there would be no escape.

"I can't believe you just inveigled all those hardworking people to do more work for you!" exclaims Sierra, shaking her head.

"They have free will, Sierra. It's not like I held a gun to their heads."

"Yes, you did. You insanely offered them work. If they were alcoholics you might as well have given them IVs of bourbon!"

"Can't you see the win-win in this? Everybody's doing something for the country, for someone besides themselves? Wasn't one of the Tools of Recovery all about serving? You can't deny that there's healing in that."

"I can't deny how you manage to pull this shit out of the bag. You're unreal."

"I can't tell if you're happy or mad," I say, as we climb inside the car.

"I can't either," she mutters. "How on earth do you do it?"

"I'm a born opportunist." I start the car and drive us out of the parking lot and back to Shutters Hotel in Santa Monica where we're staying.

Sierra turns to me, beaming. "I still can't believe you got Smitty Santos to direct My Grief Day from the west coast. You realize this makes getting financing that much easier, let alone having an accomplished director who knows what he's doing." She pauses for a beat. "Although, you completely failed at healing your work addiction."

"I'm well aware, thank you. What are we going to do about that?"

"As soon as this is over, I'm forcing you to go cold turkey."

"Now isn't that being a little harsh?" I ask, starting to sweat. I couldn't imagine what it would be like not to work. "What if it backfires? What if I become a, you know, a work anorexic?"

"Got any better ideas?"

I didn't.

Shutters on the Beach

We arrive at Shutters and Sierra retires to her room where I imagine she smoothly turns work off and Milton on. I retire to my room all the more excited by the turn of events in favor of My Grief Day. I stand on the balcony overlooking the big blue Pacific Ocean wishing Victor was with me right now. I promise myself to make it up to him as soon as he walks through the door. My thoughts drift to Arthur as I imagine the trials and tribulations he must be going through. I send him an e-mail offering my unwavering support.

Wispy clouds drift across the nighttime sky to reveal the most beautiful glowing moon I have ever seen. I stand there in my Messiah pumps mesmerized by the moon's beauty. Alas, I kick off my pumps that have carried me through yet another exhausting day and open the minibar to retrieve a bottle of wine to celebrate with Victor. I pour two glasses of white wine on the table and throw on my sexy silk white lingerie and wait, or try to.

I look at the Messiah shoes on the floor and curiously lift them up, turning them around, studying them. I notice something deep inside the right shoe that I had never seen before. There's an inscription highlighted by the glow of the moon. It reads, "For Madison Banks." I stare at it. The letters *M* and *a* have a unique flair to them. I place the shoe under a lamp. Under tungsten lighting the letters are barely visible to the eye. But under the glow of the moon, it's clear as day. I look at the shoe, puzzled. These were intended for me by someone who wanted me to have them, by someone who didn't care about developing a brand or producing thousands of well-made shoes that could have made a profit. Someone who didn't care to be recognized for their labor and design. I am deeply curious as to who would do this. It was the most confusing conundrum I had ever encountered because it worked against every principle in my capitalistic arsenal. I carefully turn the shoe upside down and around looking at its fine leather, exquisite heel and strong sole, which I surmise came from Italy. Baffled, I whisper to myself, "Who is John Galt?"

A few minutes go by as I stare out at the ocean. The lull of the waves pulls me toward a deep sleep and soon I pass out on the bed. Sometime during the night, I am awakened by a rustling noise. I open my eyes to see Victor taking his shirt off.

The light of the moon highlights the sculpted muscles on his arms and back. My senses stir to life.

"Hey, handsome," I mumble, half asleep. "Did you have a good time?"

"We had a blast," he says. "Eve is a party animal."

"Hmm. I can be a party animal, too."

Victor looks between me and the two full glasses of wine on the table. "I don't think you should try to be something you're not, Maddy."

"Who says I can't be?" I stand up, wrap my arms around his waist and offer a playful growl.

Victor takes my hands off his waist. "I think you should go back to bed. You've got a big day tomorrow, don't you?"

"Not anymore. Sierra and I went to a work addiction meeting and while we were there we got a little help. It looks like we're on our way to securing funding for My Grief Day."

Victor looks at me, disturbed. "So you worked at a work addiction meeting?"

"Sort of," I reply. "But now I can devote my full attention to you. So why don't you let me take your pants off and feed you wine and grapes?" I ask.

Victor looks suspicious. "First of all, there are no grapes here. Secondly, I feel cheated."

"Cheated? You're the one who went dancing with Eve."

"I mean by your motivation. It feels like a cheat. It feels strangely…inverted. You only want to sleep with me because you accomplished something tonight. I don't think it has anything to do with me, Maddy."

"Victor, how can you say that? So, I made some progress tonight and I want to celebrate that with you? How is that cheating?"

Victor sits down on the bed next to me and quietly holds my hand, and then he looks me in the eye and poignantly replies, "I feel like I'm constantly running in second place with you, Maddy. It's only because you fed the work monster a big enough meal to keep quiet for the night that you can devote your attention to me. It feels wrong, Maddy. I'm sorry, but I can't make love to you tonight. I don't think I can make love to you until I'm in first place. Scratch that. First place is unrealistic in today's world. I just want to be on equal ground with your career. That much I deserve. I don't care if you're president of the United States."

Normally, I'd immediately defend my actions, but Victor always knows how to disarm me with his gentle and loving approach. I owe him the courage to look honestly at myself. "Okay, Victor. I hear you. I'll keep going to work addiction meetings and I'll rise above it. I promise. And as soon as My Grief Day is over, I'll go cold turkey and detox from work for a year straight."

Victor looks at me and gently squeezes my hand. "I know you mean well, Maddy. I know you're willing to try. But I don't believe you're ready or able, and until that happens, I think we should separate for a while."

"What? Did something happen between you and Eve?" I ask.

"Nothing happened between Eve and me," says Victor. "And I'm not saying any of this because you're not a party animal. How much of that do you think I could honestly take? But tonight opened my eyes...as a symbol for the kind of interaction I crave from you."

"I can't believe I'm hearing this."

"Maddy. You know I'll always be there for you. Professionally. Personally. Any way you want it or need it. I'm there for you. But I think we should take a break for a while. You've only got room for one lover right now and that's your work, not me."

I stare at him, trying to swallow the gulp in my throat that refuses to budge. My whole life I was taught that I could do anything. That the choices available to me as a person were no longer limited by my gender as they had been for the generations of women who had preceded me and paved the path of opportunity. Here I was going for it full throttle and the man I loved, or was too afraid to love, was now giving me opposite signals. It feels cruel and unjust and at the same time, it feels like a tremendous relief for someone so single-mindedly focused as me. That, of course, does not mitigate the sting and the aftermath of loss that was sure to come, no matter how temporary it may be. "How long are we talking about?" I venture.

"I don't know…a month or two, maybe three. Let's just stay in touch but not go out of our way to get together when we really aren't…being together."

He kisses me on my lips and holds me close. Our breathing intensifies. Our hands grope for the other's body. We soulfully kiss each other for what seems like an hour. Victor finally makes a move below my waist, but I stop him.

"Victor, wait. Now I don't trust your motivations." He looks at me, waiting for more. "I don't want this to be a mercy fuck."

He tightly pulls me into his arms and kisses me all over my neck, murmuring and groaning, "This is no mercy fuck, Maddy. I'm crazy about you."

"What happened to being second fiddle?" I ask.

"We're in the eye of the storm," he says.

I know what he means. It's the gap in my armor, a moment where our love is genuine and untethered by outside concerns. The work-storm would return tomorrow. But for now, we basked in its eye and allowed our passions to take control over our reasons, our hurts and our ambitions. Our lovemaking was intensely emotional and physical, and except for one lingering question that crept in and out of my mind, I was all Victor's, all night long.

As we roll around on the king-size bed, Victor raises his head from the crook of my neck. "I can hear you thinking," he claims. "What is it?"

I hold his face closely in my hands. "Are you John Galt?" I ask.

He gives me a strange look. "You're funny," he quips, and goes back to the lovemaking at hand.

Alone

Victor's absence hurt. I thought his early morning departure would be like any other. There was the small kiss on my sleeping lips and the melodic whisper of "Goodbye, I love you." But when the hotel room door closed behind him, something else did, too. I didn't know how to define it except to call it a limbo-loss; that place of not knowing if someone or something has died or ended or not. Instead, it was a loss that lived in stagnation, an engine of love reduced to an idling existence.

Reciting the Serenity Prayer did nothing to lessen the hurt. So shortly after Victor left, I went for a long jog along the beach. Nature was the greatest healer. I focused on the low tide, the wet sand, the dark before the dawn and the brisk early November breeze. I return in time to prepare for my breakfast meeting with Sierra and Eve.

As I pass through the lobby to pick up the morning papers, I see Sierra in the outer foyer straightening Milton's tie for him and kissing him goodbye as he climbs inside a taxi headed for LAX and beyond. I find myself turning away. I should have done that for Victor; lavished him with attention, bought him ties to straighten and sent him off with a kiss each morning. I hoped a second chance was in my cards.

★ ★ ★

I'm the first to breakfast so I order a cup of Earl Gray tea and dig into the papers while waiting for Sierra and Eve to join me. The front page of the *Financial Street Journal* reads, Pintock

International under Financial Commissions investigation. Poor Arthur, I think. He doesn't deserve this.

The article was written by George Toffler. George had written the very first story about me in the *Financial Street Journal* over two years ago and he had been instrumental in unearthing the truth behind the Derek Rogers scandal with Tributes in a Box. He was a good reporter, the kind that couldn't be bribed, nor was he apt to make false judgments unless the truth had been meticulously camouflaged. I wonder what Victor thought of the article, how George Toffler came upon the story and if there really is a story or if it's been fabricated for the sake of a wild goose chase. There's the truth and then there's the truth behind the truth. I wonder how willing a journalist would be to go to find it…which reminds me to contact Brian, the genealogy software dude. I shoot him a quick e-mail from my BlackBerry asking if there's any new status on the DNA report I had given him before leaving D.C. for L.A.

I check my watch. Sierra and Eve are twelve minutes late. I scan the paper. There's another article, "President Stone meets with California Firefighters." As if not to leave the western states untouched, another disaster strikes, this time eight thousand acres has burned and charred, including two small towns, leaving another thousand Americans homeless. I sigh, shake my head, offer a small prayer for the victims and wonder if the Chinese farmer story could be of any consolation.

"Good morning," says a cheery Sierra.

I put the *Financial Street Journal* down and smile at her. "Good morning back. How's Milton?" I ask.

"Great. Do you realize how lucky we are to be with men who are willing and able to meet us across the country for a one-night rendezvous?"

"Yep," I say, and bury my head inside the menu. But Sierra doesn't miss a beat.

"Where's your promise ring?" she asks, her tone switching from light to serious.

I hesitate for a moment. "In my room," I reply, and turn back to the menu.

"I gathered that…why?" she asks.

I take a deep breath. "We separated." Silence follows. I peek at her from behind my menu. She stares at me in shock. "Not my decision," I add. "But perhaps my doing. You did warn me."

"Maddy, are you okay?"

"I'll be fine."

"Spoken like the true stoic you always feel you have to be. Can't you let down your guard, even for me?"

"Sierra, I appreciate that you're always there for me. I really do. But I don't have time to wallow in self-pity or fight to win him back. There's a country out there, our country, and no matter what you or Victor maintain, I believe the needs of the sum of the whole is greater than the parts. I trust my time will come when it's meant to, whether it's with Victor or someone else. But right now, any personal grief I may be bearing is second to the nation's. Besides, I'll have plenty of time to grieve about it during My Grief Day."

"I see. You don't think you deserve to experience your own personal feelings of grief? Is that it?"

"That is not it."

"How can you be so callous toward your own heart?"

"It's not callous. It's practical. Speaking of which, where's Eve?"

"I'm right here," says Eve, sliding into the third chair. Her eyes look dark and tired. "I need a triple espresso, please," she says to the waitress who drops off my tea. The waitress nods as she writes Eve's order down and then glances at Sierra.

"I'll have a decaf latte with nonfat milk, please," says Sierra. The waitress nods again and leaves.

Eve slips off her sweater revealing her white shirt with pink lettering that reads I PITY YOU ALI-SHI-ALI-ALI. I realize I never had time to talk to her about that.

Sierra stares at Eve. "Nothing happened between you and Victor, did it?" she asks.

"What kind of question is that?" asks Eve.

"Are you attracted to him?" asks Sierra.

"Sierra, that's enough," I say.

"Okay. What's going on?" asks Eve. "No, wait, don't tell me yet. I'm not awake. I need that triple espresso before anyone says another word."

The waitress drops it off. Eve smiles, relieved and delighted. "Thank you!" she says.

The waitress sees Eve's T-shirt. Her eyes widen with excitement. "Oh my God, where did you get that T-shirt? It's so dope. I've been looking all over for one," she exclaims.

Eve smiles at her, pleased. "No worries, the first shipment will be at your nearest high-end department store by Wednesday."

"Thanks," says the waitress. She leaves.

Eve looks at me. "Anything wrong?"

"Copyright. But we'll get to that later," I tell her.

"No, we won't. We made a deal, remember? Information in small blue package for exploitation rights of your Rose Garden speech," declares Eve.

"What are you two talking about?" asks Sierra.

"Never mind," I say.

Eve takes a giant sip of espresso then focuses on us. "So... did Victor tell you what happened *between* us?"

"No!" Sierra and I both shout. Were our hunches accurate?

"Oh, well maybe he wanted it to be a surprise."

"We don't like surprises," says Sierra.

"Sure?" asks Eve.

"Positive," I persist.

"Okay, well, first of all, let me just state for the record that that man can dance! Do you have any idea what kind of power base that represents during social engagements loaded with prestige and opportunity?"

"Ugh," I say. "You sound like…"

"You," says Sierra, shooting me a quick glance.

Eve continues, "We all rub off on each other. It can't be helped."

"Did Victor rub off on you, too?" asks Sierra, like an interrogator.

Eve beams, oblivious to Sierra's tone of voice. "He sure did."

Sierra and I look at each other in shock.

"He taught me the Appeal Approach and together we solved the Z Mas problem."

"Run that by us again?" Sierra asks.

"I took Victor to a private party at an exclusive club hosted by the Z Mas entourage. We danced up a storm and made quite an impression. Personally, I think it was a combination of our moves and our clothes. You know how impeccable Victor is, he's a total metrosexual, which really confuses the hell out of gay men, Z Mas entourage included. Next thing you know, we're hanging out in the VIP lounge with the entourage when Z Mas himself makes an unexpected appearance."

"No way," says Sierra.

"Yes, way," replies Eve. "Victor and Z Mas made friends and then at the right moment, with Z Mas sitting *between* us, Victor gave me a nod and I launched into my appeal with Victor backing me up, which was only necessary one time because—"

"And then what happened?" I ask.

"Z Mas thought about it. Victor pointed out all of the pros and cons. I get how he works. He gives full disclosure. It's remarkable. It makes the other party feel like you're not out to screw them so they give you what you want because that kind of blatant honesty trumps any reason for suspicion! So, Z Mas looked like he was about to say yes, but then he hesitated and I wasn't sure, because I have so little patience with process, unlike Victor. Z Mas kept drinking his black cherry vodka very slowly, with an actual black cherry in it—"

"Eve, please get to the point," demands Sierra.

"All right," she says, taking another sip of espresso. "I asked Z Mas if he had ever grieved for the twin brother he lost at birth, which few people know about unless you've done massive amounts of research on him."

"Why did you do massive amounts of research on him?" I ask.

"He was my thesis paper in college," retorts Eve. "Inspirations of a Fashion God! You have no idea how many fashion magazines I read from all over the world. I even had to have them translated. Anyway, he was surprised I knew that and then he confessed he had never grieved for his twin. He admitted this would be a great opportunity to pay that respect and so he said yes to design the attire for My Grief Day!"

"For free?" Sierra and I ask in unison.

"Sort of." Eve pauses. "You see, about three years ago, Z Mas lost both his parents. It was terrible. While their health was failing, he went into a year-long depression. Couldn't work. Couldn't cope. He was close to both of them. For a while, it looked like his entire business was going to go under…"

"Excuse me. What does this have to do with his fee?" asks Sierra.

"Pushy, pushy, pushy…I'm getting to that. I thought you guys liked stories. So can't a girl tell a story? Where was I? Oh, yeah, his mother had a long illness. Z Mas's father was the primary caretaker until hospice came to help, providing a beautiful end-of-life experience for his mom. Right after she, you know, died, two months later, his father became terminally ill. Hospice came to the rescue again and helped his father to a peaceful resting place while providing tons of emotional support for Z Mas. So I suggested making the National Hospice Foundation the designated charity for My Grief Day in lieu of a fee because that's his charity of choice. Well, he loved the idea! So, there you have it, and the National Hospice Foundation solves the matter of which charity to go with. It's nonpartisan with respect to a 'disease,' and it's universal, because everyone dies. And it's a no-brainer given the subject of My Grief Day. I'm meeting Z Mas at his studio to go over preliminary designs at four o'clock today," she adds. "So? Is it a go with this charity?"

Sierra and I look at each other and nod our heads in tacit agreement.

"I'm impressed," says Sierra.

Eve smiles. "I guess Victor wanted you to hear it from me, huh?"

"Nicely done, Eve. But let me get this straight," I say. "The two of you go dancing to play, not work, because we're not supposed to work anymore after a certain hour of the day, but what happens? You both end up *working* while you're out dancing. Is that right?" I ask.

"What's wrong with that?" asks Eve. "It was organic."

"Nothing," I state. "Nothing at all. One day I'll have to remind Victor of that."

"So did you get all your work done last night?" asks Eve.

"Oh, we made headway, all right," Sierra replies.

"Our first stop of the day is the Paikel PR Firm," I announce.

"Shut up," says Eve, with endearment. "They're huge. They represent all the A-list actors, singers, talk-show hosts—"

"We got it," says Sierra, cutting Eve off. "We only need one to appease a corporate sponsor. Not the whole client list."

Again, Eve smiles. "Still. I didn't know planning a grief party could be this much fun."

The PR firm

The hallway is long and drafty. People fly by in a flurry creating a wind in their wake. Eve, Sierra and I weave behind a jovial Lana Perkins, as she leads us to her office.

"Can I get you anything? Coffee, tea?" she asks.

"I'm good, thanks," I say. Sierra and Eve reply in kind.

Lana turns to a young girl in a cubicle. "Can you please get me another cup of herbal tea? Thanks," she says, then turns back to us. "I've given up coffee, cigarettes and alcohol. I've only got two addictions left now. Work and clutter."

We reach Lana's office and enter. It's tastefully decorated. I think. It's hard to see any furniture and chairs underneath the mounds of files, documents, books and DVDs. She quickly removes piles of paper from three chairs revealing sparse seating for us.

"Please, sit," she says. "Funny, isn't it? You start acknowledging one addiction only to find out it's a cover for layers of others."

"Really?" I ask, surprised and concerned. I did not want to discover any more addictions inside myself. Wasn't one enough?

"Really," says Sierra, probing for more information.

"Oh, yeah," says Lana. "Denial is the engine of all addiction. What step are you on?"

"Why are we talking about steps?" asks Eve.

"We're talking about the twelve steps," whispers Sierra.

"Twelve steps. How are you supposed to get anywhere?" asks Eve.

"It's a twelve-step program of recovery," explains Sierra, as she rolls her eyes. "Haven't you ever heard of Alcoholics Anonymous?"

"Maddy's an alcoholic?" asks Eve, shocked.

"Workaholic," replies Sierra.

Eve rolls her eyes and whispers back, "Tell me something new."

"Step? I, uh, haven't started the steps," I say to Lana.

"I highly recommend it," she declares, finally sitting down in her chair behind a desk with mounds of paperwork. "I'm on step four for both work addiction and clutterers anonymous."

"Clutterers Anonymous?" I ask. "They have such a thing?"

"Oh, there's a meeting for everything and everyone! Alcohol addiction, work addiction, overeaters anonymous, sex and love addiction, co-dependency, news junkies…" Sierra gives me a look. Lana continues, "There's shopaholics, debtors anonymous, crackberrys anonymous and there's even a meeting for people who are born Jewish with overbearing mothers." She smiles.

Sierra looks at Eve and grins. "Eve, maybe you should think about shopaholics and debt-aholics."

Eve smiles back with flaring sarcasm. "Well then, there must be a meeting for you, too, Si. Gadget addicts."

Lana jumps in. "Oh, that meeting's fairly new. It started in Vegas during the Consumer Electronics Show," she says. I roll my eyes. "So," begins Lana, "I already discussed My Grief Day at this morning's staff meeting and then ran it by a few of my clients and they're interested. I also compiled a rough draft of the press release and a strategy for print media." She hands me a pile of paperwork at least one inch thick.

"You did all this since last night?" I ask.

"I needed an adrenaline fix and this was on the front burner, so it got the attention. First of all, I think I can book you as a guest on the Torah Grant Talk Show…"

"Oh, my God!" says Sierra, who never gets excited about anything. "That would be awesome."

"It would certainly solve any need for a PR budget," says Eve.

"Well, you have no budget. That's why I thought of it," Lana points out. "And so far, I've got interest from celebrities Thom, Willy, Ellene, Nora, Mickey, Josh and…"

"Wait, stop a second," I interrupt. "This isn't supposed to be a celebrity festival. We only need one or two celebrities to help with fund-raising and host the program. If those names are the names I think you're referring to, I'm sure they're going to want fees. We need people who want to do this from their hearts."

"I get that," says Lana. "But inevitably, availability conflicts come up and you'll be lucky to have just one in this group that stays on board. Look, there's a big fund-raiser tonight at the Beverly Hilton Hotel. I suggest you go and let me introduce you to the celebrities there. I'm sure you can explain better than I what you're looking for."

"Oh, well, then, um, that sounds great."

"Does that invitation include all of us?" asks Eve. "Because there are some things that Madison just can't explain…like wardrobe sizes for Z Mas."

"That's right. You got Z Mas for this!" exclaims Lana.

"It was no big deal," says Eve.

"Nor can she explain technology," Sierra chimes in, "which is a highly integrated component."

"I think I can get you all in, if you don't mind volunteering a little, you know, like greeting guests when they arrive, that sort of thing. Would you mind?" she asks.

"Not at all!" we reply simultaneously.

"Great. Be there at six sharp. It's black tie," she informs us. "I'll be walking the room so I'll see about putting you all at Jay-Jay Lovenheim's table," she adds, just as my BlackBerry dings. I check it. It's Hampstead.

"Pardon me," I say, and answer the phone, "Madison Banks."

"I understand you're in Los Angeles," says Hampstead. "President Stone is wondering if you could be available to meet with him today. He has something he'd like to share with you."

"When?" I ask.

"Now," says Hampstead. "We're at the Peninsula Hotel in Beverly Hills."

"I'm in the middle of a meeting in Century City."

"And your point is, Ms. Banks?"

"Right. That I'll be there in fifteen minutes," I reply, and disconnect. I jump up. "I'm sorry. The president needs me," I explain. "Lana, I can't thank you enough for all this."

"Are you sure you're not binging on approval and recognition?" asks Lana. "Characteristic number fifteen of a workaholic."

"It's the president," I say, gathering my purse in a rush.

Lana looks at Sierra and Eve, then back at me. "We're aware of that," she says.

"Uh, maybe you didn't hear me. It's the president...of the United States. Where are your priorities?" I ask.

"The question is," replies Lana, "where are yours?"

Sierra sighs. "Finally, some sanity." Her voice is sweet as she asks, "Maddy, did you ever stop to think that your behavior might be enabling the president to avoid his grief instead of feeling his emotions?"

"Did you ever stop to think that maybe his grief is overwhelming and by having a grief buddy he's actually taking care of his needs?"

Lana butts in. "I think Sierra's suggesting that you simply take a moment to look at what's personally driving *your* behavior because right now it looks like symptoms of an *overly concerned-aholic.*"

"I'm sorry, but I stick by my commitments," I retort, more than irritated.

Lana leans back in her chair, and calmly replies, "Wow,

something just triggered you." She pauses. "Now is a good time to stop, extract yourself from the situation and look at what motivated that response because I assure you it has nothing to do with what Sierra or I have said. You know," she says, "there's clean energy and then there's frenzy. There's blaming others on the outside, and there's personal responsibility from the inside."

I look at her, speechless, confused and misunderstood.

"Okay, when did this become group therapy?" asks Eve. "Because two and a half hours of sleep is just not enough energy for this."

"Neither is eight," I say, and stamp out the door. "I'll see you all later."

Eve's voice trails after me. "Wait a minute, what are you going to wear tonight?"

Alone in the elevator I try not to think about Lana's words or Sierra's for that matter. Why did I resent what they were saying? Why did I feel I had to defend myself? Why was I triggered by *their* inability to see what really mattered in this moment? Clearly, we had different opinions. I wondered if all these variations on addiction meetings were really helpful. Or if they were another distraction, obsession or excuse from a society gone narcissistic with self-indulgence for self-help at the expense of helping others in need. Or had capitalism itself become some sort of distorted work ethic designed to keep the masses so busy pursuing the American dream that we had lost sight of our core selves and true desires?

But the words *clean energy, personal responsibility, approval and recognition binging* kept echoing in my mind. Until I reached my car. And drowned them all out with the start of the engine, a quick shift into Drive, and a long screech of tires as I sped up and out into the familiar urban maze of asphalt and concrete.

The Peninsula Hotel

Hampstead greets me at the door of the penthouse, impeccably dressed as usual. I notice his tie. I'm curious about where I could find one like that for Victor, assuming a second chance came around.

"Good morning, Ms. Banks," he says, looking me over with approval.

"Good morning, Hampstead. That's a really nice tie."

"Thank you. It's handmade."

"Wow. Who made it?"

"My cousin, he's a true artist."

"He's very talented. Does he have a store? I'd love to buy one as a special gift."

"You can't. They're not for sale," he says. "And besides, he lives in a remote village in Tuscany."

"Oh. Well, if he ever changes his mind, let me know."

"He won't," says Hampstead.

"Okay, well, it never hurts to ask," I mumble, worrying that my attempt to change was an omen against second chances.

"The president is waiting for you," says Hampstead, leading the way.

"How's he doing?" I ask, following him around a corner.

Hampstead shakes his head. "Let's just say grief is like a yo-yo."

"It can also be our greatest teacher…if we let it."

Hampstead glances back with skepticism, as he precedes me down a hallway. "What have you learned from grief, Ms. Banks?"

"You don't get over it. You get used to it. What's the alternative? Hide under a rock? If you don't love, you don't grieve.

And the inherent challenge in all of it is to take something negative and make it positive."

"Yes. I suppose so. Tell me, what positive deeds have you accomplished from your grief?" he asks.

Suddenly, my personal motivation becomes crystal-clear. In a moment of perfect alignment, my energy shifts from frenzy to clean as I confidently answer, "Creating meaningful experiences to remember, with personalized tributes for one, My Grief Day for another and the honor of serving the president as his grief buddy."

"How noble," Hampstead says, still unconvinced.

Yet, in that instance, it didn't matter to me if Hampstead was convinced or not because I was, although it was fleeting. I had tasted a second of sanity, where seeking approval from anyone or anything was absent. I tasted it long enough to be conscious of it and wish for more in the most tangible way possible.

I recognize the Secret Service guys as Hampstead opens the doors to a suite and leaves. The president turns away from the windows. "Ah, Madison," he says. "Thank you for coming to see me on such short notice."

"My pleasure." Yet, as soon as I say those words, the perfect alignment has all but disintegrated from behind tainted motivation. I acknowledge that it is my pleasure not only because I'm honored to serve the president, but also because I get to have an adrenaline fix, I get to rush around in a frenzy. I get to binge on recognition; in short, I get to feed the monster of inner emotional turmoil embedded in denial. Denial from what, I thought, wanting to grasp that feeling of purity again. Immediately I was sick with clarity. What if everything Lana said was on target? And how was it possible to have bouts of awareness and fog at the same time?

"Mr. President, before you begin, I think I need to tell you something." I take a deep breath and continue, "I wonder if my meeting you at a moment's notice, or rather fifteen minutes' notice, is enabling you to avoid your grief and…if that's a disservice to you."

President Stone stares at me. "Sit down, Madison." We both sit quietly. "First of all, I can't thank you enough for being there for me in a moment or in fifteen minutes. You seem to have a strong calming effect on me."

"Me? Calming?" I ask, looking around the room for the person he described as one who calms.

"Yes, you, your, uh, intensity, to see that I get well, and to remind me of what's important is what helps keep me going. I wanted to see you today to share with you a small breakthrough."

"Okay," I say, uncomfortable with compliments.

"I remembered something," he says. "I remembered what Haley and I debated about in college, that first day I met her. I remember what she was wearing now. I remember the smell of her perfume."

"That's great," I reply. "It's healing to share memories."

"That's why I wanted to share it with you. She wore a periwinkle blue shirt with a white cape or shawl of some kind. She liked to tie her shawl loosely around her neck. I always felt it accentuated her beauty. You know how she always had a sort of regal humble air about her? She smelled like crème brûlée that day, and we debated about poverty and welfare reform. In fact, some of the initiatives in her legacy of the Poverty Reform Bill are an extension of her thoughts from that debate."

"Those are wonderful images, Mr. President. Was there something that triggered your memory?" I ask.

"I started reading her Poverty Reform Bill…and it all came back to me." He takes a deep breath. "I know I have to keep talking about her, Madison. I have to get Congress to pass her bill as soon as we get through these natural disasters and the Middle East scenario. Most importantly, I have to share my memories of Haley and remember her with other folks, who are also grieving for her. That's how I'm going to keep her alive.

That's how I'm going to continue to heal. So, what I'd like to do is be a part of the lineup on My Grief Day…and tell my stories about Haley."

"Really?"

"I'll keep it nonpartisan, of course."

"I wasn't even thinking about that. I'm just honored you want to participate. That is, if I can pull it off."

"I have every confidence you can. Knock on enough doors and you get what you need. That and a little equity goes a long way."

"Equity?" I ask.

"A piece of whatever you've got to give," he adds, then pauses. "I see you work hard…all the time. Try to savor some time for living and just be."

"Uh-huh, well, um, how do you be…when there's so much work to be done? And how do you be…and not get bored?"

"You revel in the moments that make up the minutes and hours in a day. You find the beauty in the rain on the windowsill or in the appreciation for the clothes on your back, or for the honest words of a politician, should you hear them. You take pleasure in routine, in ritual. You wake up grateful for another day. You let life flow through you, not at you. Otherwise, you're in a constant state of reaction and that's exhausting." He stops. "Haley taught me that."

It felt odd to have had the tables turned. The president was now helping me. It was a role I was unfamiliar with and I didn't know how to be in it, so I nodded and closed the session. "Thank you, Mr. President."

"Anytime, Madison. I have to thank our wonderful firefighters now. I'll see you back in Washington?"

"Yes, Mr. President. Thank you, again."

"No, Madison. Thank you, again."

Ubiquitous Music

While Sierra meets with engineers at Disney Concert Hall and Eve meets with Z Mas, I decide to test the president's theory and pay a visit to an old friend. Adam Berman is president of Ubiquitous Music, which is the world's largest production music library with over a quarter of a million tracks licensed for film, TV, commercials, video games, anywhere music can be heard, even as ringtones on mobile phones. They supply music for Lights Out Enterprises' tribute films. But I had a much bigger favor to ask this time.

Inside his office, Adam greets me with a kiss and offers me a seat. "It's good to see you, Maddy. Contrary to what the tabloids say, I think your outfit looks great. Especially those shoes, those are amazing. And I never notice shoes."

"Oh, thanks," I say, "it's not me. I have a stylist, sort of."

"Really?"

"Well, more like a wardrobe Nazi...but it works. So how are you?"

"Miserable. Depressed about Haley Stone and Jonathon Darcy—they held so much optimism for our country. I hope Stone can pull us out of this economic and psychological depression."

"Well, that's what he's paying me a modest government salary to help with."

"I read about My Grief Day. Sounds interesting."

"Good, because I want to know if your company will be my strategic partner and supply free licensed music for My Grief Day's online component—the Tribute Film Festival."

"What's the Tribute Film Festival?"

"An online festival at The Tribute Network for life celebration videos. I need users to be able to add licensed music to their tribute films. The best will air on TV and as shorts in front of feature-length films in theatres. We're already in discussions with a major movie-theatre chain with exposure to forty million viewers."

"This sounds great," says Adam.

"Good…because we lost government funding. I have to ask you to help pay for this."

Adam laughs. "We're the ones who get paid, Madison."

"I'm prepared to give you equity in The Tribute Network and the Tribute Film Festival, which I plan to take global. The president is going to tell stories about Haley. And we've got celebrity interest, too. There will be in-theatre promotions and tons of online viral marketing. So, in the long run, you should come out way ahead of a mere million-dollar donation."

"A million? But we don't advertise, and we're a business to business player."

"Going to business to consumer will expand your horizons and your revenue."

Adam appears to mull it over. "It's a really good idea, Maddy. Let me talk to my board."

"Sure. I need an answer soon, or I'll have to go to your competitors."

"How much equity would we get?"

"Two percent," I reply. "And miles and miles of goodwill."

Adam nods, pleased with what I've told him. "I'll get back to you in a few days. Anything else?"

"Yes. Do you think Maurice LeSarde could write a theme song for My Grief Day, along the lines of 'What the World Needs Now is Love Sweet Love,' with a short melodic phrase for cell phones?"

"Nice thinking, Madison. I'll include that in my conversation with the board."

"Thanks. If you've got any ideas for sponsors, let me know."

"Actually, I might. There's a company called Eternal Image. They license all kinds of brands for caskets and urns. Their brands even include Star Trek and Major League Baseball."

"You mean if you're a die-hard Red Sox fan, you can rest in peace in a Red Sox urn?"

Adam nods, smiling. "And if you want the theme music that goes with the brand, you can have that, too."

"A branded music box for ashes…. Why didn't I think of that? How's their business doing?"

"Amazing. In the meantime, there's another company you might be interested in that's around the corner and is a really good fit for what you're doing. A friend of mine is one of the founders, so feel free to use my name. I'll call ahead for you, as well."

"What do they do?"

"They manufacture headstones with video monitors inside. They're called Twilight Cinema Headstones." He writes the company's address on a slip of paper and hands it to me. "Drop by. I'll tell them you're on your way. Maybe they'll help fund your project."

Twilight Cinema Headstones' offices are on my way to my next appointment, so I stop by per Adam's suggestion. Their entire staff of four greets me like a queen, as if I'm an ally in the world of personalized end-of-life celebrations. They give me a tour of the facilities highlighting various headstones with video monitors smoothly integrated into the granite, marble or limestone designs.

After signing NDAs, I explain my project to them and the need for sponsorship monies in return for a presentation credit in front of the Tribute Film Festival that will play, and in the movie theatre chain and the mobile cinemas and online at My Grief Day and The Tribute Network. They don't even bat an eye and commit to one million dollars.

"Really?" I wasn't sure if I heard them correctly.

"Are you kidding? This is a great idea," says the company founder.

"Is it the right demographic for you?" I ask.

They laugh. "Our demo is everyone. It's perfect!"

One million secured and eleven million to go! I was on my way!

As I wait for my car at the parking garage I glance at my phone. No calls or e-mails from Victor. I wonder when I might speak to him next. I want to tell him the good news, but it doesn't feel right to call him now. The parking attendant brings up my car. He greets me with slouched shoulders and a look of despair.

"You okay, sir?" I ask.

He shrugs. "Who's okay these days?" he responds. "Good folks keep on dying. The world doesn't make sense anymore, ma'am."

"It will," I say. "Have faith." I tip him well, but he smiles indifferently.

Driving from Hollywood to Marina del Rey, I pass one billboard after another. There are advertisements for everything from blue jeans to perfume. But what the entertainment billboards push aren't upbeat movies, dazzling theatrical shows, inspiring books or television programming. Instead, they feature one downer after another, from the latest new docu-dramas about Jonathon Darcy and Haley Stone to re-enactments of natural disasters and man-made ones, too. I become obsessed with the content of the billboards and start counting which ones showcase elements of death and disaster, and which ones portray inspiration, hope and healing. By the time I reach the other side of town, I've counted seventy-seven billboards promoting death and disaster and a whopping zero for hope, inspiration and healing. No wonder the nation is stagnating in depression en masse. We were being fed formulas for melancholy without an antidote in sight. What were the studio and network executives thinking? What did publishers believe? What were advertisers doing? Were they all cashing in on death

and disaster at the expense of the national psyche? As I reach
the parking lot of StoriesMakeUs.com, I hope in them and in
its CEO named Eddie, a recovering workaholic, there might
lay our salvation.

7

StoriesMakeUs.com

I glance at wispy clouds, beautiful colored boats, and not one billboard in sight.

"You like the view?" asks Eddie from behind me.

I turn around to face him. We're inside the kitchen of his modest offices on the third floor of a renovated shopping center, overlooking the marina and the Ballona Wetlands.

"It's refreshing," I agree, "and exciting to be around a start-up."

"Thanks. We've got about twenty employees building a social networking community founded on the one common denominator of all time—story, the foundation of civilization," Eddie says, as he pours us both cups of hot tea. "The Bible, the Torah, the Koran, the Book of the Dead…all stories that shape civilization. In fact, you could say that the moral fabric of a society is founded on the stories that they tell."

"So what is StoriesMakeUs and how is it different from anything else like it?" I ask.

Eddie leads me out of the kitchen and into the frugally furnished start-up space. "StoriesMakeUs embodies the process of the storytelling itself," he says.

"I don't get it," I confess.

Eddie places his cup of tea down on a table and looks me in the eye. "The process *is* the art. Storytelling becomes a gift that *everyone* can share in to bring both immediate and lasting value to a life and a legacy. That's my response to not having a mission statement. To put it in simple terms, StoriesMakeUs is a multimedia-rich online social networking site. I'll show you."

I follow Eddie into his office where I notice a well-worn paperback copy of *Atlas Shrugged* by Ayn Rand. I can't help but think of John Galt and consider whether... I glance at Eddie's shoes looking for a connection to the Messiah pumps. He's wearing a pair of scruffy dark brown leather shoes so ugly that only the most confident, albeit fashion-obtuse individual would dare to wear them. Eddie seemed to fit that bill of individuality, the Howard Roark and Hank Rearden of StoriesMakeUs.

Eddie walks me through the features of his site and its animated moving timeline that doubles as a stand-alone distributable multimedia widget. "We're licensing the timeline to corporations for their About Us page, and to online media publications," he adds. "And now political candidates are using it, embedding their timelines in campaign Web sites and blogs." A ding goes off from Eddie's watch. He turns it off. "Come with me. I want to show you something. Bring your tea."

Eddie leads me up a curly staircase to the roof. The vista is more spectacular than before. He points to a couple of chairs. We sit with our tea taking in the view.

"This is great," I say.

"I like to relax up here," comments Eddie, leaning back like a seafaring captain.

Relax? I had no idea what he was talking about. We'd been up here for two minutes and already I was getting antsy and ready to go back down and work. "Is there something you wanted to show me?" I inquire.

He nods. "The view."

I nod back, without bothering to look at it anymore. "It's very nice. Thank you." I glance at the staircase. Eddie sees this and gives no indication of getting up to leave.

"How long have you been going to meetings?" he asks.

"Well, uh, last night was my fourth meeting. What about you?"

"I've been in the program for eight years and I'm finally getting a balanced routine together. I used to force myself to come up here three times a day. Now I look forward to it. When I'm relaxed I make better decisions and end up working less. It's a strange irony, but once you get that, the road to recovery is a lot less bumpy."

"What inspired you to start StoriesMakeUs?" I ask.

"I lost my father when I was twelve and I wish there'd been a service like StoriesMakeUs to capture and preserve his stories." He pauses. "That's why I think what you're doing to heal our nation's personal and collective grief is so important."

"Sorry about your dad. It's interesting how our wounds become our gifts. So, what do you think are the opportunities to tie StoriesMakeUs into My Grief Day?" I ask.

"We're about to launch a new product called GoTribute.com. It's a collaborative many-to-one destination to create multimedia tributes to another person with a timeline for an event. I'm thinking we can co-launch with a co-revenue sharing model."

"What do you mean many-to-one?"

"Many contribute to one tribute by adding text, photos, videos, even audio voice recordings to a private url with an animated moving timeline which can then be turned into a documentary-style movie. The tribute can also be published into a book, DVD or poster for the event."

"So, if someone wants to submit a tribute film to the Tribute Film Festival they can go to you to make a video?"

"Exactly, plus we can co-brand the widget to help promote your event in advance."

"Great," I say. "Can your engineers handle the technical requirements? I'm super thin on staff."

"How are you managing My Grief Day, The Tribute Network and the Tribute Film Festival?"

"You forgot Lights Out Enterprises," I add. "I'm, a, uh, workaholic, remember?"

"Do you know what one of the major traits of workaholics is?" he asks.

"Denial," I reply, sure that I nailed it.

"That's part of it. Workaholics can't say no to work because they aren't clear on what they want."

"I'm clear. I want all my projects to be successful."

"Even at the cost of your health, family, friends, relationships…"

I thought of Victor. It was costing me all right. I was a fool to think otherwise. "You've got dreams. How are you doing it?" I ask.

"I've got a staff of twenty people. I raised ten million in venture capital so I could do it effectively. Alone, I'd kill myself. When I crashed from my work addiction nine years ago, I knew I had to change. I had to resolve *IT*."

"Information Technology?"

"No. Inner Turmoil."

"How did you do that?"

"I had to resolve past issues so I could figure out what I wanted. So I determined what stories I had made up from past hurts that I continued to believe, stories that weren't true, stories that were blocking my growth…and I changed them."

Eddie leans in and looks me in the eye. "Once I resolved my past, I could create whatever reality I wanted." He smiles. "I chose to create StoriesMakeUs."

I was blown away by his courage to face his wounds and turn them into gifts he could share with others. But it was all too much for one day. In fact, the whole day had been a big therapeutic journey and major adrenaline rush. But the adrenaline kept me going, it made me feel alive, which made me wonder if my real issue came down to a fear of stillness...the ultimate stillness being death.

"You okay?" asks Eddie.

"Yeah, I'm...fine," I say.

"Let's go back down," he suggests.

He points the way, and I think Eddie isn't the story guy at all, he's the therapy guy masquerading as the story guy. Unless you figured that therapy was in and of itself a part of story because in the stories that have moral fabric, there's therapy in there, right? My head was spinning.

Eddie walks me to my rental car. "I'll have my engineers start working on a co-branded widget," he says.

"Great." I'm about to climb into my car when Eddie speaks up again.

"Can I ask you a personal question?" he asks. I nod yes. "Would you like me to be your sponsor?"

"Really?" I'm stunned. What a trusting guy. He hasn't even seen my business plan yet. "I, uh, I'm so flattered. Are you sure?"

"Absolutely."

"Can you put in a million? Then I'll only need nine more." A perplexed look washes over Eddie's face as I continue, "Ever since I lost government funding and the president asked me to turn to the private sector to help finance this I wasn't sure how I could pull it off, but your offer to come on board as a sponsor is amazing—"

"I meant as a sponsor for your work addiction," clarifies Eddie.

"Oh…I thought you meant…for the work itself," I reply.

"Well, that is an interesting idea. Do you have a proposal I can look at?"

"Yes, of course, I'll e-mail it to you immediately!" I promise, excitedly.

"What about the other kind of sponsorship? You interested?"

"Um…what does it entail? Cuz I'm really busy."

"Think home study course and I'm your professor. We meet as often as necessary and you journal answers to questions in each of the twelve steps, starting with Step One."

"Step One?" I ask.

"That's the one where we admit to ourselves that our lives have become unmanageable because of our work addiction."

"But my life is manageable," I reply.

"Is it? Have you ever had a consistent long run of contentment?"

No one had ever asked me that before. I stare back at him. My life was beginning to feel like a conundrum that everyone else understood but me. Eddie had such a kind and gentle manner about him, how could I say anything but, "Um…okay."

Eddie smiles. "Good. You have the literature from last night and my card with my cell and e-mail. Start reading and feel free to call or text me anytime, day or night."

I nod goodbye, and laugh. "Why would I call you in the middle of the night?"

Caught in traffic as I'm driving to the hotel, I replay my conversation with Eddie. I think about the power of stories and what draws us to them. I think about characters, about people who turn their lives around, and why it is so hard. I'm not sure that kind of courage is in me. I know I have to face *IT,* to get clear on what I want. I know...I have to call Victor. Only that call would have to wait until after the Beverly Hills fund-raiser.

The Beverly Hilton

Traffic is impossible, so I drive straight to the Beverly Hilton to make it on time. Eve stands at the entrance with clothes draped over her arm as I pull up to the valet.

"I'm approachable now," I say, recalling my earlier stampede from the PR firm.

"On the contrary," says Eve. "It's black tie, remember? I figured you wouldn't get back to the hotel to change in time. So I brought an outfit for you. The bathroom is over there." She hands me the dress and pushes me along.

"What's the fund-raiser for again?"

"Autism," she says, "the nation's biggest epidemic."

"I was just at an autism fund-raiser in D.C."

"Well, it's the west coast's turn," she murmurs, impatiently. "Sierra and I will see you at the entrance to the ballroom."

"Thanks," I say. "I mean it, Eve. You really know how to cover a girl's back."

"There is no back to it," she tells me, glancing at the dress in my arms.

"Right." I smile and head to my public changing room.

Minutes later, I appear beside Eve and Sierra, as a volunteer, checking names off the guest list. Eve is beaming. "What's she so happy about?" I ask Sierra.

"Some famous movie star just said hello to her."

"Oh," I say, smiling.

Sierra looks at me again. "What are you beaming about?"

"I got a qualified one million and possibly two more today," I reply.

"Wonderful. That leaves nine to go," she answers dryly.

"Do you always have to be such a pessimist?" I ask.

"Realist," Sierra corrects me, only to be interrupted by a famous newscaster, whom she checks off the list.

Once inside the ballroom, I scan the names of companies at each of the tables. Mostly the major television networks and other related entertainment companies.

Sierra, Eve and I sit at the Significant Talent Agency table next to Jay-Jay Lovenheim and his handsome colleague, Sol Kessler.

"So what do you do at STA, Sol?" I ask.

"I'm in charge of corporate consulting," he says brashly, eyeing my naked ring finger.

"I think Sol can really help you with your project," adds Jay-Jay.

"Jay-Jay filled me in on what you're looking to accomplish," says Sol. "I'm a big fan of what you're doing…and, uh, by the way," he flirtatiously whispers to me, "I think you dress just fine."

I lift a brow. "Gee, thanks."

Eve scans the other end of the room and screeches, "Ohmygod! Matthew Martin and Lance Ranier walked in! Are *they* clients of yours?"

"Yes," Sol replies. "Jay-Jay's in the lit department and I'm in corporate consulting. McIntyre and Starr are their talent agents, but they're joining another table tonight."

"Cool," says Eve.

"What does a corporate consultant do at a talent agency?" I ask Sol.

"We consult with corporations on their entertainment initiatives."

"Oh. Who are your corporate clients?"

"Companies you'd know."

"I can help you with celebrities and Sol can help with corporate funding," adds Jay-Jay.

"That's great," I gush.

"Just give us your target list and we'll follow up," says Sol.

"Wouldn't you be the ones to provide us with a list of suggestions?" asks Sierra. "Not to pass the buck here, but we can't possibly know all your clients and relationships."

"That's not how it works," whispers Jay-Jay.

"How do you get paid?" I ask. "Do you take a commission from sponsorship monies?"

"No," says Sol.

"So you do this for a piece of equity in the project?" I ask.

"Oh, no," says Jay-Jay.

"Oh, you do it pro bono for worthy projects," I say, finally getting it.

"Absolutely not," they say.

"Then how do you get compensated?" asks Eve.

"Monthly retainer fees of thirty grand. But given your situation, we're willing to come down to twenty-five grand a month," says Sol.

Sierra, Eve and I reach for our glasses of water to swallow our shock.

"So you must guarantee a lot of results," prompts Sierra.

"Oh, no, we can't possibly guarantee results," answers Jay-Jay.

"So what would you do to help us get twelve million dollars?" asks Eve.

"Nine," I interject. "I think I'm good for three million today."

Jay-Jay and Sol look at me with surprise. A beat passes. "We're connectors," says Sol. "We open doors."

"So do we." Eve winks.

"Yes, well, we open the *right* doors and get you the *right* meetings," explains Sol.

"And how long does that take?" asks Sierra, slightly irritated.

"We can probably get you in at the top of any given department in about three weeks. It takes time to coordinate every-body's schedules," explains Jay-Jay.

"Really? That long?" asks Sierra. "How long to get to the top of a corporation and bypass the department heads?"

Sol and Jay-Jay stare at each other. "We don't usually put those kinds of meetings together," says Sol.

"But we're launching in less than eight weeks," I sputter.

Sol shakes his head. "Well, that's impossible," he tells us.

"We don't think so," says Eve.

"No, we don't," adds Sierra, suddenly transforming into an idealist.

"Excuse me," says Eve, standing up. "I feel like opening up some doors right about now."

Sierra gets up, and smiles. "Me, too. Shall we?"

The edge between Sierra and Eve disappears. Now they're comrades on a mission. Sierra glances down at me. "Maddy, are you coming?"

"Sure." I turn to Sol and Jay-Jay. "This shouldn't take too long. See you for dessert."

Eve joins the table where celebrities Matthew Martin and Lance Ranier are sitting. Sierra makes a beeline for one of the television network tables, and I ease my way over to another table where there's an empty chair. I happen to slide in right next to a chief marketing officer.

"I can't believe you're the CMO," I say. "It's such a pleasure to meet you. Your digital camera company's slogan 'Forever Your Life,' is a perfect fit for what I'm doing."

"Really? Tell me about it."

I tell him about My Grief Day and the Tribute Film Festival. I tell him about my strategic partnership with the national Royal Blue Cinema movie theatre chain, which I finalized via text after my conversation with Adam Berman. I also talk about Ubiqui-tous Music, StoriesMakeUs and Twilight Cinema Headstones.

"So you see," I summarize, "it's about celebrating life by

paying tribute to another person other than ourselves, getting out of the reality-TV 'me' bias and honoring the contributions we make to a life's journey. To that end, no pun intended, the tribute films can be in any genre—comedy, drama or slice of life, as long as they honor another person, or pet, alive or…not."

"I can't believe you're telling me this," he says. "It's exactly the kind of philanthropic project we've been looking for, to partner with. Let me introduce you to our CEO," he says.

For the next twenty minutes I schmooze with nine of the top executives of the company. Everything is perfect until I hear a familiar, discontented voice.

"Do you mind, dear? You're in my seat." I turn around and look up at Elizabeth Anderson, dressed to the nines. "You again," she says, aggravated. "I don't recall inviting you to my west coast fund-raiser, Ms. Banks. Are you crashing my event?"

"No, just your table," I come back, with a smile. Everyone laughs, which turns Mrs. Anderson's smile to stone.

The CMO chimes in, "Elizabeth, you sure do invite the most fascinating people. We've all been mesmerized by Miss Banks while you've been taking care of your other guests. We can't thank you enough for sending her over here to keep us company."

Mrs. Anderson sends me a mock grin. "It's nice to know you have one handy trait, Ms. Banks."

"Oh, it was my pleasure," I say, standing up, determined not to get defensive.

"Does Mrs. Anderson know about your project?" asks the CMO. He turns to Elizabeth. "It's terrific. We're coming on board as sponsors, it's that good."

"Really?" asks Mrs. Anderson.

"She knows a little bit about it," I comment. "In fact, I invited Mrs. Anderson to be on my advisory board."

"Is that so?" asks the CEO, shifting in his chair to address Mrs. Anderson directly. "I certainly hope you're accepting because I don't think you'd be too happy with yourself in the future if you pass on it now."

"Thank you for your opinion, Jerry," says Mrs. Anderson, who turns to privately glower at me. "Where are you sitting?"

"I'm at the STA table. So, I'd better get back to it." I turn to my newfound colleagues and wave. "It was great meeting all of you." I turn back to Mrs. Anderson. "I kept your seat nice and warm for you and I didn't touch the silverware. Have a nice dinner."

I return to the STA table at about the same time as Eve and Sierra. Sol and Jay-Jay are finishing their steaks and look up at us.

"So, how'd you girls do?" asks Sol, with cocky attitude.

"I got a commitment from DigiCams for a million. From the CEO himself," I answer. "How'd you do, Eve?"

Jay-Jay and Sol stop chewing.

"Matthew and Lance are on board and they want to bring along their friends. Their agents, McIntyre and Starr, even signed this napkin for me agreeing to bring in their publicists…and forego any commissions because it's such a worthy cause." She holds up the napkin with a manifesto written on it. "They even signed over a kill fee of twenty-five grand if they fail to make good on their word."

Jay-Jay and Sol stare at us in astonishment. "They signed a kill fee?"

Eve nods like it was nothing. "How about you, Sierra?" she asks.

Sierra smiles. "That network's new CEO loves what we're doing. She wants to broadcast My Grief Day. The behind the scenes, the performances, the president, everything." She takes a sip of wine, smiles again, and adds, "Oh, and that includes borrowing their ad sales staff to help underwrite the broadcast…not to mention future plans, since this will be an annual event."

Jay-Jay turns to Sol. "Maybe we should hire them," he says.

"Sorry, we're not available," Eve responds.

The lights in the cavernous room dim. Celebrity comic Marilyn DeMarcus takes the stage to make an announcement.

"Ladies and gentlemen," begins Marilyn. "Autism has become an epidemic and while your donations tonight help us find a cure, it's important to remember that these children have extraordinary untapped gifts. New research shows there is a level of intelligence in autistic children that exists on a scale unfamiliar with current measuring systems. Many of them are unrecognized geniuses, trapped in a prison of unsocial cultural capabilities. You might say the same thing about our keynote for this evening, a brilliant mind trapped in a different kind of prison system, but determined to use his gifts and the gifts of his comrades to help our country achieve fiscal greatness once again. Ladies and gentlemen, I give you a brilliant financialist, Mr. Derek Rogers."

I quickly maneuver to see the stage, and am sickened to glimpse Derek Rogers receive a round of applause, for duping the country. Sierra, Eve and I watch astonished as Jay-Jay and Sol join the cheers. We grimace in disgust.

"Well, I think we're about done here," I say.

And just like that, the three of us pick and leave like Charlie's Angels.

Shutters on the Beach, one more time

The next day consists of back-to-back follow-up meetings with my prospective sponsors and strategic partners to iron out the details of the agreements. It looks as if this really will happen. Exhausted yet satisfied, I return to my hotel room ready to take a long hot bath and then call Victor. I didn't notice how tired I was; and wake up in the tub two hours later.

My cell phone lies askew on the night table. I pace back and forth in my bathrobe glancing between my phone and the clock wondering if it's too late to call. It's two o'clock in the morning in New York, assuming that's where Victor is right now. He's probably sleeping. I decide to text message him. That way, if he's awake, he'll have the option to call me. Two minutes later my phone rings.

"Hi, Victor," I say. My voice is calm, sweet, quiet and terribly unsure. "How are you?" I ask.

"It's Eve."

"Oh…well, how are *you?*"

"Great. I'm so excited I think I'm going to pee in my pants. Can I show you the preliminary designs from Z Mas now?"

"Sure, stop by. But please don't pee in your pants."

Five minutes later, Eve is in my room hanging giant rolls of paper on the walls and letting them unravel dramatically to reveal crude pencil sketches, depicting a variety of designs for men's, women's and children's clothes.

"What do you think?" asks Eve, twitching and holding her legs together.

"Eve, go pee, will you? In the bathroom."

"Ohmygod, I had so much wine. I'll go after you tell me what you think, not that you have any taste or anything."

"Then why are you here?"

"Because I don't want you to look completely clueless when the big day comes, why else would I show you?"

"I thought maybe because I'm your boss?"

Eve stares at me, uncomprehending, as if that is the most ridiculous reason on earth.

"Never mind," I say, and look at the designs. "What are these floppy things all over the arms and chests and hips?"

"Memento holders," replies Eve.

"You mean pockets?" I ask.

"No," insists Eve. "We mean…memento holders, so that you can carry around mementos that remind you of your loved one during My Grief Day."

"Clever. What's the difference between that and a pocket?"

Eve looks at me with a straight face and states, "The name."

"So it's a euphemism?" I reply, rhetorically.

"No, it's a memento holder. Is there something you're not getting?"

"Right." No use arguing with her on this one. "So does one of those uh, memento holders also conveniently fit a miniature tissue packet?"

Eve stops in her tracks and stares at me.

"For when you cry on My Grief Day," I clarify.

Her eyes light up. "That is a very good idea," she says, pacing around the room. "I'll make a note of that."

"What kind of material is he using?"

"Every kind. It's fabulous. Wool, cotton, Lycra, velvet, linen, silk, satin, cashmere, fleece, bark cloth, hemp…a potpourri of fabrics to represent the potpourri of life."

"What about those things hanging behind the shoulders?" I ask, pointing. "They look like long thick ponytails."

"Those are Memory Tails. You wrap them around your head or neck like a shawl. Especially applicable for cold climates, or if you're Muslim. And they're easily removable for warmer climates."

"Memory Tails." I smile. "Nice."

The hotel phone rings. "Excuse me," I tell Eve, picking up the phone. "Hello?"

"Hi," says Victor. The low tenor of his voice, with its steady calmness, never fails to soothe me.

"Hi, how are you?" I ask, sounding vulnerable.

"Fine. I'm in Ann Arbor helping Arthur prepare for the financial commission's investigation. How are you?"

"I'm good. Do they really have anything on him?"

"I doubt it. But it feels like they're going out of their way to make it as ugly as possible. Brace yourself for a replay of the Enron scandal."

"Oh, God, no."

"Listen, Arthur still wants to help with My Grief Day. He's offered to come on board as a major sponsor and cover the cost of the mobile exhibition with five million."

"Are you serious? In the midst of his investigation he wants to do this? Won't it look all wrong?"

"The investigation is making him furious. And before they take any other action, like freezing his accounts, he sees this as an opportunity to create goodwill for Pintock International and make a statement, that the company is financially healthy."

"Arthur is so smart. Every small town in America will see Pintock International's name on the side of the mobile cinema trucks. I'll talk to Sierra about adding Pintock International's name to the presentation credit for the screenings, too. Thanks for bringing it up to him."

"I didn't, Maddy. This was all his idea."

"Oh," I say, disappointed that Victor hadn't brought it up on my behalf. I wondered if the omission, intentional or not, was part of the separation.

"You do realize that if you accept his sponsorship," adds Victor, "and the commission does find something on him or even one of his executives or managers…you could blight the image of My Grief Day on behalf of the country, yourself and President Stone."

"Ahem," says Eve, clearing her throat from the other side of the room. "Hello? I was in the middle of a Show and Tell. And I'm done peeing."

I turn around to face Eve, still reeling from Victor's warning. "Eve, can we take an intermission now? This is an important call."

"But I need to confirm these designs with Z Mas by tomorrow morning."

"Well…you don't really need me for this, do you?"

"Are you trying to pass on new information? Because that's not," she says.

"Look, you have my full support to make whatever changes you feel necessary to get this into production and distribution on time."

Eve rolls her eyes and taps her foot as I glance between her and the phone with Victor on the end of it, hoping he doesn't get impatient and hang up on me. He never has before but now, with the separation, I figured all bets were off.

"Really, Eve. I trust you."

"Now that—is something new. Apology accepted," she says, heading for the door.

"Wait, what am I apologizing for?"

"For interrupting me."

"But I didn't apologize."

"It was inside of 'I trust you.'" Eve smiles and leaves.

I immediately return to the phone conversation with Victor. "Victor?" I ask, a hint of desperation in my voice.

"Still here," he says.

I wonder for how long. "Look, I'm sure Arthur is more than aware of the consequences of his actions here. I can't believe for one second that he would consider sponsoring My Grief Day if he thought the financial commission had anything on him. In fact, this just confirms his innocence for me."

"You're willing to bank your reputation and everyone else's involved for one man and all the employees who work for him?"

"You bet," I firmly reply. The second phone line lights up with a blinking red signal. "Hold on, another call's coming in." I put Victor on hold and answer line two. "Hello?"

"It's Brian. I've got the genealogy results for you."

"Awesome. Hold on." I switch back to Victor. "Can you hold on a sec?"

"Yes," answers Victor, and I switch back to Brian.

"What have you got?" I eagerly ask.

"I traced it sideways and forwards and backwards again, and there are no blood relations between Derek Rogers and Jonathon Darcy. I went back six generations. There are no relations through marriage or adoption. The relations that Derek Rogers claims from his correspondence with Darcy are negative."

"Thanks, Brian."

"Madison. You should know something else."

"What?"

"The information in the letters…that Rogers had about Darcy's family…"

"Yes?"

"There was a lot that was highly personal. I mean, there was information about miscarriages and abortions, secret family affairs, mental illnesses and descriptive personality traits. There had to have been someone on an inside track feeding this information to Derek so that he could convince Darcy they were related."

I pause. "Okay, thanks, Brian. I can't tell you how much I appreciate this."

"If you need anything else, just call. Oh, and I'll e-mail a PDF copy of the report to you."

"Thanks." I switch back to the other line, anxious to hear Victor's voice again, to share this information with him, and to tell him about StoriesMakeUs.com and their sponsorship participation for MGD. "Victor, I just found out—" But he's no longer there. Instead there's only the dull flat line of a dial tone. My heart sinks. He had dropped the line, only I had dropped it long before he did. I resolved to try a new kind of sponsorship, and hope that my progress would restore Victor's faith in me and bring him back.

Even though Eddie said it was okay to call day or night, I didn't feel my anxiety justified waking him up. I could at least *begin* to tackle my feelings on my own. The question was how. He did say the process of recovery required journaling. So I sit at my computer, subscribe to StoriesMakeUs.com's free timeline, create a profile for myself and start writing to Eddie my answers to the questions outlined in Step One.

Scanning the Workaholics Anonymous literature, my eyes land on the following question. *What has your work addiction cost you?* I never thought of it in terms of cost. But it made perfect sense. The word *work* itself implied a monetary value, only inverted now in the strangest way. I felt a conundrum coming on, although this time I forced myself to face it and meditate on the cost of work addiction. I was losing intimacy—with Victor, with friends, and family, even with myself. There was no monetary value for the loss of life, that could never be replaced with monetary goals derived from the incessant need to work anyway, so what was I working so hard for? Or what was I avoiding through the camouflage of work?

I begin my story to Eddie online. As I write, layers of insight slowly reveal themselves. Sadness overcomes me. What I didn't know was that I incorrectly filled out the profile so that it wasn't only Eddie and I who were seeing this, but all the other hundred thousand subscribers to StoriesMakeUs.com.

Dear Eddie, I started Step One, and discovered the cost of work addiction cannot be measured. I'm exploring my anxiety and believe that I am running from my own grief, which I will attempt to unearth in following writings. This discovery is ironic, given my current role in this world as grief czar of the United States of America. In the absence of a balanced life, I know no other way to function in which to accomplish my goals. I think I may have unwittingly created a Baudrillardian hyper-reality for myself. These layers of hyper-realities have become borders of protection from loss without end. I do believe that our wounds have the potential to become our gifts in life, the gift of purpose for ourselves and for humanity. My intention is to unravel the source of my grief and…

A ding alerts me to an incoming e-mail from Brian. The temptation is too great. I immediately abandon my self-improvement work to read through his full report and consider my options. Who would take me seriously if I went public with this? Derek could easily discredit me, just as he did in the cabinet meeting. Plus, what if Brian's software was inaccurate? I had to think this through like a game of chess. I decide to sit tight and be "tao" about this, trusting the right opportunity will present itself to me.

Tired, but not yet sleepy, I flip on the TV to catch the news. The media offers several sensationalized reports on the despair of the country, including a mention of what they're now referring to as The Pintock Scandal. It was all conjecture. That a real scandal existed hadn't even been confirmed. I flip to another channel only to be bombarded by rave opinions for the Insider Think Tank from leading economists and top-level Washington bureaucrats, who claim the plan is a mastermind of financial intelligence. Not one mention is made about Derek Rogers' own scandalous background. I flip to another channel where reporters debate President Stone's decline in popularity. Most of them predict that he'll never make it to a second term in office. Even though the election is a year away, and even though the ITT was born under his regime, with all of the credit going to Tyler Simmons, which seemed odd to me. As the president's political advisor, wouldn't Simmons want the president to get credit for what the media perceived as a positive opportunity, putting my own personal opinions about ITT aside? Or did Simmons have an ulterior motive, perhaps his own political aspirations? I flip to another channel where the Middle East crisis is mounting with increased tension. In the background, it looks as if people are wearing the I PITY T-shirt, but I'm sure I'm seeing things as I fall into that delicate hypnagogic place before sleep.

Back to the Capital

Breakfast on Arthur's private jet includes waffles, pancakes and Eggs Benedict. Eve, Sierra and I dig in.

"Have you thought about what people are supposed to eat on My Grief Day?" asks Eve, as she sips her latte over a white cloth-covered table.

"Good question," pipes in Sierra. "I was wondering the same thing. I'm thinking hot chocolate and s'mores." She smiles.

"Yes, I have thought about it," I reply. "I've got it covered."

"What's on the menu?" asks Eve. "Because I think they should include these waffles. These are amazing!"

"I hired a food service company out of D.C. They're going to orchestrate it with StoriesMakeUs.com."

"They're going to orchestrate what?" asks Sierra.

"The recipes," I reply. "They're putting together a compilation of comfort food by the people for the people. Since this event is about participation, Americans get to donate their recipes and a story that goes with it. Like a story behind a famous matzoh ball recipe from a beloved bubbe, or a story behind a delicious pumpkin pie of a departed uncle…that kind of thing. People can share their comfort recipes online at StoriesMakeUs. We're going to publish it through StoriesMakeUs.com's publication partner and probably call it *The Comfort Cuisine Book*. The food service company will recreate the recipes at food stations in the theatres and mobile cinemas. What do you think?"

"Cool. Where did you find the food service company?" asks Sierra.

"Um…my east coast meeting," I mutter. Sierra rolls her eyes.

"What's the tally on the budget?" asks Eve.

"Ubiquitous Music, StoriesMakeUs, Twilight Cinema Headstones and DigiCams are all in for a million each. And Arthur's in for five. That's nine million, with three to go."

"I say we go for it," says Eve, taking another bite of her waffle.

"How firm is all that?" asks Sierra.

"Well…" I smile. "They e-mailed me confirmation this morning and their media relations people are putting out press releases later today…and wiring fifty percent of the funds into the account so we can start hiring our vendors tomorrow."

"That's awesome, Maddy," enthuses Sierra.

"But what about the rest of the budget? We still need three million…plus contingency."

"Don't sweat it," says Eve. "It will come. I have total faith."

"So do I," Sierra agrees.

"Okay, then." I smile. "We're greenlit." We all smile at one another. It seemed as if the luck we had created for ourselves was too good to be true. And in short order, it was. Two days later, after the Grief Team landed back in D.C., and after the press releases had notified the media that My Grief Day was a go, a smear campaign against me caught fire with no firefighters in sight. It was an ugly day. It was…the worst day of my life.

8

"Someone must really dislike you," says Richard Wright, in a pair of flannel long johns and a thermal long-sleeved shirt.

"Dislike? More like hate and detest," corrects Eve, shuddering inside a pink terry-cloth bathrobe. "No, make that loathe and despise, or maybe abhor…"

"That's enough, Eve," says Sierra in a flannel shirt and blue jeans.

"She's right," I agree, standing in my flannel footsie pajamas. Eve smiles triumphantly. I stare at the ten different major newspapers spread across my hotel room bed at five thirty in the morning.

The front page of each newspaper boldly prints my name only in the context of disgrace and humiliation. One prominent paper reads, "Grief Czar Brings Nothing But Grief," another blares, "Grief Czar Poses as Griefaratzi," and even the *Financial Street Journal* declares, "Madison Banks Equals Moral Bankruptcy for USA," and so forth and so on. It is relentless.

The stories inside the headlines are full of mistruths about My Grief Day and me. Some stories go so far as to say I am undermining the president and using my role as his grief buddy to ascertain my own political aspirations into the White House. Some stories suggest I am even sleeping with the president. Others claim I am stooping to the lowest common denominator to stage distasteful commercial events in the name of advertising. Awful. The whole world would be reading these stories within the next twenty-four hours and then, of course, they would be syndicated.

"Can you think of any other enemies?" asks Richard, "besides Derek Rogers and Johnny Bright?"

"Elizabeth Anderson?"

"I doubt that," says Sierra. "She knows you mean too much to Stone."

"Maybe I upset someone standing in a checkout line last month," I pose.

"Let's face it. It's someone who wants to take you down in the worst possible way," claims Eve, taking on the posture of a criminal lawyer. "And the only two people on the planet with a motive are Derek Rogers and Johnny Bright. Maybe they got wind of your Torah Grant interview and wanted to kill it…because it's dead now. Lana called to say the network executives axed it, saying you're too controversial…and Torah Grant doesn't do controversy."

"What will our sponsors think?" asks Sierra.

"What if they're threatening people's lives to write this stuff?" asks Richard. "You know. Blackmail."

"Don't be ridiculous," says Sierra. "That's not realistic… right?"

"Okay, that's it," exclaims Eve, spooked, climbing off the bed. "Too many danger flags for me. I'm outta here. I did not sign up for a life threatening spy-mission scenario." She heads for the door.

"Oh, yes, you did," I counter, catching up to her. Eve stops in her tracks and raises an eyebrow back at me. "You're a die-hard risk-taker just like the rest of us. You finagled your way into Professor Osaka's class. Why? You could've married any trust-fund baby in the entire university if you wanted. You could marry any six-figure guy right now. You could've skipped building Lights Out Enterprises into a success. You could've stayed in L.A. and expanded your Fashion Therapy 101 brand. But you didn't." Eve stares at me, speechless. For once in a long time, the tables of our dynamics turn. "You chose to join the Grief Team, Eve. You chose to come to D.C. You chose to use your assets in one risk-taking adventure after another to help launch My Grief Day. And now you want to bail…because of a worrisome theory? Your wily assets are some of the greatest weapons we have in countering these errors, the corruption, bribery, deceit, and defeating the grief that's gripping this nation. You can't possibly walk now. We need you."

Eve studies me and haughtily cocks her head. "Well, when you put it that way, I guess I can change my schedule back around." She takes her seat on the bed. "So what's the plan?"

"I have no idea," I say. "Except that I don't think I can go outside for a year, maybe two…and certainly not without some mask or transgender operation."

"First things first," Richard interjects. "Maddy, you need to be a turnaround specialist."

"A what?" asks Sierra.

"A guy who turns companies around and saves them from going under," I tell her.

"In this case, you're going to need to turn *people* around. You do that by using silence as your weapon," Richard says. "Don't be so quick to answer people. Push them to answer you and wait, in silence, until they do. Whatever you do, do not under any circumstances ever defend yourself."

There's a knock on the door. "Did someone order room service?" I ask. Everyone shakes their head no. "Who is it?" I ask.

From behind the door, I hear a low voice, "Press Secretary James Damon, Ms. Banks. May I come in?"

I unlock the chains and open the door. He enters and stares at my motley crew in assorted pajamas, while taking in the newspapers spread across the bed.

He nods at everyone. "Good morning," he says and turns to me. "We have a situation," he states.

"No shit, Sherlock," mutters Richard.

"Are we all fired?" I ask.

"On the contrary," says James. "The president would like to see you in the White House immediately."

"And my team, too?" I ask.

"Just you," he replies. "Now, while it's still dark and the paparazzi can't see you."

"But I have to change," I protest.

"We have to move quickly. I suggest you change at the White House."

"I'll get her clothes," offers Eve, leaping to her feet and jumping inside the closet to pick out my outfit, one that includes my Messiah pumps. She puts the clothes inside a laundry bag, hands it to me, and says, smiling, "You're golden."

I look at her. The last time she told me that I was beseeched by the president to solve the nation's grief crisis and so far, look where it got me and the country. "Please say something else, Eve."

"Okay. I'm so glad I'm not in your shoes," she says, chuckling.

I stare at her, and then glance at Richard and Sierra.

"Remember, turnaround specialist," whispers Richard.

"We've got you covered, Maddy," says Sierra.

"Thanks." And with that, James Damon escorts me via the fire escape out of the hotel room, into a dark limousine and back toward the White House at 5:45 a.m.

Inside the limousine, James turns to me and asks, "In my entire career, I have never seen a smear campaign as ugly as this. What on God's earth did you do to provoke a media attack like this one?"

"I have no idea."

"No idea? I find that hard to believe, Ms. Banks."

"You find it hard to believe? What about me? You think I'm swallowing this like a spoonful of sugar?"

"Surely, you must have done something or said something to instigate this, this…assault?"

"I promise you, James, I did nothing to provoke this. Nothing that I can think of, that is." Silence follows and in those minutes I remember Richard Wright's directives. Never defend myself. Use silence in my favor. So I remain silent. James glances at me. I glance back, refusing to utter another word.

Another two minutes pass. He finally says, "We're doing all we can to stop this. We've got every available press agent working on it. But I need to know a few things. Have you cheated on your fiancé?"

I stare at him in shock. "What? Of course not." Of course, Victor thought I had, only not with a human being, but with an addiction. I shudder to think what kind of implications this scandal-mongering sensationalism will mean for Victor.

I wonder if I should tell James we had separated, but I decide to keep my private life as private as possible.

"Madison?" he asks. "Are you not telling me something?"

"No," I say, believing the innocent have nothing to hide.

"Then where's your engagement ring?"

I look down at my hand. What a dead giveaway. I could lie and say I've gained weight and it no longer fits, or that it broke and is in for repairs, or that it fell down the drain or I've suddenly become allergic to diamonds. But I can't tell a lie. "We've temporarily separated," I say.

James shakes his head slowly, and stares out the window in exasperation. "Let's move on. Any drugs I need to know about?"

"No," I reply. "Unless you want to count aspirin for headaches."

"What about your history with drugs?"

"Zero," I say. "In college I tried pot and it made me fall asleep. I tried half a quaalude once with the same result. I never touched them again, never tried anything else. I'm clean."

"What about cocaine?"

I stare at him. "Do I look like I need caffeine?"

"Right. Are you on antidepressants?"

"No, but maybe I should be after this."

James smiles at me. There's a moment where he actually softens. "Let's go over enemies," he says. "Got any?"

"Two," I reply.

He looks at me, attempting to mask his surprise that I have any at all. "Who are they?"

"Derek Rogers and Johnny Bright."

"That guy running ITT? What's he got against you?"

"Um…prison, maybe?"

"You'll have to go into a little more detail than that," remarks James.

"I sort of helped expose the Tribute-in-a-Box scandal… which resulted in their time at Yankton Federal Prison," I answer.

"Huh," says James. "So you think they're behind this?"

"Maybe. Derek did pull the government funding out from under me for My Grief Day, but why he would go to this extreme is beyond me."

"Some people make a sport out of revenge, Madison. You think he's the type to do that, and risk losing what's he just built up all over again?"

I turn to James and shrug. "I don't know."

We arrive at the back of the White House to avoid any camped-out press. Still in my footsie pajamas, camel-colored Ugg boots and a navy-blue pea coat, I carry my bag of clothes and scurry after James across a crunchy, frost-covered lawn and through an entrance.

"Mr. President, I'm terribly sorry about all this," I say, standing in the library where we once broke beverage together. I'm still in my footsie pajamas doing my best to keep a defensive tone out of my voice. The president is in a long, dark robe and slippers standing near the coffee table.

James Damon stands behind the couch. "How do you want to handle this, Mr. President?"

"Handle this?" asks the president. He looks at me. "Is there something to handle?" I shrug. He walks around the coffee table. "The way to stop this nonsense is to simply disengage altogether," he insists.

"You don't want Madison or the administration to address these accusations?" asks James.

The president looks James in the eye and declares, "I don't want anyone addressing these accusations, including me."

"What's our response going to be?"

"We simply have 'no response,'" he answers.

"With all due respect, that's political suicide, Mr. President."

"I'm not spending my presidency playing muckraking games with the media or whoever's behind this."

"What about when the press asks you about it?"

"We won't be here for them to ask us," says the president. Oh, God, I note the *we* and hope he's not including me in it. "We'll be in the Middle East. We leave in three hours. I've decided to resume the peace talks myself." The president looks back at me. "It's what Haley and John would want me to do."

"We? Mr. President," asks James.

"Madison Banks, myself, and I'd like Ms. Nominos to come along. I was extremely impressed with her theories of ODD stemming from child psychology."

There's no way to hide the shock on James's face. "Mr. President," he pleads, "have you thought this through?"

"Enough to know it sounds like I'm off balance. But so was Teddy Roosevelt. And he got results."

"Um, Mr. President," I interject. "I, uh, don't belong in the Middle East peace talks. I have no background in political science and I don't remember one third of what I learned in Hebrew school."

"Yes, you do belong. You're coming as my grief buddy and the Head of the House Bereavement Specialists Committee."

"Have you cleared this through all the proper channels?" asks James.

"It's in process now," explains the president. He turns to me. "Madison, I suggest you get packed and meet me at Air Force One at oh-nine-hundred hours. Please contact Ms. Nominos and see if she's able to join us. James, see to it that no one gets wind of this until we're on our way."

"I think there's something you should know before getting on that plane with Ms. Banks, sir."

I stare at James wondering what on earth he's about to say.

"What's that?" asks the president.

"She and her fiancé have broken up."

The president turns to me, clearly concerned. "I'm terribly sorry to hear that, Madison. Are you all right?"

"I'll be fine. It's only temporary," I say. Both of them remain silent, letting their doubt linger. "Honest," I argue, falling into a tone of defensiveness I've been trying to avoid all morning.

"Now why did I need to know that, James?"

"Because we need to know *why,* sir, so we don't look foolish when the media discovers the reason before we do, or creates reasons of its own in order to fuel this smear campaign, which quite frankly, given your recent popularity polls, is not something you, nor this administration, needs right now, sir." James pauses a moment, then continues, "We can't have the press making insinuations about the two of you. I would like to ask, no, sir, make that beg, Ms. Banks to please wear her ring during this trip."

The president takes James's monologue under consideration and then softly asks me, "I'm sorry to pry, Madison. Can you tell us why the two of you have parted ways?"

"Well, sir. I have an, uh, addiction…and Victor no longer wishes to be afflicted by it."

"Oh, God, I knew it," exclaims James, slapping his hand to his forehead.

"What kind of addiction?" calmly asks the president.

"Work addiction, sir. But I've been addressing the matter by attending Workaholics Anonymous. Uh, as a participant of the program, I have to request you both keep this information private because the principles of Workaholics Anonymous include never bringing attention to itself through the news, TV, radio or movies."

"Got that?" asks the president, addressing James now. The president comes over to me and quietly adds, "One day, Madison, you'll have to explain this addiction of yours to me."

Air Force One takes off on time with the president, myself and the alias of Rachel A. Nominos inside. Eve has helped me pack a bigger bag this time. And I left the fate of My Grief Day in the hands of Richard, Sierra, Eve and a potpourri of east coast and west coast work addicts. Sierra promised to explain everything to my parents, our sponsors and strategic partners, and to contact Victor for me to let him know my whereabouts and the White House's status on the situation. She reassured me that all would be well and to take care of myself.

"I can't believe I'm here," exclaims Rachel, shocking me back into the present moment on Air Force One as it taxis down the tarmac. "Have you ever been to the Middle East?" she asks with a heady mixture of excitement and anxiety.

"When I was seventeen," I say. "United Synagogue Youth Group Tour, and you?"

Rachel shakes her head. "Never. My theories are hypothetical."

"So...you've never tested your theories in a lab, in a focus group or on a society of monkeys?" I ask nervously.

Rachel nods. "In a manner of speaking. I did test them at fifty different day-care centers and they proved to be flawless."

"Day care?"

"That's what makes it hypothetical, for this trip at least."

The president sits down and joins us. "Thank you for changing your schedule around to accommodate us, Rachel," he says.

"Oh, it's my pleasure, really," she assures him, pointing to her three bulging carry-on cases. "I brought my work along with me, so it's no problem."

A newspaper is spread across my lap with a leading article about ITT's latest idea to bring back junk bonds. The president glances at it. "Maybe we should put a moratorium on newspapers for a few hours," he suggests, smiling.

"Good idea," I say, and toss the paper out of our sight. "But I do have one question, Mr. President."

"Yes?"

"Putting my own personal opinions aside, sir, if ITT is helping your polls, why wouldn't you want credit for it?"

"I don't believe in ITT. But I do believe in letting the people I've hired try out their visions. If they succeed or fail, the accolades and/or the embarrassment, all goes to them. That kind of leadership is what makes everyone more responsible for their actions."

Okay. "Thanks," I say.

The aircraft takes off for approximately a twelve-hour flight. As the lull of the engines kick into gear, the president and Rachel quietly doze off.

Wired and anxious, I pull out my BlackBerry and read the forty e-mails I received in the last hour. There were e-mails from my parents, friends and colleagues, including Norm Pearl and Maurice LeSarde, but there were no e-mails from Victor, which only intensified my anxiety about how he would respond once he saw the papers. Or worse, I wondered if he had already seen them and chosen not to respond at all. Or maybe he's on the west coast right now where it's still six in the morning. I sigh out loud. I would have no way of knowing his reaction until we landed at Ben Gurion Airport in Jerusalem.

Eddie had also e-mailed me, responding to my progress with Step One, and telling me that the scandal in the newspapers is part of a test; that when you choose to move forward, the universe likes to challenge you. He encourages me to keep writing, to take nothing personally and to be gentle with myself. So I pull out my laptop and start working on Step Two in the work addiction program by writing another missive to Eddie at StoriesMakeUs.com.

Step One is about accepting the fact that one does indeed have an issue with work addiction. Step Two is about return-

ing to a state of sanity by giving up the notion altogether that
you yourself can fix the problem. Instead, you are to trust in
the fact that some power or spirit, greater than yourself, can
and will guide you to healthy living. For a workaholic who
needs to have a sense of control and is used to self-reliance, this
is a tough one to swallow. But I read the literature, meditate
on it, and then start writing.

Dear Eddie,

*Step Two is no doubt a challenge for me. I'm not sure how
I'm going to come to believe in a higher power. Especially after
what's happened today. It feels as though the world has turned
against me and I have no idea why. I suspect foul play and that
the people masterminding this media mess are Derek Rogers and
Johnny Bright. One has only to look at the history of our collid-
ing paths to see his footprint of unethical behavior. I have never
acted maliciously or with contempt, only out of the guiding principles that have governed my life, not to mention, our country. I
live by the Golden Rule and so it is especially painful to feel at-
tacked by an anonymous and intangible opponent.*

*I like following the paradigm that hard and honest work be-
gets success, but that paradigm seems to no longer exist. I realize
I am powerless in this situation and am unaccustomed to feeling
this kind of…humiliation. I feel as though the world has deemed
me unworthy of my right to be human.*

*But I will try to practice a new way of being. I will meditate
on this so-called higher power…without expecting immediate results.*

*I understand I have placed my faith in myself through the faith
others have in me, like Victor, who has always supported me, until*

my work addiction began to suffocate the core of our intimacy. I understand faith inside my self must come from my self and not from others. I understand, as I write these words, that I must disentangle my work from my desire to be accepted and approved by externals. I must alter the motivation that feeds it. Does any of this make sense to you? I want to do a good job for America. I want to help heal the grief of our nation and of our president…and I think I need to think well enough of myself to heal my own grief, as well.

I'm off to the Middle East now, for the continuation of the peace talks with President Stone and Rachel A. Nominos. I promise to take time out every day to meditate on my higher power. All for now, Madison Banks

In the land of Israel

Nightlife in Jerusalem is teeming with activity. The city is much more developed than what I remembered from my high-school trip seventeen years ago. President Stone, Rachel and I watch from behind the tinted windows of a high-security Hummer that transports us to the King David Hotel.

Within moments of being inside the vehicle, the BlackBerries belonging to Rachel and I begin a cacophony of buzzing and ringing without interruption. Like Pavlov's dogs, we instantly check to see who's trying to reach us, until the president gives us a look.

"Are you two expecting an emergency, or are you trying to beam yourselves to Mars?" he asks.

"No, sir," we say, and shut them off altogether.

The president stares curiously at us. "How do you two know each other?" he asks.

"We met at a...uh..." I stutter.

Rachel comes to the rescue. "We met at a meeting. I mean a lecture about organizational behavior in the workplace. And we found out we had a lot in common...about the way we, uh, work."

"I see," says the president, and leaves it at that. "We'll get settled into the King David Hotel and tomorrow morning we'll meet for breakfast before our first round of peace talks. Tyler Simmons will be briefing both of you on your responsibilities."

I mask my disappointment that Tyler will be there. I don't like Tyler Simmons, nor do I trust him. He gives me the creeps, especially given his association with Derek Rogers. Whatever respite I have had from the morning newspapers quickly disappears in the wake of this new information.

That night, restless from jet lag, I decide to walk the city streets and let the sights, sounds and smells of a different culture overtake me. It's refreshing and invigorating to see the vibrancy of life of all those who live in Jerusalem.

I stop to eat a falafel and practice some long forgotten Hebrew. "*Toda*," I say, remembering the right word for *thank you*. Mr. Falafel tries to flirt with me. I smile and continue on my way.

I pass a newsstand and peruse the publications. I'm starting to feel my old self again; a self I had forgotten existed, one of calmness and a sense of inner peace. I wish I could trust the feeling to stay a while longer, perhaps move in permanently...until my eyes land on an English-language tabloid with a photo of me on the cover, in my footsie pajamas, no less, running across the lawn of the White House. The word *mistress* is slapped across my footsies in bold print. Mortified, I quickly duck my head down, vacate the neighborhood and return to the King David to hide out in my room.

The day was finally coming to an end. I had been scorned and humiliated. Sierra was right. I had gone global, only in the most awful way possible. And the worst part was that I did not have Victor by my side to hold me or offer reassurance.

The next morning, the president and Rachel meet for coffee and a light breakfast on the heated outdoor patio of the hotel surrounded by U.S. and Israeli security. I arrive late. My stomach has succumbed to all the anxiety of yesterday and for the first time in my life, affected my ability to work.

I slip into one of two empty chairs and order hot water and lemon to play it safe. The president informs us that Tyler Simmons has been delayed, hence the empty seat. I'm glad. I had a feeling his presence would thwart whatever good might come of this trip. At the president's request, Rachel continues to explain her theories and approach to resolution for the region. I do my best to concentrate, but my feelings of self-worth have diminished to zero overnight. I wondered if Victor, whom I still hadn't heard from, might not think that I really was having an affair with the president. All through breakfast, the president glances my way, forcing me to stay as present as possible, which isn't saying much.

Once inside the Knesset, Israel's parliament, where the peace talks will resume, the president wants to have a word alone with me. He boldly stations his security guard outside an empty men's room and guides me inside for a private discussion.

"I don't think it's wise for us to meet in here," I tell him. "What are people going to think?"

He looks me square in the eye. "Do you think I honestly

give a damn what people think about my being human, Madison Banks?"

"You care about what they think of your politics, don't you?"

"Yes, because I'm in office to serve the people in the work I do on behalf of our country. I'm not in office to act like a yo-yo every time the public or the media decides to pass judgment on how I conduct myself and with whom I choose to spend personal time, for instance, if I'm with my grief buddy." He pauses. "The same goes for you, Madison. The fact that someone in the media, or whoever is behind this scam, went to the trouble to publicly bring you down, is a compliment."

I stare back at him. "Please do not use reverse psychology on me."

He smiles, pacing around the tiny space between the sink and a few stalls. "Is that what you think? I'm trying to tell you that you're doing something right. Or else you wouldn't be scrutinized or seem threatening to those with an axe to grind."

"I'm doing something right?"

"Yes, and I can't have my head of the House Bereavement Specialists Committee, nor my grief buddy, moping around the Knesset because she's doing something right and is being duped by folk who think otherwise. I need you to be you, Maddy. I like your insights, no matter how obtuse they may appear to be. I consider you a treasure."

"You do?"

"Yes. Now can you straighten your shoulders, walk tall, be proud of yourself, and most of all, be you in there?"

I take a deep breath and exhale. "Yes, sir," I say, straightening my shoulders. "Thank you," I quietly add.

"You're welcome," he replies. As we exit the bathroom he turns to me and whispers, "That felt strangely good... to help you."

"Did you feel for a moment or two, the grief subside?"

"Yes. Yes, I did. For a moment I stopped…grieving. Thank you, Madison."

"You're welcome, sir."

And with that, I proudly accompany the president, past camera crews and shouting journalists, and enter the room for the peace talks to begin.

The peace talks

Delegates from Israel, the Palestinians and all the Arab nations join the three of us at a large round table, which the president insisted on ahead of time in order to create an atmosphere of equality.

"Thank you all for coming here today," the president begins. Each delegate offers their sincere sympathies for the loss of Jonathon Darcy, for which the president is clearly grateful.

On cue, a beautifully-decorated traveling buffet, with a variety of aromas, is rolled into the room. Rachel smiles proudly at me.

"What's this?" I whisper.

"I always start my programs this way. It's a great ice-breaker. Did you get the e-mail I sent you and the president at four this morning? The president agreed to go with my alternative approach. You'll be leading the afternoon workshop."

"I will? On what?"

Rachel gives me an odd look. "On grief, silly."

The delegates take great delight in sharing the food of their culture.

The Israeli delegate passes around samples of a classic Israeli eggplant dip. "The purple eggplant symbolizes nobility and spirituality," he explains. "It is high in fiber, vitamins and minerals with many potent antioxidants, so we should all be at peak performance today," he says, smiling.

The Egyptian delegate points to the pita bread with stuffed dates and figs. "This bread is a staple of Egyptian life called *aish,* which means life. It is made with crushed walnuts, pecans and shredded coconut and symbolizes peace and plenty."

The strolling buffet lands next at the Palestinian delegate's chair. He smiles. "This is Mutabak, our favorite dessert. It is made from square dough with cheese and covered in syrup and powdered sugar. We believe it represents wisdom."

Our culinary trip down the road of Middle Eastern cuisine continues until everyone is full and has been fairly represented.

President Stone then returns to the matter at hand. "Delegates. As you can see, we're taking an alternative approach to the peace talks today. We will not be discussing specific portions of land such as the Gaza Strip or the West Bank. These talks today are about shifting our focus to listen to everyone's feelings and get to the core of what's really going on. I'm going to pass the baton over to Rachel who will lead the next phase of our workshop."

Rachel thanks the president and then confidently addresses the delegates. "Now that everyone has experienced the flavors of each other's culture, we're moving on to verbal expressions of our feelings. What we're addressing is the co-dependent relationship among your nations. Remember, we are trying something new and it's imperative that we all maintain open minds." Rachel's style is, no doubt, direct and to the point. She doesn't bother to dilly-dally with phrases of political correctness. Shock and dismay are registering on the faces of the delegates, but she keeps going. "Let's assume your nations never got over your grief going back thousands of years. Let's face it, according to the Bible stories that you all seem to adhere to in one form or another, Abraham cast Hagar and Ishmael into the desert and gave Isaac, the son of his wife Sarah, the land of Israel. And you people have been bickering about this ever since. And who would blame you? It hurts to feel rejected by a father figure and spiritually abandoned by your brother. Now, is it Isaac's fault? How do we know that Isaac didn't have terrible guilt for surviving his father's legacy? Maybe that's the origin of Jewish guilt. Who knows? Do you think you may have misplaced your anger on your brother, Isaac, for your father, Abraham? Why didn't he stand up to Sarah? Or was Hagar trying to usurp Sarah's role? Or did Ishmael have a violent disposition and pose a real threat to Sarah and Isaac? We don't know, do we? But we can get to the core of these untouched feelings that have been hardening your hearts over centuries, causing so much pain to so many generations."

Some of the delegates stand up to leave, but Rachel catches them in their tracks. "Oh, I see. You're thinking you can walk out of here in defiance and disagreement. If you do so, you will continue to deny the pain and suffering of your nations and only cause it to resurface in destructive ways. Is that what you want? You can dole out the weapons of destruction, but you can't handle a psychological breakdown with a goal of peace in sight? Go ahead, stampede out of here! Keep your people in an arrested stage of anger and denial and take the responsibility for not having the courage to sit here and deal with your feelings and the feelings of your neighbors. You don't have to agree. And you might change your feelings. And they might change theirs. That's the beauty of feelings…they can change. Or you can sit back down and try, just try to open up your hearts to understanding yourselves and each other through a different prism… because that takes a hell of a lot more courage than walking out that door."

The delegates silently sit back down. I'm impressed.

"The past is over, everyone," announces Rachel. "It's time to stop carrying the hurt of it in the present and right on into the future because of defiant behavior."

"I beg your pardon," says a delegate. "I disagree."

"Of course you do," Rachel replies. "That's a typical response. My theory is that defiant behavior stems from unresolved issues. In this case, I believe it's all about loss, loss of the father figure, loss of homeland, loss of family of origin."

Another delegate raises a hand to ask, "I would like to know what the grief czar of America thinks." All eyes turn to me.

"Me?" I ask. "I'm not really qualified to talk about historical events. The closest I came to studying history was art history and visual perception at..." The delegates continue to stare at me. I swallow and offer my humble opinion. "Okay. I think you all suffer from addiction."

"I am not a drug addict," a delegate insists. "Well, not counting coffee."

"Addiction does not have to be in the form of drugs. Trust me. I'm becoming very familiar with the subject. Addiction is a mask for denial. And I think that everyone here has a struggle addiction...and a hate addiction, too. I'm told one addiction often layers several others, so if I had to venture what the layers might be in this particular case, I'd guess those two, oh, and maybe obstinate behavior addiction, too."

"Are you actually calling us addicts?" asks one delegate, getting all huffy and puffy.

"Um, your behavior hasn't changed in over five thousand years. I'd have to say that's a very good indication we're talking about addiction in one form or another."

The president weighs in with, "I think Madison has a very interesting concept here. If we were to go with this approach, Madison, how would we solve it?"

"Sir, I'm not an expert in this matter, but according to traditional twelve-step programs, the first step in treating addiction is to acknowledge that you have one."

The president is pensive, and then asks me, "How would we get to a place of acknowledgment?"

"The first thing to do is something that Richard Wright

taught me, and that is for everyone to create a loss graph. In this case, it would be a national loss graph, from the loss of their ancestral father or brother, to the loss of their physical homeland, to the loss of their modern-day brothers and sisters. This way you can see a timeline of struggle and loss."

"Can you show us an example?" asks Rachel.

"Um…sure," I say, getting an idea. "Can I borrow your laptop?" Rachel hands it over. I quickly get online at Stories-MakeUs and demonstrate what I mean using the animated moving timeline with multimedia illustrations. Every delegate then takes a turn creating and sharing their national timeline of grief with the group. Then I ask them to consider how they want to be remembered and to write it down in detail. I then put each one of them through the paces of pseudo-dying, covering them in a white sheet, as if they are now dead, and unable to comment, while the rest of the group reads their instructions and talks about them based on what we've all learned from the loss graphs. The experience is a cathartic one and takes two days to complete.

Many of the delegates are visibly moved, opening the door for the peace talks to continue via the exploration on the topic of struggle addiction.

On my return to Washington I learn that Sierra had finally tracked Victor down, or rather his whereabouts. He was on a kayaking expedition in the South Pacific, followed by a week-long program of silence in some remote monastery and completely out of touch with civilization for ten days. This information minimized the hurt of his absence. Still, why hadn't he told me he was leaving?

In the meantime, I document my thoughts and feelings in another online letter to Eddie at StoriesMakeUs. I confide in him about the peace talks, about my battle with work addiction, and that by all accounts, the meeting of delegates had shown substantial progress. Surely, this progress during the peace talks has obliterated the damage done before I left. Unfortunately, that wasn't the case at all.

9

Sierra and Eve pick me up at Dulles Airport. I climb inside the car, glad to see them again.

"You are so persona non grata," says Eve. "I really shouldn't even be seen in the same car with you."

"Thanks a lot, Eve. It's that bad?" I ask, as Sierra speeds us out of the airport and onto the freeway.

Sierra nods. "You haven't been reading the papers in Israel? It's like round two in a heavyweight boxing match only we're the lightweights."

"President Stone asked everyone not to look at the news during the peace talks. He wanted everyone to stay focused on the workshops."

"So, now that they're over—here," says Eve, dumping a slew of headlines on my lap.

Photos from my disastrous college days of "Black Tuesdays" are spread all over the tabloids. "I think I'm going to be sick," I tell them, skimming the story. "George Toffler wrote about this in his exposé on Derek Rogers two years ago. And now, these people are rewriting history and turning *me* into the bad guy?"

"Oh, it gets worse," comments Sierra. "Keep flipping."

I flip through to the next paper pointing to my past relationships and my separation from Victor. "I can't believe this," I mutter. "What about my work during the peace talks? Doesn't that count for some good news?"

"Not on your behalf. Tyler Simmons is taking all the credit," explains Sierra. "You should hear that bloated broadcaster Bill Sutter talk about it."

"Actually, she shouldn't hear him. It might make her cry," adds Eve.

"Why? What has he been saying now?"

There's a pause. Sierra looks at me. "She can't dress but she can run...all the way to the Wailing Wall..."

"And that you're a media-chicken," adds Eve, again.

"You've got to be kidding!" I explain.

"We wish," Eve responds.

"I'm sure President Stone will speak on my behalf," I offer, somewhat hesitantly.

"He already has, but the media isn't picking up on it," says Sierra.

"Meanwhile, My Grief Day is on pause," concludes Eve. "The grief fashions will be ready to hit department stores within one week of MGD...at cost, with all the revenue going to the National Hospice Foundation. The fact that Z Mas doesn't watch the news means he's remained neutral on all of this *gossigrief.*"

"Gossigrief?" I ask, with curious apprehension.

Eve smiles with pride. "A new word I made up. Gossip plus grief equals *gossigrief.* Like it?" We stare at her. "Well, it's better than *griefsip,*" she says.

"Moving on," says Sierra, "all the event production is in place on both coasts. Smitty and I even went through two rehearsals together. Talk about a work anorexic, that guy can party! Oh, and I met with Eddie at StoriesMakeUs.com for you. Everything is set to go online as well. But there's no point in launching the whole affair because given your polls, we don't have a chance of anyone participating…including celebrities, who have started dropping out."

"They have polls on me? Doesn't our country have more important things to poll about than me?"

They both pause and look at me. "Uh…I believe that is a rhetorical question," Sierra retorts.

"What we need is a miracle," says Eve.

"What we need is the truth," I demand.

"Right, but where is it?" asks Sierra.

The three of us glance at each other and then stare out the window. Creating a national event to deal with collective grief was one thing, manifesting the simple truth was an entirely different challenge altogether. In fact, I need a universal source of truth. I could go to synagogue or search the Talmud, the great commentary of sagacious old rabbis on the meaning of stories in the Torah. Those great stories, including parables from the wise old Rabbi Akiva of the first century, usually reflected the theme that the truth is inside of us.

"The truth is inside of us," I say.

Eve rolls her eyes. "Come on, are we writing essays on the nature of truth now? The point is how do we get it out there?"

"The point is how do we get it embraced by the public?" asks Sierra, shaking her head. "I just don't think that these kinds of dirty political games are what our forefathers had in mind when they wrote the Constitution."

"That's it," I blurt out, as we approach the hill, that area in D.C. known for the location of the Capitol where the Rotunda, Senate Chambers, Hall of the House of Representatives, Brumidi Corridor, the Old Senate and the Old Supreme Court reside. "Drop me off here," I insist. "I'll meet you back at the hotel in a couple of hours."

"Where are you going?" Sierra asks.

"I'm going to have a talk with our forefathers," I reply.

Eve rolls her eyes again. "They're dead. What good is that going to do?"

"It was a metaphor, Eve. I'm going to get inspiration on where to go from here."

"Inspiration is not what we need. We need action. Can you please take some action?"

"I am taking action in order to get inspiration to know what kind of action to take," I reason.

"Is that supposed to be some sort of brain teaser?" har-rumphs Eve.

"Got any better ideas?" I ask, jumping out the door.

"Yes, wait!" cries out Eve. "At least cover your head and your eyes, so you don't attract any *griefarazzi* and make a scene." She throws me her trendy baseball hat and a hip pair of shades.

National Statuary Hall

Inside Old Congress, I tip Eve's hat low over my forehead to avoid recognition. I'm cutting a path through large tour groups on my way to the National Statuary Hall, also known as the Old Hall of the House. This is the room where for nearly fifty years the House of Representatives would meet to debate the future of this nation. Poor sound quality, however, and disruptive echoes from the tall curved ceiling necessitated creating a new House of Representatives, leaving this one to become the home of statues for exemplary citizens and politicians.

I hike across the black-and-white marble floor to the front of the room to view the statue "Liberty and the Eagle."

"What would you do?" I ask Liberty. I wait. And as I'm waiting, my gaze falls upon the Constitution denoted in Liberty's right hand. I concentrate, thinking about liberty as freedom, the eagle to her right as a symbol of strength, and the serpent as a figure of wisdom. I squeeze my eyes shut and focus on whatever energy I might derive from the icons. Nothing comes. I try clearing my mind to let new thoughts in, but Eve's comment about the need for a miracle keeps popping up. Again I stare at the carved words of the Constitution, held upright by Liberty—they're a miracle in and of themselves, a miracle of democracy, freedom and human rights. I reach out and touch the cold stone marble and whisper, "Please show me a sign that your original intentions still hold true. Please show me a—"

"Excuse me, ma'am." A security guard interrupts my prayer.

"Listen, I am not a ma'am," I politely point out. "I am way too young to be called a ma'am. Okay?"

"There's no touching the statues…miss," he says.

"That's much better, thank you, and sorry. I didn't mean to actually touch her." I turn on my heels and do a double take. Derek Rogers and Tyler Simmons stroll through the hall engaged in conversation. I can't believe my eyes. I dip the glasses down and peer above the rim. Yep, it's them. I dive behind the statue of Stephen F. Austin, exemplary citizen and politician of Texas. I'm pressed up close to the stone figure.

Derek stops to make a point to Tyler Simmons. The two of them appear to be in a heated debate.

"Ma'am. There's no touching the statues."

I look up at the security guard again and glare at him.

"Miss," he corrects.

"Thank you," I reply, backing off of Mr. Austin. "He was a good guy wasn't he? He must've been. They named a city after him, right? Okay, bye-bye."

I camouflage myself by falling into line with a pack of tourists.

"…nearly fifty years, from 1807 to 1857," instructs the tour guide. "In 1864, Congress invited every state to send two statues of famous, productive citizens. Forty of those statues are in this room."

I get tangled in the crowd while keeping an eye trained on Derek and Tyler, desperate to know what they are saying.

"Now, let's move over to the statue of John Quincy Adams. If you look at the historical marker on the floor you'll see that this is where his desk was…and legend has it that he would pretend he was sleeping at his desk after every debate. But what he was really doing was listening to the plans of his political enemies on the other side of the room. He could even hear conversations where they considered assassination of Adams himself as one of their tactical approaches. Now the reason why John Quincy Adams could hear his opponents from across the room was because of the principle of osculation, which has to do with the amplification of light and sound in relationship to the geometry and curvature of the ceiling. Not many people knew or understood this, but Adams did because he had studied the science of optics and acoustics before entering politics. Now if you all get very quiet, you can hear what people are whispering about all the way across the room."

The group goes silent, and for about ten seconds I can clearly decipher the conversation between Derek Rogers and Tyler Simmons.

"We have to keep pressuring them," Derek Rogers says.

"Your methods are too dangerous," replies Tyler Simmons.

"Then change them. I don't really care, as long as the results are in," demands Derek.

The group nods in fascination over the feat of scientific engineering that makes this possible. Their "ooohs" and "aaaahs" snuff out my chance to hear the rest of the conversation. But I realize I have the opportunity to obtain valuable information. This is my inspiration and now I need to do like Eve said, and take action.

"Any questions?" asks the tour guide.

My hand shoots up in the air. "Yes, where was uh, Stephen Austin's desk?" I blurt.

"Ah! The 'father of Texas,'" says the tour guide. "The markers are only for those members of the House who became President of—"

"Okay, well, what about, um, James Madison?" I ask. "Can you lead us to the marker for his desk, immediately?"

"Sure, that would be over here," he replies.

The tour guide moves on, and like an obedient flock of sheep, the rest of the group follows, leaving me in silence. I stay put with my back to Derek and Tyler and whip out my BlackBerry Pearl to capture a photo of John Quincy Adams. Derek and Tyler are in the background, and I can just overhear what they're saying.

"You can't keep manipulating the media," says Tyler.

"What are you worried about? The tabloids eat this up. Besides, nothing is traceable."

"Paying Paikel a retainer fee is."

"I didn't hire them. And neither did you," says Derek. "Stuart Provost did, even though he doesn't know it." There's a pause. "You keep forgetting. This is what's going to get you the nomination to your party so you can run next year. You just keep advising Stone, in public, that you're against him having anything to do with that stupid event. The fact that Pintock is sponsoring it falls right into our lap. We've basically brought Pintock and Banks to their knees. By association, Stone falls too, only it won't be your fault. You'll be on record as having advised him to do the opposite."

"How do you know the commission's going to find wrong-doing?"

"I planted a mole, that's why, right in the middle of his accounting department. If they don't find any cooked books, she'll write the recipe herself."

"Where's your sidekick?" asks Tyler. "He's late."

"Relax. He's always late."

"Where did he go this morning anyway?"

"To visit his second cousin once removed or something like that. He's the only one who can fill in the blanks on all these letters I've received about Darcy's family history. Over three hundred fucking letters…it's a pain in the ass."

I stop staring at John Quincy Adams. I can't believe what I've just heard. If only I had a witness. Next to me is a nice-looking man. "Excuse me, sir," I whisper, tapping him on the shoulders. "Did you hear that conversation?"

He smiles back at me and points to a hearing aid behind his ear. "Hold on there, gotta put the volume up. What did you say now?"

"Have a nice day," I reply sadly. I spot my adopted tour group and fall back into line with them.

"This statue is a representation of Clio," says the tour guide, "the Greek muse of history who records all the events that take place here. In fact, she helped launch the parchment industry."

The group nods and I duck past them and out the door into daylight.

★ ★ ★

I'm about to hail a cab when Sierra and Eve pull up to the curb and spring the door open. They're all dressed up in dark-colored clothes.

"Jump in!" they shout.

I hop in the backseat, breathless. "You will not believe what I just heard," I scream.

"Here," says Eve, handing me some black clothes with pink accents and a black mesh veil. "You need to change in the car right now."

"Where are we going and why are you both dressed...like you're going to a funeral?" I ask.

"Because that's exactly where we're going," says Sierra.

"Who died?"

"Charlotte Abbotsdale...who happens to be Torah Grant's great-aunt. We just read in the paper that Torah flew in for the funeral."

"Do we *know* her great-aunt?" I ask.

"We know enough to crash her funeral," quips Eve.

"Like what?"

"Like she died. Hello?" says Eve.

"Oh, God, no," I argue. "We don't need to do this. I've got proof like you won't believe. Really, like incriminating evidence against Derek Rogers and Tyler Simmons for manipulating the media, for plans to bring down Arthur Pintock, myself and President Stone, by default...and that Johnny Bright is the long-lost distant relative of Jonathon Darcy—not Derek."

"Talk about manipulating the media doesn't mean anything,

and insinuating proof does not make for hard-core evidence," says Sierra.

"This is pure confession," I plead. "I heard it with my own ears!"

"That's nice," says Eve. "But it's only your word…and no one's going to believe you anyway…unless we can get Torah Grant to believe you."

"You've got to be kidding. What's our relationship to this woman?" I ask. "We can't be funeral crashers. Hello? We'll stick out like sore thumbs."

"Ahem, I read her obituary," says Eve. She hands it over to me. "Very large crowd. Read for yourself. Charlotte happened to be a member of the Association of American Sewers and the Auctioneers Guild. The auction-thingy I know nothing about, however, it just so happens that I now have a membership card from the Association of American Sewers Guild, since they made me an honorary member. So…we're going as fellow sewers."

"That is so weak. And I don't know anything about sewing," I say.

"Neither do I," states Sierra. "But somehow, we have to get Torah Grant to believe in you, so the rest of the country will, too."

"I suggest you start changing now," orders Eve. "And don't forget the black mesh veil, or you will have a scene and it won't be pretty."

As I change, I scan Charlotte Abbotsdale's obituary to discover among other things that Charlotte had two children named Jason and Lillian, she survived her husband and she lived to be seventy-two.

Torah Grant's great-aunt's funeral

"Is that it?" I ask, as we drive past a bleak building on a country road. A freshly painted sign reads Johnson Funeral Home. We drive up and notice chain locks on the front door, not to mention that there are no cars or limos in sight.

"It looks deserted," murmurs Eve.

"That…and it's for sale," says Sierra, pointing to the for sale sign.

We move on, driving through the quaint town of Charlottesville, Virginia, about one and a half hours southwest of Washington, D.C.

"It's gorgeous out here. Such a cute…village," remarks Sierra. "It's so…little."

"Not that little," Eve retorts. "See? They have a Gap, Banana Republic, Victoria's Secret, Petco and Toys R Us."

"How much farther?" I ask.

"Well, according to the GPS, we've reached our destination and the funeral home is right here," says Sierra.

"Looks like a big outdoor shopping mall to me," comments Eve.

We scan our surroundings. And then I spot it. "Look, over there," I direct them. "Whitney & Sons Funeral Home is part of the mall."

"Wow. They do say location is everything," adds Sierra.

"I am impressed with their courage to hang their shingle in a shopping mall," I comment, glancing at my watch and the details provided in the obituary. "Meanwhile, we're forty-five minutes early."

The parking lot is packed with cars and limos. We squeeze into a spot and then hike in our high heels toward the mall.

"Uh-oh," whispers Eve, staring at the entrance.

Two beefy security guards flank the doors with guest lists in their hands, while a crowd of Torah Grant devotees circle the perimeter.

"They must be here to prevent a mob scene around Torah Grant," says Sierra.

One fan holds up a placard that reads, "Dear Torah, we are sorry for your loss and grieve with you!"

"I think it's time for a new game plan," Sierra suggests.

"Like what?" I ask.

"Like is there a back entrance?" asks Eve.

"We can't sneak in the back way," I protest.

"Why not?" asks Eve.

"Because it's rude and against funeral service etiquette," I blurt out.

"Not if no one knows, it isn't," says Eve.

I roll my eyes. "Look, why can't I just tell the media what I *heard* Derek and Tyler say in the Hall of Statues?"

Sierra and Eve stare at me like I've lost my mind.

"Because we *heard* that Hampstead is having an affair with the president," says Eve.

"That's ridiculous! Stop spreading rumors," I shout. "You could get sued for that unless you had proof..." I'm stopped short by their raised eyebrows, hands on their hips and stare-down. Unified, they are a force. "Okay. I got your point. Let's try the back door," I say, acquiescing, and wondering how the hell we're going to pull this off. Unfortunately, our thinking is totally unoriginal. We turn the corner and witness another pod of Torah fans held at bay by two more security guards.

"Now what?" I ask.

"Oh, please," insists Eve. "This is a breeze. We plow through and pretend like we belong here. I do it every time I need to go to a convention."

"And it works?" asks Sierra. "You just prance in without a badge or ID, or anything?"

Eve smiles. "Hmm, I wouldn't say I prance in without anything. I prance in with a hot outfit and an even hotter attitude. Works like a charm," and then she whispers, "I think they think I own the place." She winks at us. "Let's go."

Eve leads the way as Sierra follows and I traipse behind.

"Excuse me," I protest to deaf ears, "but we can't pretend to *own* this funeral home because the real owners will be here. Did you ever consider that?" I plead, trying to instill some reason into the situation. But neither one of them answers me.

Eve politely pushes her way through the crowd, reiterating "excuse me," a dozen times. Sierra copies Eve while pulling me along. As we reach the back door, Eve cries on cue, muttering the name "Charlotte" over and over again. I can't believe how upset she is. I almost believe that she is really grieving for this woman. Sierra follows with tears as well, but a more subdued version. They waltz through the pearly gates without a hitch. I lose contact and a large hand shoots out to halt me.

"Excuse me, ma'am, we need to check your ID," says the security guard.

"Okay, you know what? This ma'am bit has got to stop. I am way too young to be called ma'am and I would appreciate it if you would please refrain from using that particular salutation on me."

"All right, then who are you?" he asks, glancing between me and the guestlist.

"I am…um, I am…the funeral planner…you know, Lights Out Enterprises." I lift my veil so he can see me more clearly. "Grief czar, if you will," I add. The security guard looks me over with a gaze of recognition. I quickly drop the veil back down.

"Oh, hey, I know who you are. You're in all those tabloids." He leans in and whispers, "Did you really do it with the president?"

"No, I did *not* do it with the president! Shame on you for believing that crap," I scold him under my breath. "Now if you don't mind, I have a funeral to oversee."

You'd think he'd leave it at that and let me inside, but instead he turns to security guard number two and hollers, "Hey, man, the funeral planner is here!"

Guard #2 nods and waves for me to follow him for a personal escort to the grieving family. Mortified, I have no choice but to follow him through the door and down a stark sanitary hallway. He keeps turning his head around to gape at me while I frantically peek around corners for Sierra and Eve who are nowhere to be seen. He slows his step until I nearly bump into him, then he looks at me with a salacious smile and starts to pose a question, "So…did you really…"

"Don't even think about it," I quickly whisper, cutting him off.

He nods and shuts his mouth. We reach the room where the family has gathered in private. It's separated from the hallway by a large thick curtain, making it possible to hear some of their conversation. They are clearly upset, and it sounds as if there's a lot more bickering than crying.

I whisper to the guard, "I'll take it from here, thank you." He disappears down the hallway and I press my ear to the small gap where the curtain meets the wall to better hear the details of the mourners' conversation.

"I understand this is a traditional funeral home, unlike the other one, but with all due respect, Aunt Charlotte deserves to have those who knew her speak about her, not some clergy who never met her and can't talk about her," says the voice of Torah Grant.

"We do it all the time," says a placid–flaccid male voice.

"That seems so wrong," weeps a family member. "My mom always told me we should remember her for who she was. She was especially proud of being the best female bid champion in auctioneer history. She'd want everyone to remember that."

"I assure you," replies the voice of placid flaccid, "our hymns are lovely. We do them for every funeral. They have beautiful melodies and if you'd like we can have an organist accompany—"

"It's not the hymns we object to, Mr. Whitney. We'd just like to have those friends and family, who would like to speak, have the opportunity to do so," Torah explains.

"I understand," says the other voice, slightly irritated, "but with all due respect, we're the only funeral home in town now, and we have a tight schedule of services immediately following this one, and unfortunately, family members tend to go on and on and on which…"

I've heard enough from this pathetic unaccommodating funeral director and whip open the curtain for my entrance. An obvious clash of funeral practices and cultures was evident in their inability to communicate clearly to one another. This is where I come in.

"Excuse me," I say, holding out my hand to greet the mourners. "Members of the Abbotsdale family, it is an honor to finally meet you, though of course, I wish it were under different circumstances. Miss Grant, it's a pleasure to meet you, too. Oh, did Charlotte ever rave about you!"

"Uh, have we met?" asks the man with the placid voice. From his youthful appearance and inexperience, I assume he's Whitney Jr.

"No, we've never met, Mr. Whitney, Jr., I presume, but I've always looked forward to meeting you. I've heard wonderful things about your funeral home, in particular how accommodating you are to last-minute requests on behalf of grieving families, especially considering that Charlotte's funeral was supposed to take place at the Johnson Funeral Home down the road, where her requests were laid out in advance but then…they closed, and all of their business went to you, which could give you a monopoly on dictating the services you conduct, but I hear you don't succumb to that sort of practice, and I can only imagine how busy you must be given the aging baby-boomer population and all, anyway…my job is to make sure Charlotte's requests are carried out per our pre-need consultations. So many times, people record their final wishes inside their wills and well, let's face it, wills don't usually get looked at until *after* the funeral, so it's a real bummer to find out things were done…differently—than the departed would have liked, which is why, by the way, I highly recommend that my clients record their last wishes inside health directives because that's much more likely to be seen in time for the service…assuming the departed wanted a service, and in this case, Charlotte did very much want a service."

They all stare at me. "Uh, who are you?" asks Junior Whitney.

"Oh, yes, forgive me." I remove my veil. "I'm Madison Banks."

Their faces register my notoriety. "You're the grief czar!" exclaims Torah Grant.

"Yes, and Charlotte's funeral planner," I state.

"Have you really been slee—" interjects a young man, whom I surmise to be her son, Jason.

"Uh-uh!" I say, firmly holding up a hand to stop him midword. "Tabloid journalism has no business here today, or any day. And by the way, I'm innocent."

"Mom had a funeral planner?" asks the shy daughter, perplexed.

"Wow, how radical of her," says Jason. "But then, it's no surprise, is it?"

"You must be Charlotte's son, Jason. And you must be her daughter, Lillian. She always spoke so well of you two."

"She did?" asks Jason. "I thought she was mad at me for moving to L.A. last year."

"Well, she wasn't mad two years ago when she hired me but we haven't spoken for a while."

"So if Aunt Charlotte hired you to plan her funeral," says Torah Grant. "What exactly did she plan?"

"Yes, I'm coming to that. She, hmm, wanted to have a member from her sewing club speak about her."

"That would be Mrs. Rainey," supplies Lillian. "She's always telling funny stitching stories about Mom."

"Yes, she specifically requested that Mrs. Rainey tell a story or two. And…she invited Jason and Lillian to speak about her, but *only* if they felt comfortable. She understood their shyness and felt it would most likely be too painful for them to speak, but she did want both of you to speak about her together in private after the burial."

"I thought she wanted cremation after the viewing," says Jason.

"Pardon me, I meant to say, she'd like you to speak about her after the viewing, but before the cremation. She also requested that Torah tell a story about her and sing her favorite song."

"*The Wind Beneath My Wings?*" asks Torah. "We used to sing that to each other all the time, ever since she took me to see the movie *Beaches.*"

"That's the song," I say.

"What about her boyfriend, Eli? They used to cover all the auctions in the entire state together," asks Lillian.

"Right, of course," I apologize quickly, "Forgive me, my notes are with my assistants who seem to be delayed in getting here. Let's see…for Eli…one moment, it's coming to me. Eli. Eli. Eli…"

"That's my name," says an avuncular-looking fellow peeking through the curtains and entering the room. Underneath the heartbreak and sadness, I see a jovial, confident eighty-something showman possessing a voice of great clarity and presence.

"Ah, there you are, Eli. Madison Banks, Charlotte's funeral planner. She specifically requested—"

"Well, I'll be damned," interrupts Eli. "Charlotte always talked about doing something like that, she was always planning for something, even if it was a rainy day. But I never thought she'd go through with it. Now, isn't that something?"

"Yes, well, she did go through with it, and she wanted you to speak about her and to sort of, you know, lead the ceremony, maybe do a little sample 'bidding.' And, oh, I've got an id—I mean, for every adjective you use to describe her, she wanted to have those words written on paddles and then have the *paddles* passed out to the mourners so when you say those keywords that describe her so well, the mourners with the matching words on their paddles are to hold them in the air as a representation of her life, at least the auctioneer part of it."

"What a wonderful way to celebrate her for who she was and what she meant to all of us," Torah comments.

"But Mom didn't have a single drop of creativity in her bones," argues Lillian.

"She did sew," I say in Charlotte's defense. "That's creative."

"By numbers," reply Jason and Lillian.

"Right…well, this was a, uh, collaborative process."

"What about Pickles?" asks Eli.

"Pickles?" I ask.

"Her faithful dog, who's having an anxiety attack in my truck right now. Charlotte always did say if she went first, she'd want Pickles to be buried with her. Alive."

"Well, Eli, I, uh, talked Charlotte out of that."

"Impossible. Once Charlotte made up her mind there was no talking her out of it."

"You got that right," says Jason.

"That may be true, but I pointed out a few things to Charlotte…like compassion and animal rights, and in the end, she, uh, talked herself out of it."

"Then who gets Pickles?" asks Eli. "I think that dog was jealous of me."

"Yes, well, uh, Charlotte thought it would be best if Pickles…" I scan the room trying to figure out where to place an orphaned dog named Pickles. "Uh, she thought that it would be best if Pickles...decided for herself." I see Lillian's eyes brighten with hope.

I turn to Mr. Whitney. "So now, Mr. Whitney, will you please get me a pen and paper? And Eli, Jason, Lillian and Torah, can you all provide for me a list of adjectives about Charlotte."

Mr. Whitney gives me a look. I stop cold to stare at him and then hit him with a giant smile. "Oh, Mr. Whitney, are you hesitating to get that pen and paper in case I need something else? You are too kind!" I pinch him hard on the cheek, the kind of pinch that hurts. "Thank you, but I don't need anything else but that pen and paper...right now." Mr. Whitney starts to leave. I hold up a finger. "Oops, forgot one more thing. Can you please ask one of your staff members to scoot across the street and pick up a black Sharpie and two dozen toy paddles at Toys R Us? The kind with the rubber ball attached. We'll just cut those balls off and be good to go. And I suggest you pick the fastest running staffer you've got so we don't roll over into your next service. Thank you so much, Mr. Whitney. Much appreciated. Oh, and can you please pick up a bone at Petco for Pickles."

Mr. Whitney glares at me. "A bone for Pickles?"

"Yes, Charlotte did want Pickles to attend her funeral in lieu of being stuffed in the casket with her. The bone is an insurance policy for you, Mr. Whitney." He's not getting it. I whisper, "To counter the anxiety attack...so Pickles doesn't chew your furniture." He nods. "Bye-bye," I say.

"What about the clergy?" asks Mr. Whitney. "He should be here any second."

"Oh," I say, looking to the family members. "He can handle the intros and outros? Everyone good with that?" The family members nod in grateful appreciation. I turn to Mr. Whitney. "There's your answer."

Security Guard #2 peeks his head through the curtains. "There's a Lizzy here, says she's part of the family."

"Send her right in," Torah tells him. He nods and leaves.

Lillian approaches me. "Did Mom want Lizzy to speak?"

"I'm sure she's going to want to say a few words. They were tight," adds Torah.

"No, no, no," cries Whitney, Jr. "There's absolutely no time. This isn't a marathon," he whines.

I stare at him. "Excuse me, Mr. Whitney, Jr., but you're breaking the law."

"I am?" he asks, stunned.

"As a licensed funeral director familiar with the psychology of grief and the rituals of funeral service in America, you know full well that the funeral service is the last place of public expression where a community can come together to mourn its dead, and how crucial that is for society. How a society treats its dead is exemplary of how a society treats its living. I shudder to think how you must treat the people in your personal life if this is an indication of how you always behave. Not to mention that this is a rather public funeral, given the presence of Ms. Grant. I'd hate to see you get bad press for this. Trust me. It's no picnic."

"I believe I've heard enough and there's no need to panic," a new, yet oddly familiar voice says. "Charlotte understood my personal feelings about not speaking at funerals. But I do appreciate the effort you've gone to on my behalf, as well as that lovely bit about how society treats its dead and living."

I slowly turn to face Elizabeth Anderson, aka, Lizzy. "My pleasure," I reply.

Mrs. Anderson's polite demeanor quickly vanishes at the sight of me.

"This is Mom's funeral planner," says Lillian.

"Charlotte?" Elizabeth chokes. "I highly doubt that. She would have told me."

"Mrs. Anderson, with all due respect, why would Charlotte tell you if she knew how you felt about public displays at funerals?" I ask.

"Don't feel bad, Lizzy," says Torah. "She didn't tell me everything, either."

Mr. Whitney fumes under his breath and stomps off. The immediate family and I draw up a list of adjectives together so that no one person feels left out. Because they participated in helping to create the content for the service, Lillian and Jason decide they would be more comfortable listening and grieving than speaking in public. That leaves the podium to Mrs. Rainey, Torah Grant and the beloved boyfriend Eli, who will lead the service.

While Mrs. Rainey tells stories about Charlotte and her valiant yet futile attempts at back-stitching, I peek through the curtain of the family room to search among the mourners for Sierra and Eve.

The funeral home is packed with over three hundred people. Charlotte was well-loved. How did she have time to constantly travel around the state as an auctioneer, be a mother, a partner, and have time to keep up with family and friendships with that many people and for God's sake, have time for a hobby like sewing? Maybe workaholism was a myth and life was really about time management.

I spot Pickles seated in the front row on the lap of a mourner. She's some sort of dachshund. She chews the bone, then stops cold when she hears Mrs. Rainey imitate Charlotte. Pickles stares with sad eyes at Mrs. Rainey, abandons the bone and whimpers for her beloved master. The bone lies untouched between her paws. I wonder how she got the name Pickles just as Mrs. Rainey starts to tells the story. Oddly enough, it has to do with time management.

"Charlotte believed in the pickle jar theory," says Mrs. Rainey. "You put pickles inside a jar, and when you can no longer fit any more in, you add pebbles, and when no more pebbles fit, you add sand, and when no more sand can fit, you add water. If you try to do it backwards, you fail miserably. Well, that was how Charlotte lived her life. She took care of the big things in life first. She always used to say, 'If you focus on the little stuff, then there's no room for the big stuff.' Pickles were big stuff, and that's why she named her four-legged best friend Pickles. It was how Charlotte accomplished so much and had time for everyone and everything."

Mourners dab their eyes with tissues and smile in remembrance. Mrs. Rainey passes the microphone to Torah Grant when I finally spy Sierra in the back row and Eve in a middle row. Both of them hold paddles in their laps. I see Mrs. Anderson looking skeptical.

Torah Grant mesmerizes the folks with tales about Charlotte and then sings "The Wind Beneath My Wings" a cappella. That's when I notice some dissention in the crowd. Most respond positively to Torah's actions, but others look perturbed by the lack of tradition. Sierra and Eve ham it up for the positive side with nods and whispers of approval to their neighbors.

Eli takes over from Torah with a command of the crowd the likes of which I have never seen before. I'm thinking they should get this guy for an awards show. He's charming, poignant and down to earth. He shares humorous, heartwarming stories about Charlotte using the auction-bidding format. It is nothing short of brilliant. As he says the keywords, mourners raise their matching paddles in the air in honor of Charlotte's memory and a life well lived. Even Mrs. Anderson is responding with a blend of smiles, laughter and tears.

As the ceremony reaches its conclusion, I surreptitiously place a dog bone in Lillian's purse, my insurance policy that Pickles reaches out to her. I start looking for my escape out the back door when Elizabeth Anderson quietly intercepts me.

"Ms. Banks, I owe you an apology. You truly honored Charlotte's memory for all of us. I dare say I now see the value in what you're doing."

"Coming from you, Mrs. Anderson, that means the world to me."

She smiles and one brow is raised. "I still wonder—if you don't have a penchant for crashing fund-raisers and funerals, though."

"Well, if I do…it's on par with your penchant for supporting the ethically depraved, Mrs. Anderson."

"What do you mean by that?" she asks.

"I was hoping the right opportunity would show up because I really wasn't sure what to do with this," I say, "but maybe you will know." I reach inside my purse and hand over a thick manila envelope with the genealogy information Brian had supplied me. "If you decide to dig further, I suggest you talk to George Toffler at the *Financial Street Journal,* and watch out for Simmons," I warn her. "Have a nice day, Elizabeth."

I slip down the hallway and am about to duck out the back door when Torah Grant catches up to me.

"Madison. I can't thank you enough for what you just did," says Torah. "I am so deeply touched and so grateful. I will never forget this. Now may not be the best time, but would you be interested in coming on my show?"

Before I can answer, Eve and Sierra materialize and introduce themselves as my funeral-planning colleagues at Lights Out Enterprises, then proceed to negotiate the terms of my appearance.

"An exclusive one hour straight on Madison," says Eve. "She appears as your solo guest in order to have time to delve into the issue of grief. This, of course, has to be followed up with reruns as well as your radio show for two weeks following the initial interview."

"Plus, she'll need thirty minutes devoted to talking about My Grief Day," adds Sierra. "For full disclosure, she'll also need to talk about The Tribute Network and our sponsors, Ubiquitous

Music, DigiCams, Twilight Cinema Headstones and Pintock International."

"I'm sure we could give each audience member a free copy of *Grief Tributes,* our grief guide," adds Eve.

"I'm loving this," says Torah, beaming.

"One more thing," mentions Eve, raising a finger. "No one knows in advance. No network executives, no advertisers, no one. Maddy comes on as a surprise guest two days from now."

"Wait a minute," I protest. "What if she's sitting shiva?" I turn to her. "Will you be sitting shiva?"

"I'm a mix of a lot of things, and I was named after my Jewish great-grandmother, who broke tradition to study Torah, but no, we won't be sitting shiva," Torah explains. She turns to Eve. "I'm good with all this."

"Then that settles that," Eve states smugly, as if there was nothing to it. Sierra beams and pats me on the back. And that's how I came to secure an hour-long exclusive appearance on *The Torah Grant Show.*

10

In my shower at the Hay-Adams, a strong stream of warm water cascades over my fatigued body. I wonder if it's possible to exfoliate jet lag. I wonder, too, about Victor. Why didn't he tell me he was going on a walkabout in the remote regions of the Himalayas…followed by a visit to a medieval monastery amok with monks. And furthermore, did he go alone? Or did he take some hiker-meditation chick with him? We never discussed whether or not our separation included the right to date other people. When I eventually spoke to his parents, they didn't tell me if he went solo or not. They only told me he went off to sequester himself for ten days. I feel empty without him, and abandoned, though admittedly he knows nothing of what's happened during the last seven days.

Seven days, I think. According to the book of Genesis, it took God seven days to create the planet and all the living beings on it, before he rested. It took Derek Rogers one day to destroy my good name. What could happen in seven more days before

Victor returned to civilization…if he ever returned? Maybe he would turn into a monk? It's possible. He had a transformation-seeking streak in him. Maybe it wouldn't be a week or a month before I heard from him again, maybe it would be…never? Maybe he was done with us. Maybe we were two big pickles I had neglected to put in the jar first. The best thing I can do, I decide, is to stop making assumptions because I could be totally off base here, and the second thing I can do, is learn from this. If Victor reenters my life, I promise to work less and love more, that I will change by…that's the tricky part. Creating change. But work addiction meetings have given me the answer—take different actions. Ah, that's the rub. Like what? I think, rubbing my neck. I know! I've never spent a day shopping for Victor, let alone for myself. I could change by making up for all the gifts I've missed giving him. Perhaps I could enlist the ever-impeccably-dressed Hampstead to help me, that is, if the opportunity ever presents itself again.

Exhausted and peckish, I wrap the cozy hotel bathrobe around me and proceed to unpack from Israel while packing for New York, where my live interview with Torah Grant will take place in one and a half more days.

"What am I doing?" I mutter. "I better let Eve handle this." I boot up my computer. I should order some food, but decide to put it off until after I e-mail my sponsors and strategic partners that My Grief Day is back on. I'm putting all my ducks in line when there's a knock on the door.

"Room service," a male voice calls out.

"I didn't order room service," I say, as I open the door. There's an exquisite table setting for two, with delicious steaming aromas, lit candles and an ice bucket with a bottle of champagne. Suddenly, I'm starving. "Are you absolutely, positively, one-hundred percent certain that *that* is for *this* room?"

The room-service guy double checks his ticket. "Filet mignon with peppercorn sauce, Caesar salad with grilled chicken, sautéed brussel sprouts, tiramisu and decaffeinated tea. Yes, I'm absolutely certain this is for your room."

"Filet mignon, wow…rare or medium?" I ask.

"Medium rare leaning toward juicy pink," he reports, matter-of-factly.

"Okay, so if I let you in and you find out you made a mistake, then what happens?"

"You get to keep it." He grins. "Especially if it's in your stomach."

"Oh great, then." Someone in room service made a big mistake, or else Sierra, Eve or Richard must have wanted to make sure I ate a good meal. One of them is sure to barge in any moment to join me and go over the to-do list, or the wardrobe for *The Torah Grant Show,* or discuss grief etiquette during My Grief Day. Meanwhile, there was no use in letting this culinary delight get cold. I take a bite of the filet and it melts in my mouth. This is the best filet mignon I have ever had, I think to myself, when my BlackBerry rings. It's Hampstead.

I quickly answer, "This is Madison Banks."

"Greetings, Ms. Banks. Welcome back to Washington, D.C.," says Hampstead. "Are you dressed?"

"Uh, I can be," I reply.

"Then I suggest you do so."

I realize I've just provided a mental picture of myself naked for Hampstead. "I'm not naked or anything," I blurt, "just in my bathrobe."

"Lovely," comments Hampstead. "The president will be stopping by to see you in a few minutes."

I'm about to jump to my feet and repeat my patterns, when I catch myself, remembering the insights and admonishments of Sierra and Lana. Change starts with taking different actions. So I do.

"I can't meet the president right now," I say, shaking. They never said change was easy. There's a pregnant pause on the other end of the line from Hampstead.

"When can you?" he asks.

I swallow hard. "Um…in about thirty minutes," I reply.

"I'll tell him," says Hampstead. "He's rather hungry after the long flight from Jerusalem, so I've taken the liberty of ordering dinner for him…and you."

I stare at the food. Well, that cleared up that little mystery. "Thank you, Hampstead. It's very, very good…of you," I acknowledge, and quickly toss my fork on the table and cover my plate so as not to be rude when the president arrives.

"Please do remember to dress appropriately, Ms. Banks," adds Hampstead.

"Would that be casual or dressy?"

"Casual nice will do," he replies.

We hang up and I scurry around my hotel room towel-drying my hair and trying to figure out what to wear. I look up "casual nice" in my pocket fashion planner provided to me by Eve. But that outfit is all wrinkled from my suitcase. There's a knock on my door. They're early.

"Secret service, Ms. Banks. We need to check the room first," they say.

I throw on a faux-dressy flannel shirt with a pair of corduroys and socks and let them in. They search the room, then leave. A moment later, President Stone enters.

"Good evening, Madison. Thank you for accommodating my schedule. I won't be long. Mind if I sit down?" he asks.

I shake my head. "Please," I say. "Sit wherever you like."

President Stone sits down at the room service table and smiles. "That was quick of Hampstead, looks like he went all out. Mind if we eat now?" I shake my head no, and sit down to join him. "I wanted to thank you again for your help in Jerusalem," he proclaims. "Rachel has enthusiastically agreed to stay on board and oversee a recovery program." I squint, feeling guilty for enabling her habit. "Don't worry, Maddy. I'm forcing her to take weekends off."

"Thanks," I say, nodding in appreciation.

"Thanks to your input, we've entered a new era where conversation just might lead to transformation."

"That would be nice."

"Listen, Maddy, I don't want you to think I've forgotten about what I brought you here to do in the first place. I'm still totally supportive of My Grief Day and I appreciate you keeping the ball rolling with sponsors from the private sector."

"Uh, about one of those sponsors, Mr. President—"

"Yes, I know all about the so-called Pintock scandal," he says. "Innocent until proven guilty, and until that day comes, his association to me through this national event doesn't scare me. I'm sure you know my political advisor Tyler Simmons is completely against my appearance on My Grief Day. He's made everyone aware of it, especially the media... he's convinced it will kill my chances for reelection."

"What did you tell him?"

"To shove it, so to speak."

I smile at him. The president was certainly finding his core strength again. It was a very attractive trait.

"Madison, I'd like to run by you the full story I plan to tell that day."

"Shoot," I tell him, enjoying how good the food tastes.

"It's the story of how I met Haley on the debate team."

I put my fork down and look at him. "That's a great story, Mr. President."

"Good, because I'm thinking if we truly honor Haley for what she believed in, maybe it will help get her Poverty Reform Bill passed in Congress before I leave the presidency, with or without a second term. I know I said I'd keep my story nonpartisan, but I believe it honors her memory, and if I'm going to change my word, I do it up front. What do you think?"

"I think it's perfect, Mr. President."

"Terrific," he says. We finish our meal and then he stands up to thank me profusely for my time, and leaves with his security detail. Truly exhausted, I change back into my bathrobe and turn the sheets down. I'm about to climb into bed when there's another knock on the door.

"Who is it?" I ask.

"Elizabeth Anderson," says the voice.

"Oh, um, hold on a second. I have to get dressed." I abandon the bathrobe and scurry around my room for some decent clothes to put on. I throw on a wrinkled dress. It looks horrible. I rip it off. At a loss, I simply throw on my blue jeans and a blouse and open the door.

"Hi. Please, um, come in," I say, holding the door open for her. She nods, looking me over, and then walks in. "Please, have a seat," I offer.

"In a moment," she says, gazing around the room.

"So, uh, to what do I owe the pleasure of your visit?"

She turns to me, looks me in the eye, and states, "Ms. Banks. I've come to accept your offer to be on the advisory board of The Tribute Network on behalf of the Tribute Film Festival and My Grief Day, if the offer still holds and depending on what the responsibilities of its board members are."

"Sure, the offer still holds," I confirm for her. "That would be great. The only responsibility is to offer advice on an occasional basis."

"That's it?"

"Well…I'm three million short on the budget for My Grief Day, so any suggestions or leads on financing would be greatly appreciated."

"Very good," she says, "I accept your offer."

"Really? Awesome." And again there's a knock at my door.

"Room service," announces the voice.

I glance at the door. This is starting to feel like a foodie's wet dream. Turns out, it's the same room-service guy with another dinner for two. This time there's a bottle of wine and a bottle of champagne on ice.

"I didn't order this," I say.

"Someone did. And it's all yours." He quickly wheels the fresh table of food and departs with the expired one.

Elizabeth sees the table for two. "Are you expecting someone?"

"They left. So if you're hungry or thirsty, please help yourself."

"Very well," she murmurs, and sits down at the table.

I join her and the two of us have the red wine and some steamed broccoli.

"By the way, I read those documents you gave me," she says, stopping to take a sip of wine. "And I took your advice to do a little more digging. I also met with George Toffler from the *Financial Street Journal* and I'm having a thorough check done on the veracity of that genealogy software program."

"Wow. You work fast."

"I don't waste time. I've also hired a private detective to look into the matter more closely. And now that I'm on your advisory board—I have some advice for you, Madison." She carefully sets her wineglass down on the table and then continues, "Stay away from the likes of Derek Rogers and Tyler Simmons until this is sorted through."

"I know, and thanks. I'll be sure to follow that advice."

"Good," she says, and rises from her chair. "I have to go. We'll be in touch," she promises. On her way out, she notices my Messiah pumps and stops short. "Those are striking shoes," she remarks. "May I see them?"

"Sure," I reply, and pick them up to show her.

She carefully studies them. "I've never seen anything like these. Catchy name, Messiah. The rare type of kidskin would indicate that these must have come from somewhere in Tuscany. Where did you buy them?" she asks.

I shrug my shoulders. "I didn't. They were sent to Eve

Gardner, as a sample, but the designer never made any more, at least not that we know of," I answer.

"What a pity," she says. And then I'm finally alone.

I shed my clothes and climb into bed, feeling a tremendous sense of redemption, recognition and understanding. As I'm starting to doze off, there's yet another knock on my door. I traipse over to it, thinking it's room service again, and open it.

Victor stands there, gruff, unshaven and unkempt, with worry lines around his eyes and mouth. His hair is long and askew. Even his clothes are disheveled. And yet, I've never seen him look more attractive. I want to hug him and then tear his shirt off. But the energy between us was thick with unanswered questions.

"Maddy, are you all right?" he asks, with a depth of concern I've never heard before.

"Victor…um, what are you doing here? Your parents said you were in some monastery in Asia."

"I was…until two diplomats in the program broke their vows to talk about the current peace talks and the scandal with you in the middle of it all. I left immediately and it still took me three days to get here. I tried to catch up with you in Jerusalem first, but security was insane and then I learned that you'd left, so I changed course. I tried leaving word with you, but your mailbox was full. I tried getting hold of Sierra, too. So, I figured I'd just get here and see you in person, but then there were airport delays." He glances inside the room. "May I come in?"

"Of course, you must be drained."

"And filthy," he says. Seeing the table of food he adds, "And starving."

"Please, have it all."

He looks at the table setting for two, then at me, and asks, "Are you expecting company?"

"No, room service keeps sending me food I didn't order."

"Lucky for me," he jokes, and sits down to eat.

I pour him a glass of wine and another of water. "You must

be dehydrated from all that traveling. Would you like me to run the shower for you?"

"I'd prefer a nice hot bath, if you don't mind…but in a minute. What happened, Maddy? I've been worried sick about you. Why didn't you contact me?"

"Contact you? You disappeared without a trace. I had no idea you'd even left the country."

"Did you not get my gift? It should have been delivered here eight days ago. I left a complete itinerary for you in case there was an emergency."

I shake my head. "No gift. No itinerary."

"That's awful. You must have felt…I'm terribly sorry, Mad. I should have been there for you."

"It's okay, Victor. I know if you knew you would have been. And maybe it was good that you weren't here, you know…it forced me to develop faith in myself."

"Have you been getting through this all right?"

"Do I have a choice?"

"I read all the tabloids I could get my hands on. I think it's abominable. Clearly, someone wicked is behind this."

"I know. I've taken care of that, why don't we make you a nice hot bath now?"

"Hold up a minute. Go back a sentence," says Victor, eyeing me. "What did you do?"

"Nothing…I followed a hunch, proved I was right and handed the information over to the appropriate person."

"I see." Victor munches, still eating. "Does the investigation happen to involve Derek Rogers?"

"Maybe," I reply. "Now what about that bath? And are you staying overnight? Because if you are, I was thinking maybe we could watch a movie…in bed…that is if our jet leg doesn't get the best of us, and if it's not breaking the separation rule, which I was never quite clear on to begin with.

But no political dramas, I think I've had enough of that in real life. Would you like to watch a comedy?" I ask.

"Something's wrong," he says, scrutinizing me. "You're avoiding conversations about work."

"Fancy that." I smile, until my computer dings several times alerting me to multiple e-mails. I pretend not to hear them and tightly grip the arms of my chair to remain stationary.

"Aren't you going to check those?" asks Victor.

"Check what?" I ask.

"Those very important e-mails," he says, in between bites of steamed broccoli.

"They can wait," I say through clenched teeth. "So, would you like that bath hot or warm? Bubbles or no bubbles?" Again, I smile.

He smiles back. "Hot, with bubbles." I stand up to prepare the bath when he reaches out for my arm and stops me. "About that separation thing. I don't much care for it, how about you?"

"Ditto," I whisper. "But you were right to care in the first place. I do have a problem and I'm addressing it. I even have a sponsor now."

"Yes, I know," he says. "I've been reading about it on Stories-MakeUs.com. You've got quite a following."

"What are you talking about? My sponsor is the only one who can see that," I respond, shocked.

"I think you mistakenly made your stories public, not private."

I sigh and shake my head. "How do you know about Sto-riesMakeUs.com?"

"I'm an early investor," Victor replies.

"What? How come you never told me about it?"

"I didn't think you wanted to hear about the details of Winston Capital," he says.

"First of all, I do want to hear. So, please don't make assumptions on my behalf. Did you ever stop to think that if you shared your world a little more with me, I might not have to be in mine all the time?"

Victor stares at me. "Fair enough. And I will share more." He advances, inching slowly towards my lips.

I'm about to kiss him, then stop myself. "I like the way you think and move, Victor. But, I...don't know what kissing you means right now." I duck away from his spell and go to fill up the tub. Victor follows me.

"Madison," he says, joining me on the edge of the tub as I check the water temperature. I turn to face him. "I missed you."

"I missed you, too," I state. "But what does ending the separation mean?"

"It means you're committed to working on your work addiction," he says.

"That's sort of one-sided, don't you think?"

"It means that I'm committed to sharing more of myself with you," he adds, taking my hand in his and doing a double take on my ringless finger.

"Anything else?" I ask.

"It means my fiancée can put her engagement ring back on," he says, smiling.

"Okay, then, separation is over. Let's reunite."

Victor kisses me gently on the lips and declares, "I love you, Maddy."

I look at him and feel the love I have for him more intensely than ever. "I love you, too."

He winks. "While I get cleaned up, why don't you check those e-mails and then hurry back."

"Thanks for that." I take off, but I spin on my heels and turn back to ask him, "Victor, out of curiosity. What was the gift you got me that I never got?"

He grins. "Airline tickets to New Zealand, in case..."

"That's sweet," I say. "I'd love to go with you."

"I'll track them down and see what happened to them," Victor offers.

I smile and walk, not run, to my waiting e-mails.

E-mails confirm that all the pieces are now neatly falling into place for My Grief Day and the Tribute Film Festival. I'm about to scoot back into the bathroom when an e-mail arrives from Sierra. It reads as follows: Hope you don't read this until tomorrow. I received a message from Victor that he was on his way to see you. I took the liberty of ordering a romantic dinner with champagne for both of you. Love, Si. The value of true friendship hit home. I say a silent prayer, grateful for Sierra. With that, I turn off my computer, unplug my BlackBerry, and join Victor in the bathtub and in the bed for a very long, uninterrupted romantic evening.

The Torah Grant Show

"Ladies and gentlemen, let's welcome our surprise guest, a talented young woman who makes death sexy, our very own funeral planner, CEO of Lights Out Enterprises, head of the House Bereavement Specialists Committee, our nation's grief czar…Ms. Madison Banks!"

That was just my introduction. Once Torah began clapping for me, the audience in the studio followed suit and then, just as Eve and Sierra had predicted, so too, did the audience watching on television and online. It was a good thing Eve and Sierra negotiated a surprise appearance because I heard that throughout the show, network executives were trying to order the producers to stop it.

"So tell us all about My Grief Day," invites Torah. "As I

understand it, there are many components to this. You've got live performances going on simultaneously from coast to coast, is that correct?"

"Yes. Musicians are writing original songs about grief that they'll perform at the Disney Concert Hall and the Kennedy Center," I explain. "Everyone is welcome to share their tributes about loved ones and pets who have contributed to their life's journey. And President Stone is making an appearance to share a very special story about Haley Stone."

Torah and her audience react positively to this news. "Wouldn't we all love a good story about Haley," says Torah. "God bless her soul. Besides these venues, where else is this taking place?"

"We'll be broadcasting online at TheTributeNetwork.com, on network television, at Royal Blue Cinemas everywhere nd at mobile cinemas throughout rural America," I reply.

"Now how are you paying for all this?" asks Torah, "because I understand you lost government funding as a result of the Insider Think Tank program."

"That's true," I admit. "But we were able to get generous help from sponsors who are truly committed to the positive message of My Grief Day."

"God bless corporate America," Torah chimes in with a big smile. "So people are invited to send in their two-minute 'trib vids,' as you say. And what do they do if they don't have one or are completely clueless on how to make one?"

"They can go to the Tribute Film at TheTributeNetwork.com to create one in a few simple steps. The highest viewer-rated trib vid will play for a month as will shorts at the Royal Blue Cinema chain across the country and in a new TV series called *America's Greatest Tribute Videos.*"

"That's wonderful," says Torah. "Everyone can participate. I know for me, sharing my grief with the support of a community, helps me heal." Then she notices my Messiah pumps. "Oooh. Love those!"

"Thank you," I reply. "We're also inviting people to post their loved one's favorite recipes at StoriesMakeUs.com, with a story to go with it. StoriesMakeUs will publish the recipes into what we're calling *The Comfort Cuisine Book.*"

"Now that is a terrific idea." Torah seems genuinely delighted by it. "Those famous recipes that your favorite aunt or uncle or grandmother refused to give up…unless it was over their dead body…and in this case, it will be." The audience smiles.

"This day is about community support," I add. "So it's our hope people will gather together at the Royal Blue Cinemas, at the mobile cinemas, everywhere and anywhere, really. You can check for locations at TheTributeNetwork.com. And of course, we have My Grief Day attire."

"You have attire specifically designed for this day?"

"We do. In fact, I'd like to have one of my colleagues from the Grief Team present it to you now. Eve Gardner, can you step out here, please?"

Eve sashays onto the stage like a runway model wearing the pastel pink-and-black clothing.

"Now why is pink in there?" asks Torah. "I thought grief was associated with somber moods and that it would be all black."

"We want to shift people's perception from mourning a death to celebrating a life. So we chose pink because it's the color of celebration," I explain.

"And who designed these?" she asks.

"Grief Day wear was designed by Z Mas," I reply.

"How on earth did you get a fashion icon like Z Mas to design these?" asks Torah.

"I didn't, Eve Gardner did." The audience hollers.

Eve politely bows in acknowledgment.

"You may know her as founder of the company Fashion Therapy 101, and she's responsible for the 'I PITY YOU' T-shirts."

Eve smiles at me and the audience, and proceeds to exhibit the layers of attire per my description, including the Memento Holders, and Memory Tails.

"This is fabulous," says Torah. "Where do we get these clothes and how much are they?"

"These are available in department stores next week. All one-hundred percent made in America with donations of time and energy from the Association of American Sewers, which allowed us to keep the price down to nineteen ninety-five."

"Nineteen ninety-five for a Z Mas piece? How did you manage that?" she asks, truly floored.

"We've included Z Mas's preferred charity in our project; so all revenue will be donated to the National Hospice Foundation. You can learn more about the National Hospice Foundation and their mission to provide quality end-of-life care at www.nationalhospicefoundation.org."

"Well, I have to say that I don't think I can wait a week for a Z Mas designed Grief Day outfit. Can any of you out there?"

The audience hollers back, "No!"

"Good, because Eve Gardner on the Grief Team helped make it possible for everyone in the audience today to receive one right now!"

The audience flips. I glance at Eve and salute her with a smile. She offers back a knowing smile in return, and sashays off the stage.

Torah's tone downshifts and she brings up the matter of my missives on StoriesMakeUs.com and how it's attracting a following.

"Tell us more about your battle with workaholism," she says. "I understand it's hurt your relationship."

"Not anymore," I reply. "We've reunited."

"Mazel Tov," says Torah. The crowd cheers.

"How did you do it?"

"I'm not cured or anything. But it starts with awareness. For me, that awareness is accepting that life is…a process."

"As opposed to what?" she asks.

"A report card," I reply. The audience cracks up. They seem to be relating and finding this to be amusing at the same time.

"Now isn't that the truth, ladies and gentlemen!" Torah is thrilled with my answers and boasts throughout the show about the funeral planning that took place for her great-aunt Charlotte.

"So what else can we expect on My Grief Day?" she asks. "Can I join your broadcast? Maybe I could tell a story?"

"Of course! Why don't you tell a story about your great-aunt Charlotte?"

She smiles softly at the thought and turns to her audience. "Do you all want to hear a story about my great-aunt Charlotte?" The audience cheers in approval. "Okay, I'll appear on My Grief Day, Maddy. Any final comments?"

"I just want to add that there's no right or wrong way to grieve. But sometimes grief can be debilitating. It's not only personal, it's collective, and encompasses all things, from natural disasters to terrorism, to deaths of beloved leaders. We are in a state of global grievance, and instead of shoving our emotions under the rug of denial, we hope this event will make it okay to talk about grief, by sharing our grief…

and in that, there is healing. In fact, I want to introduce a new national volunteer program for the purpose of those people who have no one to grieve with."

Torah looks at me, impressed and intrigued. "Now how does that work?"

"People will offer to serve in small towns and big cities throughout America to basically keep solo grievers company during the first seven days after a death occurs, so that no one has to grieve alone."

Without any prompts, the audience stands up and cheers. Eve and Sierra give me two thumbs up. My persona non grata status has vanished. Sure enough, the next day, two major news shows call for interviews, our public relations campaign is finally underway, with Lana orchestrating, and our sponsors are back on board.

My Grief Day

My Grief Day attire sells out across the nation as people prepare for the holiday. Thousands of heartwarming and meaningful tribute videos are submitted to the Tribute Film Festival, rated and selected for theatrical distribution.

My Grief Day kicks off without any hitches. President Stone tells a funny, yet poignant story of how he fell in love with Haley Stone, which later results in record-breaking popularity polls securing his reelection campaign and Congress' approval for Haley Stone's Poverty Reform Bill.

Torah Grant tells a story about her great-aunt Charlotte's favorite recipe that becomes a popular staple in *The Comfort*

Cuisine Book, which receives so many orders that the Delicious Network creates a show based on the book.

But the biggest coup of My Grief Day occurs during the live performance at the Kennedy Center...I'm sitting in the director's booth with Sierra when comic celebrity Marilyn DeMarcus introduces a surprise guest.

"Whoa. What surprise guest?" I nervously ask Sierra.

"You got me," she says, then pushes a button that feeds her voice into the ears of Smitty on the west coast at Disney Concert Hall. "Smitty, know anything about this?"

"Nope," Smitty replies. "But we're live, ya gotta go with it."

"Copy that," says Sierra. She pushes more buttons. "Camera one, give me a medium shot," she says. The screen moves in on Marilyn DeMarcus.

"This is indeed a national honor, for she rarely makes public speeches," announces Marilyn, to the audience and cameras. "Let's welcome one of our precious political bastions, Elizabeth Anderson."

"Wow," I say. "This is big." The audience cheers.

"Give me an audience shot...go tight on Mrs. Anderson," Sierra directs. "Pull back as she takes the podium...now give me a close-up."

"Thank you, America," says Mrs. Anderson. "I find myself equally surprised to be standing here today. I've always believed grief to be a private matter, but a few weeks ago I attended a dear friend's funeral, planned by our grief czar. It was indeed a celebration of Charlotte Abbotsdale's life and my grief was assuaged by the personalization of the service.

I've since come to believe in the merits of this program. So I'd like to do something I've never done before."

"Uh-oh...here comes another surprise," I mutter.

Mrs. Anderson pauses, and then declares, "I'd like to grieve for my husband, the late Alexander Anderson. It's something I never did because...well, I was angry at him—for dying. Many of you remember him as a titan of the steel industry. I remember him as the young boy from across the tracks who didn't have a penny but used his integrity and honor to win my heart. I have tried to honor his memory by helping others with the same kind of integrity and honor that Alexander always displayed to achieve greatness and benefit society. But I fear I have made a grave mistake on behalf of the American public."

"Oh, man," Sierra interjects. "I think we're in for another surprise."

"I put my faith in the Insider Think Tank...but as of today, I am withdrawing my public support for this organization as it lacks the criteria by which I honor the memory of Alexander."

"Wow!" I exclaim, as the audience stands up and cheers.

"Holy shit," says Sierra. "Give me angles from every camera we've got."

"Bye-bye, Derek Rogers...and Tyler Simmons." I give a little wave to the screen.

Fifteen minutes later, Mrs. Anderson stops by the director's booth to find me. I step outside to talk to her in private.

"How was I?" she asks.

"Amazing on so many levels," I answer. I stare at her in humble appreciation. "I really don't know what to say, Mrs. Anderson."

"Madison, you meet the criteria I'm looking for. I've

decided to make a private contribution to cover the remaining monies you'll need to pay for all this. So, if you'd like, you may say, 'thank you,' and keep it between us."

I stare at her in shock and wonder. "I…uh…thank you, Mrs. Anderson. Thank you very much."

She's clearly pleased, and turns about to leave, then stops and turns back. "Hampstead was right about you."

"Excuse me?" I ask.

"He's the one who vetted your character and approved your hire at the White House. He seemed to have faith that the position would become you, the way a good pair of shoes mold to the feet…I do believe that was the analogy he made."

My Grief Day…the conclusion

The result of Elizabeth Anderson's public appearance brought the Insider Think Tanks to its end, at the same time, clearing all accusations that had been brought against Arthur Pintock and Pintock International. Derek's faux relationship to Jonathon Darcy became public and he returned to Yankton Federal Prison. Tyler Simmons resigned immediately from his post as political advisor to President Stone with investigations to follow. And my work addiction buddy, Brian, received a slew of offers from venture capitalists to further develop his software.

As for my sponsor, StoriesMakeUs.com, My Grief Day helped Eddie initiate an IPO, the likes of which had never been seen before in the technology sector. It appeared that one commodity Americans loved more than anything else was a good story demonstrating that the American spirit could heal from grief, and that folks could catapult themselves out from under the grief cloud. Spirits rose, and the gross national product began to climb.

Eddie sent me a generous check in appreciation of my efforts and I decided to put it to good use. First, I made a long overdue trip to visit my family and my beloved dog, Siddhartha, and took everybody, including the canine, out to a five-star restaurant for dinner. Second, I bought vacation packages to Fiji for my Grief Team and my fellow work addicts, complete with preplanned activities and an onsite WA sponsor for emergencies. And third, I purchased two extra weeks at a luxury hotel in New Zealand for Victor and myself. I included a stopover in Fiji for a reunion dinner with my Grief Team and fellow work addicts, as well as a tune-up for myself with the WA sponsor to keep me on track during my "vacation."

Outtake

One week prior to the aforementioned activities and vacations, Eve and Sierra accompany me on a shopping mission for Victor. We're standing inside a futuristic tech store and I am like a kid surrounded by candy, completely overwhelmed by all the amazing inventions.

"Whoa! Check this out!" I hold up a contraption for a remote control key locater. I skim the description. "Hey, you can use this to find all kinds of items. Do you realize how this could revolutionize the way people save time? Not to mention doing away with feelings of inadequacy when you can't find what you're looking for. What if you could take this technology and find intangible things, like…memories. Do you think the company is working on that in their R and D department, because maybe I could—"

"Ohmygod! She's impossible!" says Eve. "Will you please talk to her?" Eve asks Sierra.

Sierra turns to me. "Maddy, sweetie, I think you're seeking an adrenaline fix right now."

"No, I'm not. Look, this is amazing. And I just got this idea…"

"Will you please stop with the ideas?" begs Eve. "And think about using that remote control finder to *find* a gift for Victor, not a new business venture."

"Right. You're absolutely right." I immediately replace the contraption on the shelf and refocus. "Victor gift, Victor gift, Victor gift," I repeat. "What should I get him?"

Sierra picks up a rabbit corkscrew wine opener and looks at me. "How about this?"

I hold the contraption in my hand and play with it a little. "This is a blast," I tell them. "Look, it flips up and down. Like a rabbit! Isn't that clever?"

"You really need to get out more," says Eve.

I smile at the rabbit. "I think I'll take this."

Eve and Sierra sigh with relief. Sierra checks her watch. "Well, that only took six hours."

"While you spend the next twenty minutes buying it in that line over there, I'll be next door checking out the new spring collection of Manolo Blahniks," Eve informs us. Then turns to Sierra and asks, "Are you coming?"

"Sure," answers Sierra. She looks at me and smiles. "Think

you can stay focused enough to buy the thing? They gift wrap, too."

"Piece of cake," I say.

"Good, then we'll meet you next door," she instructs me, and they both leave.

I am waiting in line to purchase Victor's gift when a knowing sensation rumbles in my gut. A wine opener, with or without rabbit-ear-like levers, didn't seem special enough on its own. I wanted to get Victor something truly unique. And that's when I see Hampstead on the other side of the store picking up the remote control key locater. I complete my purchase and walk over to where he's standing.

"Hi, there," I greet him.

Hampstead turns and smiles. "Ms. Banks, pleasure to see you. Now that you've accomplished your objectives and are taking an extended vacation, I want you to know that we'll miss you at the White House."

"Thank you, Hampstead. I'll miss you guys, too."

"I trust your relationship with your fiancé is back on track?" he asks.

"Yes, except for one thing. And I thought you might be able to help me. I'd like to get him something special. He's got impeccable taste like you."

Hampstead pauses. "I have an idea," he suggests and puts the remote control key locater back on the shelf. He starts to take off his tie. "I think he'll like this."

"You're giving me your handmade tie? But your cousin made it for you. It's special," I protest.

"So are you, Ms. Banks. Consider it a gift from me to you to Victor. May I add that the polite thing to do is accept."

"This is too…kind of you, Hampstead. I really don't know what to say…except, thank you. Thank you very much."

"You're very welcome." And he hands the tie to me.

I stare at its beautiful craftsmanship and notice the artist's signature on the back side. "Mark."

"That's an unusual M and A," I say. "It's got a unique flair to it." I pause and look at Hampstead again. "Hampstead, can I ask you something?"

"Ask away," he answers.

"In your position at the White House, you would have access to all kinds of information about someone before hiring them, like their financial records and even a history of where they spend their money. Is that right?"

He nods. "That's right."

"So, you would know if someone has a strong character but no sense for fashion, since their records would indicate they never shop for those things. Is that right?"

He nods again. "I suppose you could conclude a scenario like that." He grins ever so slightly.

"Hampstead, one more question. Does your cousin in that remote village of Tuscany also make one-of-a-kind shoes?" I ask.

"I believe he likes to dabble in women's shoes from time to time," Hampstead replies, still smiling.

"I see." I smile back. "Please tell your cousin if he ever

manufactures women's shoes for the U.S. market, I'd be his biggest customer."

Hampstead bows. "Consider the message delivered." He then checks the time. "Well, I'd better be going. Enjoy your vacation, Ms. Banks, and try not to work."

"I will. Thank you, Hampstead…for everything."

"You're welcome," he replies, and exits the store.

I continue to smile, overcome with a feeling of inner harmony, and most especially, with relief, because I finally solved a blessed conundrum. "Who is John Galt?"

"We believe creating meaningful ways to pay tribute to a loved one begins with compassion and is shaped by the understanding that each life is truly unique."

As North America's largest provider of funeral, cremation and cemetery services, the Dignity Memorial® network is the name families turn to for compassionate and professional final arrangements. Dignity Memorial providers care for more than 300,000 families each year and understand the importance of thoughtful, personalized arrangements. Offered through a network of more than 1,600 funeral, cremation and cemetery providers in the United States and Canada, the Dignity Memorial brand is your assurance of quality, value, caring service and exceptional customer satisfaction.

We believe creating meaningful ways to pay tribute to a loved one begins with compassion and is shaped by the understanding that each life is truly unique. For us, there is no greater responsibility than honoring and preserving the story of one's life.

www.dignitymemorial.com

Legacy.com®

Founded in 1998, Legacy.com is an innovative online media company that collaborates with more than 900 newspapers in North America, Europe and Australia to provide ways for readers to express condolences and share remembrances of loved ones.

As the leader in the online memorial and obituary market, Legacy.com is visited by more than 14 million users each month. It partners with 124 of the 150 largest newspapers in the U.S. and features obituaries and Guest Books for more than two-thirds of people who die in the United States.

Legacy.com® *Where life stories live on.*®

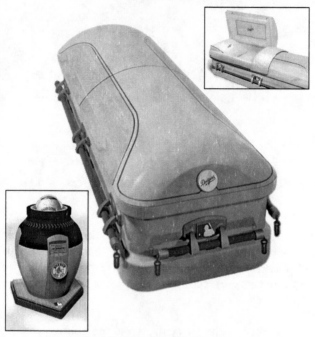

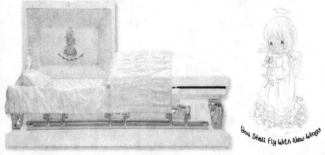

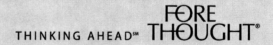

EchoSign

Maddy Banks is one smart cookie, and as a small business owner she can't spend a lot of time waiting for her business contracts to be signed. So Maddy uses EchoSign -- the fastest, easiest and most secure electronic signature service. Whether Maddy needs to sign a contract herself or get documents signed by her customers such as estate planning documents, a pre-need arrangement, or a contract for a celebrity appearance at a life celebration, Maddy always uses EchoSign, the web's #1 esignature application.

Click below to try EchoSign for Free and see how you can get your contracts signed, tracked and filed in minutes.

Free Trial

Want to learn more? Click below for a Free Online Demo.

Free Online Demo

877-324-6744   **www.echosign.com**

**Increase Your Online Sales Using Maddy Banks'
Favorite Web Marketing Tool & Save 20% Off ***

Small business owners agree with Maddy Banks – Heardable.com
is the easiest way to improve your online business.

• Drive more traffic to your website
• Increase sales and improve your ROI
• Get expert advise on how to optimize your brand

How? With Heardable.com, the world's first and only brand
optimization platform. We provide a powerful suite of marketing
tools to help you rapidly assess, analyze, and share key website
and brand performance metrics so you can optimize & meet your
business goals.

Try it for FREE! Paid subscription plans start as low as $19.95 per
month. Go to www.heardable.com and sign-up today!

* Use Promo Code: 10777 to save 20% off any paid subscription
plan. Discount good through the first 12 months of service.

www.Heardable.com

Expires 1/1/2015 or at the discretion of Heardable, Inc. management.

EAGLES NEST RESTAURANT

PROUDLY PRESENTS
10% OFF YOUR NEXT MEAL OR OUR SIGNATURE HAMBURGERS

BOOK LAUNCHING PARTY AT EAGLES NEST

EAGLES NEST RESTAURANT IS PROUD TO BE FEATURED IN
THE COMEDY NOVEL

THE FUNERAL PLANNER,
ABOUT A WOMAN WHO BRINGS LIFE TO A DEAD BUSINESS.

THIS IS THE RESTAURANT WHERE HEROINE MADDY BANKS
EXPERIENCES A TRANSFORMATION OF SELF WORTH!
COME CELEBRATE LIFE AND EXPERIENCE YOUR OWN SELF
WORTH OVERLOOKING BEAUTIFUL CLARK LAKE WHERE
THE AUTHOR WROTE THE TRILOGY OF NOVELS!

EAGLES NEST RESTAURANT
1368 EAGLE POINT DRIVE
CLARK LAKE, MI 49234
517.529.9520

UPON MAKING RESERVATIONS AND PRESENTING THE NOVEL WITH THIS INSERT
RECEIVE 10% OFF ON YOUR NEXT MEAL OR
SIGNATURE HAMBURGER AT THE EAGLES NEST.

PORTION OF PROCEEDS DONATED TO THE CLARK LAKE SPIRIT TRAIL FUND.

Jay, Janet, Alec, Zackary, Alec, and Parents Irene
and Robert Newman Honor the memory of
Nancy Hope Newman
In Loving Memory of a Beloved Sister, Sister-in-Law,
Daughter, Aunt and Friend
We miss you and love you!
We send you love and light on your journey!
You are not forgotten…
and Loved Always…

FIRST CAPITAL FUNDING
www.fcapfund.com
512.692.4195

Special Note from the Author:
*After completing the manuscript for THE FUNERAL PLANNER I went on a walk
with Tao (my four legged daughter) who befriended a white lab named Casey.
That's how I met Jay Newman, Casey's dad. There was an instant connection
between us. As our dogs played, we chatted about movies; both of us having
worked in the film business sharing common experiences. We quickly became
dog walking buddies and I discovered his wife was from my beloved hometown
in Michigan and that his work in real estate sparked my love for investing in the
tangible. One day Jay invited me to meet his father to discuss investing
opportunities. Upon seeing the address I realized our paths had crossed before.
"Do you have a sister named Nancy who died ten years ago?" I asked. Jay was
shocked. "How do you know my sister?" "We used your parents' house as a
location on a film I produced. I remember getting to know Nancy who was my
age and was dying. Six months later I attended the funeral and never forgot it--
it was unique." And then I remembered a flash of Jay walking past me as night
fell during Shiva and everyone gathered around a campfire to take turns sharing
stories about Nancy. I never experienced that kind of collective healing before
so in addition to the loss and experience of my father's and brother's funerals,
it was Nancy's "life celebration" that set the stage for THE FUNERAL PLANNER.
Since then, Jay has become a brother to me and I a sister to him. Four years
later I sucessfully invested in First Capital Funding, his real esate private
finance comapny with great faith, which is a great passive way to supplement
the income of an author! Though Jay now lives in Austin we continue to share
our unique connection. And so it is with great pleasure that I share this tale to
remember the spirits of all of our loved ones and the mysterious ways in which
they unite humanity. **Lynn Isenberg**, Author of "The Funeral Planner" series*

National Hospice Foundation

Committed to compassionate care at the end of life

We are the National Hospice Foundation--committed to compassionate care at the end of life.

We envision a world where everyone facing serious illness, death, and grief will experience the best that humankind can offer.

NHF supports the National Hospice and Palliative Care Organization's quality and research initiatives; hospice/palliative care provider education activities; consumer engagement and caregiver services; and the FHSSA Impact Fund.

In partnership with NHPCO, we work to improve care at the end of life throughout the United States. We raise funds from individuals, foundations, and corporations to fund programs that make a difference in the lives of the patients and families served by NHPCO's membership of more than 3,400 hospice and palliative care providers.

Through our support of Caring Connections, a program of NHPCO, NHF funds the development of resources, tools, and information to educate and empower individuals to access advance care planning, caregiving, hospice and grief services, and information.

National Hospice Foundation
1731 King Street, Suite 200
Alexandria, Virginia 22314
703/516-4928 (General NHF Information)
877/470-6472 (Donations)
703/837-1233 (Fax)
www.nationalhospicefoundation.org

CPSIA information can be obtained at www.ICGtesting.com
Printed in the USA
244991LV00001B/14/P